Choose Wisely

Practical Insights from Spiritual Traditions

GARY J. BOELHOWER

Paulist Press
New York / Mahwah, NJ

Cover image by Bruce Rolff / Shutterstock.com
Cover design by Sharyn Banks
Book design by Lynn Else

Library of Congress Cataloging-in-Publication Data

Boelhower, Gary J., 1950–
    Choose wisely : practical insights from spiritual traditions / Gary J. Boelhower.
        p. cm.
    Includes bibliographical references and index.
    ISBN 978-0-8091-4814-1 (alk. paper) — ISBN 978-1-58768-098-4 1. Decision making—Religious aspects. I. Title.
    BL629.5.D43B64 2013
    204`.4—dc23
    2012042670

ISBN 978-0-8091-4814-1 (paperback) — ISBN 978-1-58768-098-4 (e-book)

Published by Paulist Press
997 Macarthur Boulevard
Mahwah, NJ 07430

www.paulistpress.com

Printed and bound in the
United States of America

CONTENTS

To
Susan Griffiths
and
Virginia "Ginny" Gilmore
Servant-Leaders

GRATITUDE

I am deeply grateful for the precious insights and learning through the years from colleagues at Marian University: Jerry Burns, Fr. Dan Crosby, Dan DiDomizio, Ann Egan, Sud Ingle, Sr. Donna Innes, Mike Ketterhagen, Mary Klein, Jeff Reed, Richard Ridenour, David Schimpf, Sr. Susan Treis, and Bill Zierdt; from colleagues at The College of St. Scholastica: Ron Berkeland, Bill Campbell, Elyse Carter Vosen, Larry Goodwin, Bob Hartl, Mary Bridget Lawson, Steve Lyons, Sr. Kathie McLaughlin, Carleen Maynard, Jay Newcomb, Steve Ostovich, Randall Poole, Denise Starkey, Cecelia Taylor, Sr. Mary Josephine Torborg, Lon Weaver, and Marty Witrak; from fellow leaders and searchers in Servant Leadership and other learning circles: Barbara Cecil, Jack Christ, Sr. Joyce DeShano, Ted Drewson, Don Frick, Andrea Gelb, Mike Kipp, Nancy Lanyi, Jack Lowe, Ann McGee Cooper, Judi Neal, Ron Pevny, Martin Rutte, George SanFacon, Sr. Sarah Smedman, Richard Smith, and Deborah Vogele-Welch; from my trusted friends in our long-term leadership circle: Gary Baltz, Timothy Haukeness, and Barry Mulholland, from fellow board members on the Sophia Foundation Board: Rob Casper, Ginny and Jim Gilmore, Valerie Graczyk, Dick Kleinfeldt, Sandi Roehrig, Terri Sexton, Ginger Timchak, Christa Williams, and Cathy Wolfe; from fellow adventurers on the Figment and other courageous outings: Dan Hill and Carolyn Polodna; and from fellow writers and artists in writing projects and groups: Sam Black, Karen Cannizo, Ellen Kort, Cele Lieder, Kathy McTavish, Joe Miguez, Sheila Packa, Tricia Pearce, John Pegg, and Mike Vogl. I also owe a great debt to Parker Palmer and Dean Fowler who guided and challenged me with their mentorship. My immense appreciation goes to Pamela Mittlefehldt who reviewed and made insightful suggestions for every chapter of this book. Thank you to The College of St. Scholastica for a sabbatical semester, which facilitated the final revision of these chapters. Finally, I cannot begin to express my depth of gratitude to my sister Susan Griffiths, my brother Bill Boelhower, my children Matthew, Joel, and Rebecca, and my partner, Gary Anderson, for the innumerable ways in which my learning and my soul have been nurtured and expanded.

PROLOGUE

$\mathcal{T}$his is a book about practical wisdom: How can we make wise choices in the concrete situations of our lives? It is a book that explores the intersections of philosophy, theology, spirituality, and leadership studies. Without pretending to be comprehensive, I draw a set of core principles from diverse spiritual traditions of the world and apply these to the hard work of making good decisions in both personal and organizational contexts. Each core principle is translated into two operating procedures that address the method by which good decisions are made, and two criteria for judgment that deal with the standards upon which good decisions are based. It is impossible to speak of choosing wisely without identifying some basis for determining what is wise and what is not. The five core wisdom principles that are the backbone for this wise decision-making model are commonly held across many religions.

These principles focus more on right doing than on right thinking. Even religions that have very significant differences in understanding the divine and the afterlife concur on key moral principles for acting in the world. I do not claim to be an expert in comparative religions, nor do I attempt to provide a comprehensive overview of the religions of the world in relation to these principles. The scope of this book does not allow for such treatment. However, in my study of spiritual traditions over the past forty years, and in my work with leaders and organizations interested in nurturing spiritual values, these five principles have consistently caught my attention and the attention of others. I provide some brief examples of where and how each of the principles is embedded in several spiritual traditions. My examples are mainly drawn from the major religions of Hinduism, Buddhism, Judaism, Christianity, Confucianism, and Islam, and understanding that these terms identify sets of very diverse traditions that have as many differences as they have common theological and spiritual underpinnings. I also occasionally provide examples from other spiritual traditions in order to suggest that the principles are broadly held. My examples are an attempt to indicate that these are common principles that are broadly shared in the human community and that have humanizing results when they are reflected upon and applied.

Assumptions of the Model

This model for wise decision-making based on five principles drawn from diverse spiritual traditions of the world makes three fundamental assumptions. First, the spiritual traditions of the world have much to offer in the way of wisdom, even though they have sometimes used their particular understanding of the divine and revelation to condemn and wreak violence on others. These traditions have been instrumental in raising questions of ultimate value, in advocating for justice for all, and in providing a moral sense of the preciousness of life and the dignity of the human person. They have been significant guides for countless persons throughout the centuries in living a meaningful and responsible life. Since we have access to these great treasures of wisdom, it makes good sense to build our model for wise decision-making on their time-tested, profound principles.

Second, our most important values and solid critical inquiry must be applied to every dimension of life. We find it hard to live with ourselves when our actions don't match our expressed values and priorities. If we divide our lives into a "spiritual" part and a "secular" part, we soon create an unhealthy, divided life that leads to physical, mental, and spiritual "dis-ease." Try as we might, we can't help but be whole persons. Every aspect of our lives affects every other aspect. What we do at work and how we are treated there affects who we are at home and how we treat our families and vice versa. Since there are no areas of life off limits to wise decision-making, the model for making wise decisions must be general enough to be applied in many different circumstances.

Finally, this model for wise decision-making assumes that the work of practical wisdom is critical for both individuals and organizations if the human community is to prosper. We cannot afford to allow decisions made in the realm of business and government to be somehow immune from the scrutiny of these wisdom principles. Organizations, as well as individuals, must be focused on more than self-interest, must respect the dignity of all persons, and must be responsive to the needs of their local, national, and global community and the planet's ecosystem because our lives are inextricably interrelated.

Decision by Decision We Make Ourselves

We make hundreds of decisions every day. Some of them are simply a matter of taste and have nothing to do with wisdom. However, there are many more decisions we make with little or no reflection that have very important consequences. We pay more attention to the process of deciding wisely when we recognize that decision by decision we become ourselves, and that decisions are our everyday opportunity to live out our values and our vocation. When we recognize that every important decision within our organizations has an impact on a diversity of stakeholders, and that decisions are our everyday opportunity to live out our values and our mission, we also become more purposeful and careful in our decisions.

This book is intended as an exploration into wise decision-making. I make no claims this is the only relevant model or that the principles I have identified are the best ones for your own reflective decision-making process. I hope the model I propose here will get you thinking about the most important principles, methods, and criteria that you might apply to your own wise decision-making. This model is not appropriate for every situation, especially circumstances in which decisions must be made quickly and with limited data. In such situations, there isn't time for the kind of reflective processes that are central to this model. However, I propose that a regular use of this model over time, or your own version of it, will inform those situations when decisions need urgent resolution. As far as possible, one must identify the kinds of emergency situations that might occur and use the reasoned and reflective processes of this model to clarify the best steps for wise action in such situations.

Even when there is time for reflection, research, and in-depth conversation around a decision, it is generally not feasible to apply every suggestion in the operating procedures and criteria for judgment. Especially at the outset of using this model, it is important to pick and choose a few dimensions of it to implement. Depending upon your organizational culture or your own familiarity with the skills and processes related to this model, there may be some discomfort when initially implementing aspects of the model. My suggestion is to stay the course and use the operating procedures and criteria for judgment with an attitude of experimentation.

Structure of the Book

Before I launch into the model itself, I have provided some preparatory reflections in the Introduction on the importance of our decisions and the shifts in attitude that we need if we are to take seriously the challenge of deciding wisely. Each successive chapter is focused on one of the wisdom principles: (1) Respect all persons; (2) appreciate the wholeness of being human; (3) recognize the interconnectedness of all reality; (4) value inner wisdom and personal experience; (5) attend to preservation and transformation. In each chapter, the process of explication is similar. First, examples are given of how the principle is embedded in several spiritual traditions. Second, two operating procedures that emanate from the principle are identified and concrete suggestions are provided for how the principle can be embodied in the methods for decision-making. Third, two criteria based on the principle are explained and examples and suggestions are provided for applying these standards to the decision. Each chapter then ends with a few key questions and an assessment of one of the central dimensions of the chapter. If you are serious about developing your own wise decision-making capacities, these questions and the assessment can be very helpful in identifying a way forward. Finally, a brief Epilogue provides my reflections on how the five principles and the correlative operating procedures and criteria for judgment are related to the development of instrumental, interpersonal, imaginal, and systems skills.

I am less sure about any one dimension of the model than I am about the need for us to be as reflective and wise as we can be in our decisions. My ultimate motivation is quite simple. My desire to live with greater authenticity and wisdom comes from that moment when my newborn daughter wrapped her tender, tiny fingers around one of mine. The world was suddenly bigger, the horizon of my hopes more far reaching. When my sons were born, my resolve was strengthened. Every visit with my grandchildren brings a deeper realization of our need to be wise stewards of a world I hope they will enjoy and pass on to those they name with hope and love. The final lines from my poem "Everything We Can" attempts to communicate the "why" behind this model, the "why" behind our persistent efforts to decide wisely.

> If you've ever watched a baby's chest
> rise and fall or cut the cord to free the child
> completely or let his small hand curl
> around your finger or noticed his eyes
> scanning until they met your face, you know
> why we have to do everything we can.

MAKING WISE DECISIONS

*P*ractical wisdom is about finding our way in the world—a way that makes sense, a way that we can live with, a way that brings meaning and hope. We make our way one decision at a time, making choices that matter, and attempting to do the right thing. Often we have the good fortune of being able to follow a trail that others have made, the way clearly marked out before us. More often, there are several paths that have been worn in the earth by human beings who have struggled over this same ground and left diverging trails. Then the question becomes, "How do we choose among these competing paths? Which way forward is the best one for me in this circumstance?" However, there are many times when we are not on solid ground at all but on the shifting seas.

How do we find our way when all is fluid, when nothing seems constant, when there are no visible markers? The people of the Aleutian Islands were expert navigators well before there were astrolabes or the global positioning system (GPS). They were able to make open-ocean crossings by chanting in rhythm with the waves and observing how the wave patterns changed as they approached the various islands. Similarly, the Polynesian people who inhabited islands across seventy million square miles of Pacific Ocean watched the flight patterns of birds and used the stars to sight on as they made their journeys across the water. This idea of using the stars to guide us is embedded in our language, the word *desire* literally means "of the stars." In our most difficult decisions, we must be guided by our stars. We must chart our way by reference to our deepest desires.

Sometimes even the stars are clouded over and we are surrounded by sheer darkness. David La Chapelle tells the story of Nainoa Thompson, who "was instrumental in guiding the first modern ocean-going canoe from Hawaii to Tahiti without the aid of any modern devices. The journey became a symbolic and literal reempowerment of the indigenous Hawaiian people."[1] Remembering and practicing these old ways of navigating became a way of reconnecting to the heart of their culture. The most difficult part of the journey for Nainoa and his crew was experienced in the doldrums near the equator where the seas are calm and the sky is often cloudy. He couldn't see the moon or the stars; there was no reference point for finding the way. Nainoa tells the story.

> It was getting very intense and I was extremely tired. I was so exhausted. I turned to the rail and I locked my elbows on the rail and tried to get rest standing up. In doing that, in all the rain and all this cold, I felt this warm sensation and my mind got very clear. And I could feel the moon. I knew the moon was up, but I didn't know where it was because I couldn't see it. But somehow I could tell the direction.[2]

Good Choices in Concrete Circumstances

Wisdom is making good choices in the concrete circumstances of life, sometimes in the middle of what feels like an endless sea without a star in sight. Even in the most difficult situation, there are cues and clues in the rhythm of the waves and in the yearnings of our own hearts. We face unique situations but not without hints, directives, cautions, advice, and wise tales passed down from generation to generation in every age and on every continent. Ultimately, wisdom isn't a set of principles, commandments, or teachings. It isn't an immense collection of facts, maps, or directions. Although wisdom requires knowledge and information, it is much more than the accumulation of data. In the heat of decision-making, we face the challenge of incarnating our character and identity. Wisdom requires conscious, intentional, and reflective living based on our values and priorities. It means practicing in words and actions who we want to be.

To make a wise decision, we must be adequately informed and fundamentally free. Wise decisions are made from a close consideration of creative alternatives. One of the most important skills in the decision-making process is the ability to conceptualize multiple viable options that preserve the values at stake in the situation. The ability to "break set," or think beyond the usual boundaries and envision new possibilities, is a critical asset to wise decision-making. Certainly, we can't foresee every alternative or consequence or digest all of the relevant data, so we need to understand when our searching and researching is enough.

Once we have an understanding of a real set of creative possible choices and their foreseeable consequences, we must be free to choose among them. We cannot be coerced by actual or perceived authorities. Although there may be pressures and persuasive voices, if we don't really have a choice, we cannot choose wisely. Perhaps the most difficult authority to free ourselves from is our own assumptions or the unquestioned presuppositions that are accepted by the group or organization. When we are able to see our own automatic judgments, we have a better chance to truly choose wisely.

Wisdom, then, incorporates our mental, affective, and physical aspects as human beings. It includes the cognitive function of thinking rightly or accurately, and the affective function of desiring right relationships and a purposeful and meaningful life. Finally, wisdom does not end with right thinking or even right desiring. It goes the final step of putting thought and desire into physical action or choice. This in-depth understanding of wisdom has its roots in Aristotle. Thomas Groome in *Sharing Faith* traces the philosophical roots of the concept of wisdom to the English word *conatus*, related to the original Greek concept of *kinesis* meaning movement or motivation. Groome states:

> It is a constant cohesive structure at the heart of human existence that prompts us not to remain in a state of passivity, isolation, or ignorance but rather disposes us for meaningful and responsible action, affection, and cognition. Our conatus for 'being' has an innate ethical disposition that tends to move and subsume our reflection, desire, and will to appropriate the good and the truth by doing them.[3]

Wisdom is ultimately about doing the good. Wise actions, of course, are grounded in good information and good thinking. They are moti-

vated by sincere desire and emotional connection. Thinking about
the good and desiring the good are not enough, however; wisdom
includes the concrete choices that move conceptualization and
vision into practice.

Common Principles of Wisdom

The search for wisdom, to find the right way, echoes through
every epoch of human history. Philosophers, kings and queens, poets
and shamans deliver treatises, give advice, sing songs, and create rituals to communicate the foundational principles of wisdom and
apply them to the uncertain circumstances and troubling times of
their community. Every religious tradition tries to put into words the
deepest meanings of life, to tell a story that gives direction and purpose to each person's existence and joins them together with a larger
sense of community. In my years of studying the religions of the
world, I have been startled again and again by the commonalities of
practical wisdom across the traditions even when there are clear differences in understanding ultimate reality. Stephen Hall in *Wisdom:
From Philosophy to Neuroscience* speaks about this commonality.

> As distinct as these schools of thought are, it is their
> deeper congruences that begin to coalesce around a time-
> tested, culturally heterogeneous, geographically far-flung,
> yet surprisingly universal concept of wisdom. East or
> West, they all embrace social justice and insist on a code
> of public morality. They embrace an altruism that benefits
> the many. They try to dissociate individual needs and
> desires from the common good, and strive to master the
> emotions that urge immediate sensory gratification.[4]

Sages and seers around the world and throughout history have articulated fundamental principles of wisdom that are as common and
critical as breath.

In our own age, there seems to be a renewed recognition of the
importance of spirituality and spiritual wisdom. Many organizations
are making space in symbolic and practical ways for the insights of

religion and the values of spirituality to be brought into the work-place. Martin and Hafer in "Models of Emotional Intelligence, Spiritual Intelligence and Performance: A Test of Tischler, Biberman, and McKeage" assert that "workplace spirituality is now a mainstream management and leadership research interest" that includes diverse dimensions such as "a team's sense of community, alignment with organizational values, sense of contribution to society, enjoyment at work, and opportunities of inner life...."[5] These dimensions and others are being explored in numerous ways by scores of authors writing about the integration of spirituality in work.

This explosion of interest can be seen in academic centers and non-profit institutes around the world doing research and providing training to support spiritual integration in organizational life. Examples include the Centre for Spirituality and the Workplace at Saint Mary's University in Halifax, Nova Scotia; the Yale Center for Faith and Culture, with its Ethics and Spirituality in the Workplace program; Princeton's Faith and Work Initiative; the Tyson Center for Faith and Spirituality in the Workplace at the University of Arkansas; The Center for Spirituality at Work in Denver, Colorado; the Center for Workplace Spirituality at Seton Hall University in New Jersey; and the Center for Spirituality and Leadership at Marian University in Wisconsin.

The mounting interest in spirituality and cross-cultural wisdom doesn't mean the process of decision-making is made easy. It is never like applying an infallible formula or following a precise recipe. However, the common principles of wisdom provide guideposts and cairns and stars to help us see a way forward. Wise living requires we do the difficult work of applying these common wisdom principles to the concrete and unique circumstances of our individual and organizational lives. Ultimately, practical wisdom is making decisions with deep reflection and care, living on purpose.

Stay Awake

I can't count the number of times I have found myself on the wrong road or the wrong freeway exit because I was operating on autopilot. I was supposed to be going somewhere else, but my unconscious mind was taking me on my usual route to work or to the grocery store. This also happens in my reactions to events or persons. Sometimes I reply without thinking based on my limited perceptions and assumptions. Occasionally, I recoil in a situation, reacting out of past wounds or hurtful experiences. I take one of the basic reactions of fleeing, fighting, or freezing that has been inbred in my animal body. For example, growing up as the youngest child of four with an alcoholic father, I learned early on not to make too many waves. The really big and scary issues weren't talked about and certainly not confronted. When I am on autopilot, I tend to flee from scary questions; I don't confront inappropriate words or actions. I learned to survive by ducking, so, when I am in default mode, I duck.

If we're honest, sometimes we find ourselves living in our default setting; we don't really think about what we are doing or saying. However, we know that to live wisely, we must be conscious, present, and mindful. One of my favorite ways of thinking about this challenge to live consciously comes from the Persian mystic poet Jelaluddin Rumi, who advises us to be awake in our lives.

> The breeze at dawn has secrets to tell you.
> Don't go back to sleep.
>
> You must ask for what you really want.
> Don't go back to sleep.
>
> People are going back and forth across the doorsill
> where the two worlds touch.
>
> The door is round and open.
> Don't go back to sleep.[6]

When we live consciously, we choose our words and actions on purpose. We respond rather than react. We make decisions by observing the uniqueness of a situation and the persons involved, recognizing alternatives, weighing options, reflecting on values and principles, and taking a decisive step into our future. Sometimes this all happens in an instant; other times, it is a lengthy reflective process involving significant research and cross-functional team input. Whatever the personal or organizational context of the decision, we are faced with the challenge of deciding wisely.

What is the right decision? What will lead me as an individual or my organization down the right path? Some decisions are very important—hiring a new key leader, enrolling a child in a specialty magnet school, stepping into a board position of a non- profit agency in the community, or developing a new product. Even the small decisions—taking time to attentively listen to an employee who has a new idea about the production process, walking down the hall to have a conversation with a colleague rather than firing off an email, making a date with your partner in the middle of a busy stretch of work, doing homework with a child—can have a significant impact on another's life. Making decisions is a little like planting seeds. We don't know for sure what will come up and we don't know how the weather will affect the growth and health of another life.

Plant Seeds

Whenever I think about the consequences of decisions, I am reminded of the story that Tom Wiig, a dedicated surgeon, told at a retreat I facilitated. When Tom entered Hastings College in Hastings, Nebraska, he was set on becoming a physician and declared the logical major in biology. His academic adviser from the science department was very encouraging and committed to helping Tom and the others assigned to him as advisees. As Tom progressed through his biology classes, he found them less engaging than he thought they would be. In the middle of his sophomore year, Tom switched majors to theater arts but continued to hold his vision of becoming a physician. Tom's adviser kept in touch with him to make sure that he was still completing the courses he needed to maximize his chances for admission into medical school. He met with Tom a couple of times a semester to ensure that he was on track.

Tom recalls that his adviser "never dissuaded me from switching to theater arts, never raised his eyebrows, he never gave me a cluck or a sideways glance. He accepted me and my unique path but reminded me of my responsibility to keep my nose to the grindstone and get as many of my prerequisites done as possible."[7]

Tom graduated with a theater arts major and minors in biology and chemistry. He took another year to complete his prerequisites for medical school and, as he was doing so, he learned his adviser was terminally ill with a very aggressive malignancy. Tom was admitted to medical school a year later and started into his basic sciences in chemistry, biology, histology, and gross anatomy. As usual, his gross anatomy class was taught with cadavers that are treated with a great deal of respect. The bodies are not identified and the faces are covered. Often, a toe tag indicates where a body needs to be sent if the remains are to be returned to the family. Tom's gross anatomy class focused on the trunk, chest, and abdomen before moving to the extremities. About mid-way through the course, he noticed the toe tag of his cadaver indicated the body should be sent to Hastings. Tom continued with his story:

> As the days passed, my curiosity got the best of me. One evening after most of my lab partners had left, I removed the face cover and found that my cadaver was the body of my former adviser. For me it was an extraordinarily profound moment that basically changed my life, my commitment. Suddenly it just washed over me that this person whom I had respected in college, who had spent a great deal of time advising me, shepherding me, encouraging me, was still mentoring me after his death. And that experience has guided my life ever since. His commitment to guiding and educating science students was so total that he spent his life learning it and teaching it and, then, committed his physical remains to do the same task after his death. That indicated to me the ultimate level of commitment that we can obtain.[8]

Tom's adviser had no way of knowing whose life he would touch by his decision to donate his body to the medical school. From Tom's perspective, his adviser's donation was simply another decision consistent with his care for students and genuine passion for learning. It is interesting to note the Latin root of the word *decision* (de-cido) means "to cut." With every decision, we cut. We keep certain things, values, behaviors, and promises and then cut out others. The image of decisions as making a cut conveys the difficulty of the experience and its importance. This word is still used when talking about sports team members or performers making the cut. When we make a decision, we are doing surgery on our own lives and the lives of others. Tom's surgical practice, his own dedication to patient care and communication, is deeply informed by his adviser's commitment.

Before initiating any surgical procedure, a close weighing of the risks and benefits is required. The ultimate risk or harm to ourselves is that we waste our life, cut out something of our soul, or fail to respond to our true calling. Mary Oliver in her poem "The Summer Day" poignantly conveys the importance of decisions.

> Doesn't everything die at last, and too soon?
> Tell me, what is it you plan to do
> with your one wild and precious life?[9]

This is the larger question we face in every moment of decision-making. By our decisions we become ourselves, we create our character, our life. Clearly some decisions are more important than others. However, I often find I only understand the significance of some of my decisions in hindsight. I look back and see a decision I thought was insignificant turned into a major fork in the road of my life. If we see our small decisions, or those we think are small at the time, in the context of the largest questions of life, we are more apt to make a wise decision. Oliver's lines also remind us of our mortality. Since we have a short span of years on this planet, how can we use them most wisely? How do we decide in such a way that we won't have regrets?

Living without regrets is one of the lessons that John Izzo heard repeatedly from the elders he interviewed for his book *The Five Secrets You Must Discover Before You Die*. Izzo calls his second secret "leave no regrets" and offers this shorthand criterion for living this wisdom: "…live with courage, moving toward what we want rather than away from what we fear."[10] When people over sixty offered their wisdom, they often spoke to Izzo about critical decisions that required them to risk, to put their lives on the line in some way, to try something larger than the present shape of their lives. Izzo notes that "Not one person said they regretted having tried something and failed."[11] When we face our mortality, we see we have no time to waste in embracing our own unique vision for life. We have no time to waste in putting flesh on our values and hopes. Those who leave no regrets seize the moment of decision as an opportunity to incarnate their dreams.

Live Whole

When we make decisions that are consistent with our values and the core of our identity, we experience integrity. Our decision is integrated or consistent with what we know to be true in our heart. It fits with the whole of who we are. We can sleep at night because our decision makes sense in terms of our priorities and beliefs. Parker Palmer, author of *Let Your Life Speak* and *A Hidden Wholeness*, calls this "living divided no more."[12] We aren't thinking one thing and doing another, speaking one set of values and acting out of a different set.

When we live divided, there is "dis-ease" between our actions and our beliefs, between the role we play and the soul of who we are. The major long-term diseases that account for more than 60 percent of healthcare expenditures are significantly affected by the stresses and anxieties of living divided. When we make decisions that create dissonance within us, our body and spirit may react with high blood pressure or depression. We may attempt to flee from our own inconsistency and feelings of disharmony by self-medicating with alcohol, drugs, gambling, or more work. From Palmer's perspective, the greatest loss from living divided is the loss of soul. We are at risk of losing our center, that point where things come together, where we make sense out of the various dimensions of our lives.

When we listen to our souls and act with integrity, the ripples of wisdom are felt by others as well. Often, when I take the risk in a meeting to speak from my heart and say what I am really feeling, others share their experiences and values. Often, when I speak about my own questions in the classroom and take the time to really understand another's perspective, my fellow learners reflect more deeply and listen more openly to each other. In *A Hidden Wholeness*, Palmer talks about the effects of integrating soul and role.

> If our roles were more deeply informed by the truth that is
> in our souls, the general level of sanity and safety would

rise dramatically. A teacher who shares his or her identity with students is more effective than one who lobs factoids at them from behind a wall. A supervisor who leads from personal authenticity gets better work out of people than one who leads from a script. A doctor who invests self-hood in his or her practice is a better healer than one who treats patients at arm's length. A politician who brings personal integrity into leadership helps us reclaim the popular trust that distinguishes true democracy from its cheap imitations.[13]

Living whole doesn't mean we have to be perfect. It does mean that we need to acknowledge those places in our lives where there are significant gaps between our values and our decisions, between our soul and the role we play, between our best selves and the particular reaction that sometimes arises from the shadow self. Those gaps are places for reflection and growth. When we practice living whole or living undivided, we are able to confront those places of inconsistency with greater resolve. We are able to step into our challenges and recognize the new territory where we are pioneers of our own interior geography.

It is important to note that this kind of reflection and growth also depends on recognizing our own talents, skills, and particular unique contributions that we bring into the world. When we pay attention to our own preciousness and celebrate the abilities and passions that we have, we are able to face the gaps not as dark places to fear but as edges of opportunity. I was in my late forties before I took my first backpacking trip in the Wind River mountain range in Wyoming. It was a fairly easy hike (twelve miles roundtrip) from Dickinson Creek Trailhead to Smith Lake (elevation gain and loss: +1,100, -500 feet). For me, camping in the Smith Lake basin with its soaring cirque headwalls was like being drenched in beauty and awe.

The next year, I thought I was ready for greater challenges and took my daughter and son-in-law on a more difficult hike (16.2 miles roundtrip) from the Worthen Meadow Reservoir trailhead to Stough Creek Basin (elevation gain and loss: +2,100, -400 feet). After several hours of challenging climbing, my daughter and I were at the point often called "the wall," or a place within yourself where you don't think you can go any farther. We stopped for a short rest to consider our options and, for some reason, I began to enumerate the challenges we had previously faced and conquered. Then we began listing our strengths and convictions and we were soon smiling despite the pain in our legs. Our previous accomplishments gave us the strength to go on, to face the difficulty we were experiencing and push forward. I often think of this hike when I am faced with my own gaps. The process of personal growth requires this paradoxical attention to weaknesses and strengths, accomplishments and failures, terrain already traveled and edges yet to be explored.

Working with seasoned teachers in professional development courses for several years convinced me of the importance of holding this paradox. I had the good fortune of taking Teacher Perceiver Interview training, a certification program based on the work of Donald Clifton.[14] Through extensive interviewing of the most effective teachers, Clifton identified the key strengths of excellent teachers. His work with thousands of teachers through the years convinced him that persons grow best by continuing to develop their strengths. To live fully and wholly requires our recognition of failures and the need to continue to grow, but it also requires the confidence to keep trying, knowing that each of us has unique skills and traits.

Listen to the Call

The challenge to make a fitting and ethical decision consistent with our authentic self is another way of speaking about vocation. Parker Palmer's definition of vocation in *Let Your Life Speak* rings true for me when he says it is "a gift to be received. Discovering vocation does not mean scrambling toward some prize just beyond my reach but accepting the treasure of true self I already possess."[15] We don't often think of vocation when we are in the decision-making process. However, we actualize or enact our vocation in our day- to-day decisions.

As we determine our specific actions in our families and workplaces and communities, we literally put flesh on the spirit of who we are, on the unique character that we have. Again, we are involved in a paradox. Do we have a spirit or character out of which we act in the world or do our particular decisions and actions create our spirit and character? I prefer to let the essentialists and constructivists continue their arguments against each other. As with many other core questions, I find the "both/and" perspective to be most revealing. For many persons, there seem to be gifts given at birth that direct and shape their life decisions. Some would say these gifts seem to be passed on from previous generations as if a family line includes core ways of being in the world, genetic proclivities for certain kinds of work or particular ways of seeing. At the same time, character and calling are developed and heard on the journey, through an often twisting and turning process that includes much experimentation.

However you think of vocation at the macro-level—one's direction for life or unique way of being in the world or calling—it also includes the micro-level of everyday actions. One doesn't become a teacher by getting a degree in education or the certification to instruct in a particular subject. For me, the vocation of teaching requires those everyday decisions to be present to my fellow explorers, to try new methods that meet the needs of diverse learners, to continue to invest in my own learning so the passion of discovery is still alive in my teaching. Similarly, we can outline the micro-level of the vocation of partnership or marriage in the daily decisions to be attentive to each other's needs, to listen deeply to each other's concerns, to set aside time to share each other's joys and burdens.

So it goes with any vocation or calling. Certainly there are key decision points when we decide on our profession or accept a particular job offer or propose to our partner. Those macro-level decisions are simply the beginning of a vocational commitment that is shaped and molded in our daily, micro-level choices. After we have reached some clarity about our core values, our primary direction in life and our fundamental priorities, we are challenged to live out those values, to take concrete steps in our chosen direction, and to implement our priorities in our everyday decisions. Ultimately, we embody our calling one decision at a time in our everyday personal and organizational life.

Every decision is a threshold, an entrance into the life and fullness of personhood we dream and desire. At the threshold, we come alive with creative newness, taking all the gifts and baggage of the past and recreating ourselves in dialogue with the possible. In the threshold moments of attentive decision-making, we have the opportunity to go beyond the complacencies of repetition and mindless sameness, to dream something bold into being.

Guidelines without Guarantees

Ideally, in each decision we make, we seek wisdom. It would be easy if we could just point to some list of commandments or precepts for our answers in the complex situations of our lives. But we know there isn't any recipe to follow or any checklist that guarantees wise decisions. Rather, we often feel as if we are in a mist, cautiously making our way forward and sometimes totally fogged in. Some days, the waves are high and the winds are strong and it takes all we have to remember the basics of navigation. In these situations, as well as in less difficult circumstances, it is important to have some ground rules for considering our options, some ways of asking ourselves key questions that might give us a glimpse of the way forward.

The search for wisdom is ultimately the challenge to live with meaning and joy, to find the deep satisfaction that comes from answering our particular call, and being responsive and responsible to others. It means finding a purpose that is certainly bigger than our own pleasures, a "true north" that gives us a direction in tune with a larger and deeper story of persons and community. To seek wisdom requires we sail on that heading or as close as we can get given the winds and waves of our circumstances. I hope this book might provide an exploration of key wisdom principles and questions that help us navigate toward "true north." I am easily blown off course and often distracted by wants and illusions and easy fixes. The common wisdom themes explored in these chapters come from my own desire to sail closer to that heading which brings greater meaning and joy in my life. As I was caring for my partner in his final months of life, what was most important became very clear. I didn't have to agonize over prioritizing a long list of projects, errands, and activities. I spent most of the last month of his life sitting by his bed, holding his hand, and listening to his few words. Here is one of my reflections on that profound experience:

BY BREATH

If you hold the hand of a dying man
it will change you. You will learn to count
each breath, sit in silence in your own soft skin

and let time take as long as it wants.
You will learn the sun's ritual, the round path
it walks each day, the discipline and the bright wonder.

The tick of the clock will not annoy you
and if there is a word or two, you will listen as if
your life depended on it. Not much else will matter,

the dishes, the laundry, the paint
peeling in the summer heat. Sitting at the side
of his bed even when he is sleeping will be enough.

You may not be able to say exactly what
has changed but you will pronounce your name
as if it were hyphenated, wedded to river, orbit, earth.

You will watch trees bow and grasses lie
down before the wind as if it were your own story
and sometimes you will quiet the constant questions

and even the voice of wishes and wonder.
You will breathe one breath at a time as if your
life depended on it, your whole life depended on it.

Each of us has moments in life when things are crystal clear,
when a decision or action seems to flow from us effortlessly. These
times and our responses are important indications of the way forward
in other circumstances of our lives. The clarity of direction in these
times helps us to see how we might better respond to our own core
values in other more ambiguous situations.

Wisdom Principles, Operating Procedures, and Criteria

In this book, I focus on five wisdom principles that are consistent, clear threads in several religious traditions. These wisdom principles are found in the teachings, scriptures, rituals, practices, and exemplars of major religions. At the outset, I want to acknowledge that our explorations into the religions will be like dipping the tip of an extra-fine paint brush in the ocean. I can only hint at how these principles resonate with some small aspect of a few religious wisdom traditions. Although we will be using the common terms for the major religions, it is important to recognize that often these terms were created by observers from outside who oversimplified the diversity of religious practice and understanding.

The five principles are: (1) Respect all persons; (2) appreciate the wholeness of being human; (3) recognize the interconnectedness of all reality; (4) value inner wisdom and personal experience; (5) attend to preservation and transformation. From each of these principles, I develop two procedural suggestions for a wise decision-making process and two criteria to help in making judgments. The procedures for wise decision-making open us to creative alternatives; they are not envisioned as a fixed, lock-step regimen. Rather, they suggest certain considerations, helpful ways of asking questions, methods for deep listening, and practices for exploring concrete reality that might be instrumental in reaching a wise decision.

I also suggest criteria for making wise judgments. A criterion is a standard or test that needs to be met. Whereas the operating procedures help us identify *how* we might go about making wise decisions, the criteria identify the ultimate measures for *what* is wise. Applying these criteria often requires weighing risks and benefits, sensing what is good and appropriate, being attentive to fundamental rights and duties. Sometimes, the criteria will seem to be in conflict with one another. One criterion may have more weight in a particular situation than another. Sometimes all ten of the criteria will line up in support of a particular decision. As I have noted previously, having a set of standard operating procedures for wise decision-making and a set of criteria for judging the wisdom of a decision does not make the work of practical wisdom less difficult. However, it grounds this work of making tough decisions and gives it a sure footing. When we use these procedures and criteria, we know we are asking questions and considering values that have been proven to be helpful across the ages and among a broad diversity of peoples and faith perspectives.

Although I delineate five core principles of common wisdom, I am not suggesting these are the only central threads of the wisdom traditions across cultures and religions. Rather, I hope the operating procedures and criteria here articulated will be an effective starting point for discernment that might open out into further considerations and integrate spiritual traditions into everyday decision-making. On both an individual and organizational level, these principles and their related procedures and criteria help us weigh options, search for truth, and make judgments among competing possibilities or ways of thinking and acting. For many, this process of wise decision-making is seen as the attempt to hear the creative, transformative call of God luring us into the best possible future. However you articulate a higher power or encompassing reality, the aim of this model is to help you move forward individually or organizationally using a respectful, reflective process that welcomes and engages the world's spiritual traditions. As you become acquainted with this model and use it in several situations, you may wish to add principles and questions. You may articulate additional operating procedures that help you access the wisdom of our common humanity. You may identify other criteria that integrate other dimensions of the history of human wisdom.

Wisdom as Transformation of Consciousness

Ultimately, practical wisdom is not about following a procedure or applying a criterion; it requires the transformation of our consciousness. Cynthia Bourgeault in *The Wisdom Jesus* articulates this transformation with these "timeless and deeply personal questions: What does it mean to die before you die? How do you go about losing your little life to find the bigger one? Is it possible to live on this planet with a generosity, abundance, fearlessness, and beauty that mirror Divine Being itself?"[16] Of course, this transformation of consciousness is a lifelong process. It takes practice and more practice and more practice to learn to respond in our everyday circumstances with deep listening and unconditional love, openness and healing, deep sensitivity and clear mindedness, fully present in the moment and open to the new.

For organizations, this transformed consciousness means that decisions will be made with an expanded set of criteria that include not only financial considerations, but measures of employee satisfaction and well being, as well as the assessment of the organization's impact on the human and natural communities. We can no longer focus on one bottom line; organizations must be responsible to provide not only dividends for shareholders but also respectful workplaces for employees and caring, sustainable communities.

The kind of wise decision-making envisioned in this model is consistent with the idea of *The Servant as Leader* envisioned by Robert Greenleaf (1970, 1991),[17] who listens deeply, looks for the transformative possibilities, asks about the wellness and autonomy of the whole community, takes time to hear people's stories, and keeps learning. When we make decisions using this comprehensive model for wise discernment, we will transform the organizational structures and practices that keep us focused on the financial bottom line without an equal focus on the heart of employee wellness and communal and environmental well-being. If organizations continue to opt for an either-or attitude, the plight of the human community looks bleak. Leaders with more holistic models of leadership have the possibility of being a leaven in their own communities and areas of influence. New models of leadership, such as servant leadership, authentic leadership, compassionate leadership, and primal leadership are essential to healing the gaping wounds that the old models of leadership have inflicted and are still inflicting on persons, communities, and the earth.[18]

The transformation of consciousness comes over time as we practice using the procedures and criteria for wise decision-making. Years of disciplined application of these methods and standards leads to their internalization, so it becomes natural to approach decisions in this way. In the meantime, the operating procedures for wise decision-making are important in both personal and organizational contexts because when we are in crisis, our vision often narrows. We need a procedure that opens us to creative alternatives and allows us to see the full complexity and possibility of the reality before us. As the importance of a decision increases, so also does the tension and anxiety of those who are making the decision. If a short timeframe for consideration is added to the situation, there is often tremendous pressure to stay within established paradigms and mindsets. When we are worried or nervous or fearful, we are also prone to acting out of our shadow side.

Understanding the Shadow

To understand the *shadow*, we look to the work of Carl Jung, the eminent Swiss psychologist. He identified the shadow as the aspects of individuals that are denied or not expressed, the qualities or impulses that often go against what we desire or judge acceptable. For example, if you feel an overwhelming rage coming up in you when a friend mentions a particular fault, you can be fairly sure that a deeper look at your reaction and what's behind it will lead you to face a part of your shadow.[19]

Our shadow side is often revealed in circumstances in which we exhibit an immediate, deep reaction. When we see this happening in others, we often talk about it in the following terms: "Who pushed his buttons?" "What got into her?" "He just exploded!" In these kinds of situations, some aspect of the dark side has erupted to the surface. Our anger may be out of proportion to the offense. When we are unaware of our shadow, it can have tremendous power in our lives. It can drive decisions without our awareness. As long as it remains hidden, the shadow will do its destructive work, often wreaking havoc on our ordered existence, taking us down the wrong roads.

Persons with significant power in organizations may cast a large shadow or may shine a great light. A powerful teacher can kindle the light of learning for children or create shadowy conditions that stunt exploration and growth. This is true for the leadership in every kind of organization. Parker Palmer poignantly describes several key shadows of leaders and how they may be transformed.[20] According to Palmer, one common leadership shadow is the "belief that ultimate responsibility for everything" rests on the leader.[21] Such a leader will have great difficulty in trusting others to do important research that might impact a decision. Another shadow is a pattern of inner insecurity in which the leader denies others their own strength by filling up every discussion with his or her words and ideas without hearing the diverse and insightful voices of others. Using procedures for wise decision-making will ensure that these kinds of shadows don't keep us from important considerations.

Often it is easier to see the shadows of others than it is to face our own. It is difficult to shine the light on our personal insecurities and fears, our own blind spots. We all have shadows, but we often don't realize their impact on our lives and organizations. One of the great gifts of serious reflection is being able to see our own shadows. Reflection allows us to be aware of our true motivations. With the light on, there is nothing to fear and I am not taken by surprise. Without reflection, we may find ourselves making a remark in the heat of battle and asking ourselves later, "Where did that come from?" With practice, we can catch ourselves trying to deny, steamroll, manipulate, or use other maneuvers. The procedures for wise decision-making help us face our shadows. They help us reflect on our deepest motivations, the effect important relationships have had on our interpretation of reality, and the ways of responding to life that come from our childhood. Shining light on the shadow in the course of the decision-making process means we do less reacting and more responding. Having a set of operating procedures for wise decision-making can open us to the diversity of possibilities and get us beyond our blind spots by providing a structure for rich input and deep consideration.

To make wise decisions, we also need criteria for deciding, or a basis for judgment. I have identified two key standards that flow from each of the five wisdom principles. These can be thought of as the basic building codes that our decision must meet. These criteria help us test our decision and look at it from a larger perspective. The criteria keep us in touch with core values across the wisdom traditions as we consider our best possible decision in the present moment.

The following chapters will explore in turn each of the wisdom principles and the operating procedures and criteria that flow from them.

WISDOM PRINCIPLES	OPERATING PROCEDURES	CRITERIA FOR JUDGMENT CHOOSE WHAT...
Principle 1. Respect all persons.	OP 1A. Expand the listening process.	C 1A. Contributes to the common good.
	OP 1B. Create seats at the table for the marginalized.	C 1B. Takes into account the poor and powerless.
Principle 2. Appreciate the wholeness of being human.	OP 2A. Explore all the ways of human knowing.	C 2A. Values the whole person.
	OP 2B. Make room for silence.	C 2B. Brings balance and integration.
Principle 3. Recognize the interconnectedness of all reality.	OP 3A. Consider how systems will be impacted.	C 3A. Responds to needs of the whole community.
	OP 3B. Research effects on community and environment.	C 3B. Attends to the long term health of the earth.
Principle 4. Value inner wisdom and personal experience.	OP 4A. Reflect on experience deeply and broadly.	C 4A. Addresses the full reality of the present experience.
	OP 4B. Inquire into values, vision and best practices.	C 4B. Is most constructive to life.
Principle 5. Attend to preservation and transformation.	OP 5A. Be attentive to origins and foundations.	C 5A. Preserves the core focus and vision.
	OP 5B. Practice radical creativity.	C 5B. Moves toward the boldest possibility.

Decide with Humility and Confidence

Before investigating each of these principles of practical wisdom and how they might be concretized in operating procedures for decision-making and in standards for judging among competing alternatives, it is important to consider three insights that set the proper tone for this exploration: (1) Be humble; (2) seek confidence, not certainty; and (3) love the questions. The first insight is that we approach wise decision-making with deep humility because our human knowing and understanding is always imperfect. The English word *humility* shares the same root as *humus* and is derived from the Latin for *earth* or *soil*. We are earth creatures, even if the image of the divine shines in us. We see things from the earth, not from some heavenly perspective that is infallible. This insight cautions us against stubbornness and authoritarianism.

All of our decisions will be limited and based on incomplete knowledge. The insight of humility asks us to be careful of idolatry—of making a god out of our models or policies or structures. The great monastic traditions of the middle ages understood the spiritual life as a journey of humility. Saint Benedict, the author of one of the first comprehensive monastic rules, identified twelve degrees of humility, a process of letting go of self-centeredness and opening oneself to the fullness of wisdom through patience and subduing pridefulness.[22] When we recognize the limits of our perspective, we might be tempted to postpone unnecessarily the making of decisions until every contingency and possibility is considered, until every piece of research is in, until there is no ambiguity. But there's the rub: There will always be ambiguity in human decision-making.

The second insight balances the first: we must seek confidence, not certainty. It is right and proper for individuals to choose to act without waiting for an incontrovertible answer. In fact, there may not be an uncontestable resolution to many of the key questions that face us. On the one hand, the pressure to decide and act quickly should not prevent a regular practice of discerning more deeply and broadly. On the other hand, the lack of a conclusive answer should not prevent persons from acting, from making the best judgment possible with the given information after wise consideration. Any decision must be based on the individual's or group's web of experience, the interwoven strands of human influence that affect each person's way of seeing the world. The decisions will stand the test of conscience as long as that web of experience is being continually expanded by analyzing data, clarifying principles, listening to experts and authorities, stretching one's vision beyond its present scope, and living with integrity based on one's present worldview. Expanding the web of experience requires searching beyond one culture, beyond one discipline of expertise, and beyond the present time. With this broadening of the web of experience, persons become more fully informed as they seek coherence among the many considerations in the search for truth and make decisions with forethought and good will.

It is difficult to express this idea of deciding with confidence but without certainty. Yet, it is so crucial to not get stuck in the decision-making process with a false notion that no stone can be left unturned. A wise process will be comprehensive but not exhaustive; it will entail listening to a diversity of stakeholders and those who are often left out of the conversation, but not necessarily everyone. It will include serious reflection, but there will be limits to the "gestation" period. The closest I've ever gotten to adequately expressing this paradoxical aspect of wise decision-making is in my poem "Morning Glory."

MORNING GLORY

The morning glories climb
forever, spiral around anything
that will stand still and listen

to their lusty trumpets blare
the essence of amethyst and azure.
Where their flesh touches

trellis or branch, supple cells
rush to twirl, coil, circle
like the gathering of elders

and children around the campfire,
always creating the round circuit
of faces facing each other, telling

their stories and knowing how
to hang on and reach upward.
Oh, to have such simple wisdom,

to have it live in your body,
to have such green flesh
that everywhere it touches

creates a circle, spiral of hope,
so the lush feast of the flower
can give itself away for the only

day it will ever have. Take
the next step without knowing
everything, without certainty,

on the steep climb feeling for footholds.
Look for the circle, listen to the dream
calling in your marrow, muscle, blood.

Spiral toward hope, truth, bread,
like the morning glories with their wise
green hands climbing toward the light.

Love the Questions

A final insight is important to set the proper tone for the exploration of our five wisdom principles. Wise decision-making is best
approached with an attitude that loves the questions and values the
balance between reflection and action. In articulating this insight, I
rely on the beautiful words of Rainer Maria Rilke in his *Letters to a
Young Poet*:

> I would like to beg of you, dear friend, as well as I can, to
> have patience with everything that remains unsolved in
> your heart. Try to love the questions themselves, like
> locked rooms and like books written in a foreign language.
> Do not now look for the answers. They cannot now be
> given to you because you could not live them. It is a ques-
> tion of experiencing everything. At present you need to
> live the question.[23]

This attitude of "living the question" seems contrary to the sense of
urgency that is often experienced when persons are faced with critical issues that need to be decided. But time and again, maturity
requires living in the tension between polarities, embracing the par-

adox, rather than running full speed ahead in one direction. Rilke's words point to a respect for the questions themselves. It is not only patience that he espouses here but also an attitude of acceptance and valuation regarding the questions. Participants in a wise decision-making process must respect the questions and be willing to live with them. Even within the context of urgency, we must be able to create an open space where we can truly consider, converse, and reflect. I offer the following chapters as the beginning of a conversation about wise decision-making, a conversation that I hope continues within yourself and among your family, friends, and coworkers as each of us attempts to live more wisely.

Questions for Reflection

What is one of the best decisions you ever made? What was the process you went through to make this decision?

What is one of the worst decisions you ever made? What was the process you went through to make this decision? How could the process have been improved?

What two concrete actions might you be able to take in your personal or professional life in the next three months that would enlarge your perspective and open yourself to more creative possibilities in your decision-making?

An Assessment of Shadow Awareness

The following assessment may help you understand how aware of your shadow you are. As you rate yourself, try to think of concrete examples in the last month of each of the areas that you are rating. If you are unable to recall specific examples of your self-knowledge, you may wish to rate yourself on the lower end of the scale. If you are able to articulate for yourself specific instances of clear self-awareness, you may wish to rate yourself on the higher end of the scale.

I face what is painful in myself.

High 9 8 7 6 5 4 3 2 Low

I know what pushes my buttons.

High 9 8 7 6 5 4 3 2 Low

I deal with conflict openly and constructively in my
workplace/family/etc.

High 9 8 7 6 5 4 3 2 Low

I say what's on my mind.

High 9 8 7 6 5 4 3 2 Low

I am trying to be more deeply aware of my blind spots.

High 9 8 7 6 5 4 3 2 Low

RESPECT ALL PERSONS

WISDOM PRINCIPLE	OPERATING PROCEDURES	CRITERIA FOR JUDGMENT CHOOSE WHAT...
Principle 1. Respect all persons.	OP 1A. Expand the listening process.	C 1A. Contributes to the common good.
	OP 1B. Create seats at the table for the marginalized.	C 1B. Takes into account the poor and powerless.

*P*aul came into the leadership course in the Doctor of Nursing Practice program with a passion for nursing. He had been a nurse practitioner for several years and he was deeply satisfied with his role in a collaborative orthopedic practice. When we focused on the art of listening in the servant leadership model and the importance of each person in a circle of support, I began with a poem that came out of my own passion for creating a community of learners in which each voice matters. "In Circles" begins with the following lines:

> We place ourselves in circles and huddles
> knowing somehow that this way of being together
> signs the shape of our dreams and longings.
>
> From space we see ourselves round,
> connected to one another, facing each other,
> with all our differences, dancing around the sun together.
>
> For centuries we have been trying to bring
> the circle down from mystery skies,
> to set it stone solid in our hearts, to memorize
> the knowing of each preciousness
> equally gift to the circle of whole.

When I asked the group to share examples of deep listening to the preciousness of their patients or fellow team members, Paul shared a simple, powerful story. He told of a young teenager who came in with two broken fingers and a smashed knuckle on his right hand. When he asked the young man what happened, he brashly said he had punched a wall pretty hard. Paul picked up on the edge of anger in the young man's voice and asked why he punched the wall. After a shrug from the boy, his mother added, "His father just told him about his cancer diagnosis and I guess Brett was feeling pretty mad about that." Paul suggested that the family might find it beneficial to have a few sessions with a family counselor. He went on to tell our class how important it was for him to really listen to his patients, to make the time to hear their story. When the young man and his mother returned several weeks later, they thanked Paul for his suggestion and talked about how much the family counseling had helped all of them get their feelings out on the table. Without articulating this first core theme of spiritual wisdom, *Respect All Persons*, Paul was carrying it out in his workplace. He felt positive about his work because he was integrating his own spiritual values into his profession. This theme of respect for all persons is at the heart of religious traditions across the world.

Respect for Persons in Spiritual Traditions

This central thread of seeing the preciousness of persons is woven throughout the writings and practices of religions throughout the world. Hinduism, Buddhism, and Jainism share the central guiding principle of nonviolence or nonharming because they recognize the value of every sentient being. In these spiritual traditions, respecting and loving oneself and others is the first guideline for right living. Nonharming is understood as a universal principle, applying to everyone, no matter the time, place, or particular nature or character of the living being. All are to be acknowledged and respected. As a person learns to live in this nonharming way, relationships include fewer conflicts and less anxiety; they become more truthful, forthright, and marked by true listening.

Nonviolence does not mean being passive or disengaged from life's concerns. Rather, it requires inner and outer balance and courage. Nonviolent persons create space in their lives for silence, play, and self-caring. When we experience imbalance or "dis-ease," we often lash out at others because we feel hurried, pressured, or anxious. Perhaps you've had the experience of a very difficult, conflict-filled day at work followed by a lack of patience when you got home. When we haven't taken time out for ourselves for a while, we often find we get angry more quickly and react instead of respond. Thus, nonviolence requires balancing action and contemplation, service and rest, outward focus and inward focus. Lack of care for self often leads to subtle forms of violence—controlling behavior, over-protection, and worry.

Nonviolent persons have the courage to confront their own fears and apprehensions. It is not unusual for us to create distance between ourselves and that which we fear—other persons whom we don't understand or situations that are outside of our experience. To be nonviolent means we proactively close the distance between ourselves and others, between ourselves and experiences that may seem uncomfortable. Deborah Adele in *The Yamas and Niyamas: Exploring Yoga's Ethical Practice* calls this softening "the boundaries that keep us separated from what we don't understand."[1] This idea of softening the boundaries seems full of wisdom. It suggests that nonviolent persons are gentle with themselves and with others. They practice a way of openness that invites rather than demands, that allows rather than controls. Concretely, nonharming may require the courage to start up a conversation with someone with whom we feel ill at ease, or to apologize to someone who seems hurt by something we said.

Nonharming also requires the courage to confront injustice, to respond when others are being treated poorly, and to address structures and policies that keep those at the margins of society powerless. Such courageous actions arise out of listening deeply to the stories of the disenfranchised and having the heart to feel their plight through empathy and compassion. These courageous actions are best carried out in collaboration and conversation with those who are being oppressed.

THE VOW OF THE BODDHISATTVA

A deep respect for all persons is also revealed in the Buddhist vow of the bodhisattva who is committed to the awakening and welfare of all beings. The bodhisattva vow takes many forms. A beautiful form of the vow was authored by Shantideva, a monk in the seventh-eighth centuries CE who wrote a guide to the bodhisattva's life. A few verses will give you a sense of the scope and intention of the vow.

> May I be a protector to the helpless,
> A guide to those travelling the path,
> A boat to those wishing to cross over;
> Or a bridge or a raft.
>
> May I be land for those requiring it,
> A lamp for those in darkness,
> May I be a home for the homeless,
> And a servant for the world.
>
> May I act as the mighty earth
> Or like the free and open skies
> To support and provide space
> Whereby I and all others may grow.
>
> Until every being afflicted by pain
> Has reached Nirvana's shores,
> May I serve only as a condition
> That encourages progress and joy.[2]

This seemingly unrealistic and impractical promise states the radical nature of the bodhisattva's regard for every sentient being. Jack Kornfield, in *The Wise Heart: A Guide to the Universal Teachings of Buddhist Psychology*, explains the perspective of the bodhisattva.

> Does this mean that I am going to run around and save six billion humans and trillions of other beings? How can I do so? When we think about it from our limited sense of self, it is impossible. But when we make it an intention of the heart, we understand. To take such a vow is a direction, a sacred purpose, a statement of wisdom, an offering, a blessing. When the world is seen with the eyes of a bodhisattva, there is no I and other, there is just us.[3]

Kornfield expresses the first principle of Buddhist psychology as "See the inner nobility and beauty of all human beings."[4] The popular story of the Sukotai Buddha expresses the depth and challenge of this principle. Tradition has it that in Sukotai, Thailand's ancient capital, a massive, ten-foot high, clay seated Buddha was created sometime between the thirteenth and fifteenth centuries, a period of great artistic development. Later, the statue was moved to Bangkok and installed as the principal Buddha image in the main building of the Choti-naram Temple during the reign of Thailand's King Rama III (1824-51). The temple was deserted around 1931 and the clay Buddha was moved to a temporary shelter, since it was thought to have very little value. When the clay Buddha was relocated to a new temple in Bangkok in the 1950s (during the expansion of the Port of Bangkok), it slipped from a crane and fell into the mud. According to folklore, in the morning a monk, "who had dreamed that the statue was divinely inspired, went to see the Buddha. Through a crack in the plaster he saw a glint of yellow and soon discovered that the statue was pure gold...."[5] The golden Buddha had been camouflaged to protect it from being ransacked and destroyed. In a time of threat, its true beauty was covered with clay. The camouflage was so thorough that when those responsible for covering it died, so did the knowledge of the true nature of the Buddha image inside.

Buddhist practice requires more than not harming other beings. It requires that we recognize the gold under the clay, the preciousness of every ordinary person and every being. In her insightful exploration of the Buddha, Karen Armstrong says, "*Ahimsa* could only take one part of the way: instead of simply avoiding violence, an aspirant must behave gently and kindly to everything and everybody; he must cultivate thoughts of loving-kindness to counter any incipient feelings of ill will."[6] One of the central texts of the Pali Canon, the earliest writings based on oral traditions about the Buddha's life and teaching, is the *metta sutta* on universal love. This teaching of the Buddha says,

> Just as a mother would protect her only child even at the risk of her own life, even so let one cultivate a boundless heart towards all beings. Let one's thoughts of boundless love pervade the whole world—above, below and

across—without any obstruction, without any hatred, without any enmity.[7]

The teaching of universal love evident in the Buddhist, Hindu, and Jain traditions is shared by many other spiritual traditions as well, as can be seen by how they express the Golden Rule.[8]

THE GOLDEN RULE IN
DIVERSE SPIRITUAL TRADITIONS

Baha'i Faith:

Lay not on any soul a load that you would not wish to be laid upon you, and desire not for anyone the things you would not desire for yourself. (Baha'ullah, Gleanings)

Buddhism:

Treat not others in ways that you yourself would find hurtful. (The Buddha, Udana-Varga 5.18)

Christianity:

In everything, do to others as you would have them do to you; for this is the law and the prophets. (Jesus, Matthew 7:12)

Confucianism:

One word which sums up the basis of all good conduct...loving-kindness. Do not do to others what you do not want done to yourself. (Confucius, Analects 15.23)

Hinduism:

This is the sum of duty: do not to others what would cause pain if done to you. (Mahabharata 5:1517)

Islam:

Not one of you truly believes until you wish for others what you wish for yourself. (The Prophet Muhammad, Hadith)

Jainism:

One should treat all creatures in the world as one would like to be treated. (Mahavira, Sutrakritanga 1.11.33)

Judaism:

What is hateful to you, do not do to your neighbor. This is the whole Torah; all the rest is commentary. Go and learn it. (Hillel, Talmud, Shabbath 31a)

Sikhism:

I am a stranger to no one; and no one is a stranger to me. Indeed, I am a friend to all. (Guru Granth Sahib, 1299)

Taoism:

Regard your neighbour's gain as your own gain and your neighbour's loss as your own loss. (Lao Tzu, T'ai Shang Kan Ying P'ien, 213-218)

Unitarianism:

We affirm and promote respect for the interdependent web of all existence of which we are a part. (Unitarian principle)

Zoroastrianism:

Do not do unto others whatever is injurious to yourself. (Shayast-na-Shayast 13.29)

Although we cannot explore all of these traditions here, a few examples will help to demonstrate how these different articulations of the fundamental rule of reciprocity or mutuality are embedded in the spiritual traditions.

LOVE OF NEIGHBOR IN
JUDAISM AND CHRISTIANITY

In the Jewish tradition, love of neighbor is grounded in the creation story; the human being is made in the image of God. Many scholars recognize two creation stories in the Book of Genesis. The first one comes from the time of the monarchy and presents an all-powerful God who creates human beings by word. God *says* and it happens, male and female God creates persons in the divine image. In the second creation story, written much earlier, God creates by hand and forms the human being out of the clay of the ground and blows into the nostrils the breath of life. The human being is literally inspired and, therefore, becomes a living, spirit-filled being. In both stories, the person is created uniquely and bears the mark of God.

The Christian tradition centers on the value of each person as created in God's image as well. Responding to the preciousness of persons, Jesus in his ministry and teaching constantly reaches out to the poor and the rich, the sick and the well, the powerless and the powerful, and the sinner (that's everybody). In the gospel parables, Jesus repeatedly turns his listeners' assumptions about who is saved, who is good, and who knows the truth upside down. He tells them to follow the example of little children, for "...it is to such as these that the kingdom of God belongs" (Mark 10:14). In Luke's gospel, when the lawyer asks Jesus, "...what must I do to inherit eternal life?" (Luke 10:25), Jesus answers with the story of the Good Samaritan. The Samaritan, a member of a people that was judged by the Jews of the time to be unclean and unrighteous, is held up as the one who truly understands the law and does it (Luke 10: 25-37). A learned Jewish lawyer fully versed in the law with the confidence and skill to challenge this teacher who has been drawing crowds of people is told to follow the example of the people he has been taught to despise. Again, in Luke's gospel, when Jesus tells the parable of God's king-dom in the banquet story, he tells the servants to go out not just to the "streets and lanes of the town [to] bring in the poor, the crippled, the blind and the lame" but "out into the roads and lanes" to fill the banquet hall with all manner of people (Luke 14:21-23). Jesus eats with sinners and tax-collectors. He forgives the woman accused of adultery. At the heart of Jesus' message and ministry are a radical inclusiveness and an empathic identification with a broad diversity of persons, especially with the oppressed.

RESPECT FOR ALL PERSONS IN ISLAM

The welfare of the poor and the disenfranchised is also a cen-tral concern of the Quran. Many of the earliest recitations that Muhammad revealed were clearly focused on the universal moral duty to respect all persons, especially the hungry, orphaned, or needy.

In summing up the early message of Muhammad, Reza Aslan in *No god But God* says:

> In the strongest terms, Muhammad decried the mistreatment and exploitation of the weak and unprotected. He called for an end to false contracts and the practice of usury that had made slaves of the poor. He spoke of the rights of the underprivileged and the oppressed, and made the astonishing claim that it was the duty of the rich and the powerful to take care of them.[9]

Muhammad's teaching and actions reveal a thoroughly egalitarian perspective. His social and religious reforms were centered on closing the huge gap between the rich and the poor. His tax-free market in Yathrib and institution of a mandatory tithe, the *zakat*, are examples that struck at the roots of inequality in his societal milieu. Perhaps his focus on equality is most evident "in the rights and privileges he bestowed upon the women in his community."[10]

Principle One
Operating Procedures and Criteria

The wisdom principle of respect for all persons is embedded throughout many spiritual traditions. How might we put it into practice in the decision-making process? Here are two implications of this principle for the process of wise decision-making. First, because everyone is to be respected, we must expand the listening process when making decisions. Listening to a diversity of stakeholders has a twofold benefit: (1) It allows us to access the broader wisdom that comes from hearing and integrating multiple perspectives, and (2) it provides a powerful message to those who are heard. They are valued, their voice and perspective matter. The root meaning of the word *respect* comes from the Latin meaning "to see again." Literally, to respect someone means to see them, to recognize their preciousness and inestimable worth, to take account of them. Ultimately, there is no greater gift we can give another person than our undivided attention.

Second, the principle of respect for all requires that we provide seats at the decision-making table for those who come from the margins, whose voices often go unheard. A wise discernment process will listen attentively to those who are assumed to have nothing important to say. Such a process for decision-making values the voices of difference and takes time to hear the stories of those who have diverse experiences, assumptions, and ways of seeing. In order for the discernment process to fruitfully serve the wise decision, it must be marked not by exclusion but by intentional, hospitable, and attentive inclusion.

UNDERSTANDINGS OF TRUTH

These operating procedures that focus on expanding the listening process rest on a particular approach to truth that I call the searcher perspective. In my experience, there are three basic mindsets regarding truth: absolutist, relativist, and searcher. The absolutist asserts that the truth is unchanging and is the same for all persons at all times and in all cultures. The absolutist also asserts that he or she knows the truth because it is revealed through sacred writings, prophetic utterances, or some divine or revered authority. Some absolutists refer to personal revelation or keen, exceptional knowledge as the source for knowing the truth. Absolutists are generally not interested in enlarging the listening process with diverse perspectives, since they are not seeking new insight. They believe they have the right answer and, therefore, listening with true openness to change is not possible.

On the other end of the spectrum from the absolutist is the relativist perspective which understands the truth as plural. For the relativist, there is no such thing as the truth; because there are many truths dependent upon the experience, upbringing, and societal context of the individual. The truth changes from age to age, culture to culture, religion to religion, or even person to person. Although the relativist position seems antithetical to the absolutist, both positions are fundamentally closed to a sincere investigation of alternative viewpoints. For both the absolutist and the relativist, the question of truth is closed. The absolutist has the absolute truth and the relativist has his or her relative truth. Generally, relativists are not interested in enlarging the listening process since the truth of each culture, tradition, or person is equally valid.

Both the absolutist and relativist positions seem limited for different reasons. The absolutist perspective fails to take into account the experience and wisdom of caring, thoughtful, and intelligent persons who take very different and sometimes even contradictory positions. The relativist perspective fails to take into account that truth is more than a mental exercise. How we understand the truth really has an impact on the decisions we make and how those affect others in our community. In theory, it may make sense that everyone has their own truth and everyone's truth is just as valid as another person's truth. In real life, if you are a relativist and rocket-propelled grenades are landing in your back yard, you are probably not willing to assert the equal validity of all positions. The searcher position takes into account the real diversity of perspectives held by kind and reflective persons, and it encourages the fact that we human beings inhabit one planet and rely on the inextricably interconnected web of life together, requiring us to recognize common values and rules to guide our behavior.

The searcher takes the perspective that there must be universal truth or we would have no way of judging among the multiple positions that often confront us. Searchers believe there is some common truth that provides the foundation for identifying growth and advancement in ethical reasoning and choosing. Without some universal truth, we would have no foundation for recognizing some human actions as better than others. There would be no basis for identifying positive social change regarding civil rights or historical progress regarding humane structures of governance or healthcare.

The searcher also recognizes that we do not know the absolute truth at present. We may have glimpses and hints and important indications of the truth, but we are still searching to expand our knowledge and insight. That search requires us to listen deeply and openly to a diversity of perspectives. As far as possible, the searcher explores human experience and thought across disciplines, cultures, religions, and historical periods. Interdisciplinary investigation brings together the insights from experts who see and understand reality from multiple perspectives, including philosophy, science, theology, sociology, and so forth. An interreligious investigation takes seriously the multiple spiritual perspectives from traditions throughout the world. A cross-cultural perspective requires sympathetic experiencing of different human ways of being in the world. Languages, rituals, and customs in one culture may allow certain aspects of reality to appear that may not be seen in other cultures. The searcher is also involved in a macro-temporal quest, reflecting on past human experience and imaginatively envisioning future possibilities.

Radical openness to the experience and insights of others is at the heart of the searcher position. Paradoxically, at the same time, the searcher must be willing to voice his or her best understanding of reality in the present moment. Only when persons have the courage to articulate their most closely held insights and to listen with an openness to be transformed is the quest for truth served, according to the searcher position. Together searchers create a learning community where there is both respect for diversity and rigorous attention to differences of understanding. They look for consistency of values and rules across areas of investigation. They note how a reasoning process exhibits coherence or lacks harmony among its parts. Searchers are attentive to confirmation of an idea or insight from several traditions or disciplines.

Implementing a decision-making process that respects all persons requires a searcher perspective on truth. Although each person involved in the process clearly formulates and articulates his or her position, together the searchers create a spacious place where diversity and creativity are welcome. As mentioned in the introduction, this doesn't mean the process is interminable. Sometimes decisions must be made within narrow time constraints. Nonetheless, when a searcher perspective on truth is the underlying understanding, persons will believe there is a best answer and they can get closest to that best answer by deeply listening to each other.

OPERATING PROCEDURE 1A:
EXPAND THE LISTENING PROCESS

At first glance, this operating procedure of expanding the listening process seems easy. It may take the form of cross-functional teams in an organizational context, bringing together persons with diverse expertise and roles. In a personal decision-making context, it might mean intentionally inviting the perspective of someone who is older or younger or with different kinds of experience. In both the personal and organizational contexts, it takes time to create conversations or participate in research in which multiple perspectives are explored and evaluated. The most difficult challenge, however, is to actually hear the perspectives that are different from our own, to get beyond our own assumptions and mental models. There are particular ways in which deep listening to difference can be enhanced through the process of dialogue. Through the pioneering work of David Bohm and the efforts of William Isaacs and the Dialogue Project at the Massachussets Institute of Technology, there is a growing body of literature exploring the practical strategies and procedures for hearing the deep wisdom that can emerge from a community of persons.

The dialogue process facilitates attentive listening to the voices of difference and focuses the energy of the group toward a collective intelligence that goes beyond polarization. In *Dialogue and the Art of Thinking Together*, Isaacs describes dialogue as

> a conversation in which people think together in relationship. Thinking together implies that you no longer take your own position as final. You relax your grip on certainty and listen to the possibilities that result simply from being in a relationship with others—possibilities that might not otherwise have occurred.[11]

To access the deeper wisdom that comes from attentiveness to difference, dialogue practice involves three basic rules: (1) speaking one's voice with honesty and integrity, (2) listening to the voices of others and to the voice of the whole with genuine openness, and (3) suspending one's own presuppositions, assumptions, and judgments to allow new thought to happen.[12] To follow any one of these guidelines deeply takes courage and sustained energy. To say what we really think always involves risk. What will others think of me? What if I'm the only one who thinks this way? Will telling my truth cost me a promotion or my job?

Speaking with Honesty and Integrity

This first guideline is very difficult to practice unless there is a climate of openness and respect. When I think of creating this kind of accepting culture, I am reminded of the story that supervisor Thom Creed often tells at TDIndustries, an employee-owned national mechanical construction facilities and service company headquartered in Dallas. TD's culture is founded on servant leadership, "which means we do everything with your best interests in mind."[13] Here is how TD explains putting flesh on that philosophy of service:

> Every TD employee (or TD Partner) completes Basic Servant Leadership training. Those that aspire to lead will spend many more hours in the classroom and get regular feedback on their performance. Our commitment to this philosophy has created an environment where partners trust leadership to listen to their thoughts and ideas. And, in turn, leadership has learned to trust the judgment of partners.... Leaders see things through the eyes of their followers. They put themselves in others' shoes and help them make their dreams come true.[14]

Thom tells the story of a particular supervisor's meeting when, as usual, there was significant discussion about the ideas presented by the founding president, Jack Lowe Sr. After the meeting ended, Thom and Jack stayed seated as the others filed out of the room. Across the circle of chairs, Jack mentioned how Thom had countered nearly every point he tried to make during the day-long meeting with a different perspective. Here's how Thom told the story:

> "Well," I said, "I hope I wasn't too hard on you." He said, "No, that's all right, Thom. Everybody had a chance to hear a different side of things, and I appreciate that. And on some of those points, I wasn't too sure which way to go anyway." So, he gets up and comes over behind me and puts his hand on one side of my face and he puts his face against mine and he says, "I love you, Creed." Then, he just walks on out of the room. ... So, I went and got in my goddamn truck and I said to myself, "That old bastard just told me he loved me." And I knew he did, and that he loved others, too. And I cried. That was the first time a grown man ever said that to me.[15]

Jack Lowe Sr. left a clear legacy for TDIndustries and this story continues to be told as a way of establishing the culture of openness, trust, and care that has repeatedly made it one of the 100 best companies to work for in *Fortune* magazine's annual rating every year since the rating was begun in 1998.[16]

Listening to Others and Suspending Judgment

The second and third dialogue rules involve listening to the voices of others and to the voice of the whole with genuine openness and the possibility of transformation. To truly hear another perspective requires that we drop our own assumptions and ways of looking at the world. It requires no less than stepping out of our own skin. This authentic speaking, deep listening, and open suspension of assumptions is facilitated by specific, simple guidelines such as sitting in a circle so the architecture of the gathering symbolizes the equal value given to each voice. The very way in which a group is arranged physically says something quite profound about how persons are invited into dialogue. The circle is an ancient technology for deeper understanding in community. Many indigenous peoples use some type of gathering circle, council circle, or circle of elders as part of their religious and/or political process. In the final stanzas of the "In Circles" poem mentioned at the beginning of this chapter, I recall those ancient traditions and the importance of the circle as a symbol of the equality of voices.

> Spirals etched in red rock canyon story the journey
> out of and into the center that holds all things together.
> Stonehenge pillars and lintels dragged for miles,
> scraped into meaning, set in sacred formation with sun and
>   moon.
> Conical mounds heaped into remembrance
> ritual the lives of elders who circle the fire of the tribe.
> Everywhere and ancient the circle
> is repeated, shaping us to its original wisdom.
>
> Give us each day our daily hunger
> to be more than we are now,
> to be less solitary selves doubting our place,

to be more a circle of connection and acceptance,
spherical harmony of the heavens.
Each one a single voice, a sacred story,
but always in the larger circle of meaning and mystery.

Other guidelines that serve the openness and valuation of difference in the process of dialogue and discernment include (1) allowing
space between speakers so the rhythm of exchange facilitates respect
and deep listening, (2) using "I" statements to limit the projection of
one's ideas and meanings onto others, (3) speaking to the center of the
circle rather than to specific individuals to soften the identification
between ideas and persons, and (4) reflecting on the common understandings arising in the group.

My experience with many dialogues with many different groups
has convinced me that it is one of the most valuable tools for accessing communal wisdom. I often suggest to my fellow learners that they
try out a couple of the guidelines at a time and attempt a deeper kind
of conversation with a friend or parents or a work group. I recently
received feedback from Scott Gradin, a creative restaurateur and
chef who took a leadership course with me. He reported that occasionally he and his managers lie on their backs in a circle with their
heads almost touching and gaze up at the stars and talk about their
hopes, dreams, and challenges. Scott says their dialogues help them
do very creative and high-pressure work together with a deep sense
of trust and care.[17]

However you integrate the guidelines articulated above into
your conversations, the exchange will usually become slower, deeper,
more open to radical newness, and more respectful. As with any
important skill, dialogue becomes more honest and fruitful as it is
practiced. It is best used, from my perspective, as a way of exploring
a topic or an issue before concrete visioning or planning is started.
Whether the business of the gathering is to create a vision or articulate action steps to solve a knotty problem, the work often goes much
more quickly after an open, honest dialogue has raised the real issues
and the multiple perspectives that people have about them in a non-
threatening environment.

My colleague, Bob Hartl, has become a strong proponent of dialogue as a fruitful tool in process consultation. Edgar Schein is the

originator of process consultation, which focuses on helping clients understand their own reality and create their own solution to any problems they identify through the consultation process.[18] The consultant does not presume to be an expert in solving the client's problem but only in facilitating processes that help the client understand their situation and create ways to improve it. In this context, Hartl sees dialogue as a "way that we can learn together and maybe, most importantly, become clear about our own thoughts, about whatever we are talking about in the dialogue. I often use it as a prelude to other things."[19]

Dialogue in Practice

Hartl tells of working with a government agency that was trying to make a decision about what to do with a state-funded museum and historical records site that was created and owned by the state, but had not been doing well financially for a number of years. They had a variety of consultants who tried to help them develop marketing plans and come up with strategies for making it more financially viable. None of the plans seemed to work very well. So the person who headed the government agency decided to put together a task-force of people that represented all of the stakeholders. The group was made up of twenty-five government officials, community leaders, and business people—people in favor of continuing the site, as well as those who thought it should be closed or its mission should be modified in some significant way. As Hartl met with the various individuals to ask them their viewpoints, it was clear the group represented the full spectrum of perspectives, from "it's a boondoggle and it should be shut down" to "this site is something the state owes us" to "this museum can be a wonderful resource for the surrounding communities."[20]

After these meetings with individuals, Hartl thought the consultation might be a long and arduous process of attempting to reach consensus, and he wasn't even sure that goal was realistic from listening to the conflicting opinions. One thing was very clear to him. He needed to create a process in which people could hear one another, a forum to simply listen to what other people had to say and, in the process, become clear about what they thought as individuals. He continues the story:

So when I met with the group, I put them in a dialogue circle. And I described a little bit about what the dialogue process is and talked about active suspension and used pretty much what Ed Schein would recommend. We don't look at each other when we speak, we look at an imaginary camp fire in the center and we talk to the campfire, not to each other. Don't feel compelled to seek clarity on issues that may sound fuzzy or funny to you at first. Let them stand and don't feel compelled to respond to questions whether they are directed to you or simply implied. You don't have to say a thing; you are empowered to remain silent. So, I think most of them found it to be kind of an odd experience at first. But after five minutes, it really started working. People were speaking from their hearts about how strongly they felt about whatever their viewpoint happened to be. And it went on almost uncontrolled for a long period of time, much longer than I had expected it would. And when it was done, after everyone had checked out of the dialogue, I just said, "Well, how did that go?" And someone said, one of the members said, this is the first time that I have understood that other viewpoint. I've always turned it off and started arguing my case before. I don't agree with it but I think I understand it. And one by one people said, this was a very good experience. We like this and we want to do more of this. So I worked with that group for several months. We had several meetings, one or two meetings a month and at the end of that time, that group came to a consensus about what to recommend to the state and the state followed through on their recommendation. So it's a very powerful way of people becoming clear about what they think and they do that based on hearing the perspectives of other people. And that was a wonderful experience and it really underscored to me the importance of dialogue.[21]

When the practical guidelines of dialogue are used to create a safe container for in-depth, honest sharing of difference and inclusive listening, the possibility for effective, authentic decision-making is enhanced. Allowing the voices of difference to be fully heard requires deep courage and open-mindedness. If the process of decision-making invites all the significant voices, especially the perspectives of difference from the margins, one's own perspective and worldview may be radically challenged.

A focus on deep listening to difference is one of the most practical applications of the inclusivity of the message and ministry of Jesus in the Rule of Saint Benedict which has been the guiding force for monastic communities as well as for countless lay persons since the sixth century. Benedict's purpose was to write a practical house rule for his extended family as they attempted to live a life based on the gospel. When he articulates rules for community decision-making, he advises that the abbot listen to everyone in the whole community. The rule states explicitly what process should be followed and why:

> Whenever any important business has to be done in the monastery, let the Abbot call together the whole community and state the matter to be acted upon. Then, having heard the brethren's advice, let him turn the matter over in his own mind and do what he shall judge to be most expedient. The reason we have said that all should be called for counsel is that the Lord often reveals to the younger what is best.[22]

Even when the decision is not of major consequence, several in the community should be consulted. Benedict also identifies the way in which this community counsel is to be given. Monks should speak their own perspectives but "with all the deference required by humility, and not presume stubbornly to defend their opinions...."[23] Benedict's guidelines for making community decisions with a deep respect for others provide noteworthy recommendations for us today.

The business case for decision-making that invites a diversity of voices is summarized well by Andre Delbecq in "Bureaucracy, Leadership Style and Decision-Making."

> These studies suggest that leadership-sharing results in group performances generally regarded as "better" in our society. When performance is measured, it is, in the long

run, higher; when cohesiveness is measured, it is stronger; and when interpersonal effect is measured, it is more friendly. Further, such ego-involvement as is provided by participation purportedly has important corollary benefits for fulfilling motivational needs.[24]

OPERATING PROCEDURE 1B: CREATE SEATS AT THE TABLE FOR THE MARGINALIZED

The second key operating procedure that emanates from this principle of respect for persons is the decision-making process must invite and listen deeply to the voices of the marginalized and unheard. Attention to the disenfranchised stems from a fundamental sense of "justice as fairness," the core concept and primary contribution of John Rawls, arguably one of the most influential contemporary philosophers of justice.[25] One need not agree with his entire theory to grant a preeminent place to the idea of fairness in social justice. Rawls, in his famous thought experiment, asks us to consider being in the "original position" of not knowing our class or economic status in society, our good luck or lack of it in natural assets, talents, IQ, physical strength, emotional balance, family security, and so forth. Rawls proposes that when the fundamental principles of justice "are chosen behind a veil of ignorance…no one is advantaged or disadvantaged … by the outcome of natural chance or the contingency of social circumstances."[26] From this position of ignorance, according to Rawls, two core principles of justice for society would be chosen:

> …the first requires equality in the assignment of basic rights and duties, while the second holds that social and economic inequalities, for example inequalities of wealth and authority, are just only if they result in compensating benefits for everyone, and in particular for the least advantaged members of society.[27]

Rawls argues against a utilitarian perspective that would put the aggregate benefit of all above the rights and benefits that are due each person. A just society requires that basic rights be shared by all and that these rights not be sacrificed to provide greater advantages for some portion of society.

The institutions of society and structures of organizations ought to be so arranged that when some achieve greater benefits beyond those basic rights or are more fortunate in their social position, those benefits and good fortune are shared with those who are least fortunate. Rawls reasons from both a "rights" perspective and a pragmatic perspective for this second principle. The accidents of particular talents or natural abilities are arbitrary from a moral point of view. They do not give an individual the right to political and economic advantage. Therefore, if chance smiles on some, their greater good fortune must also produce good fortune to some degree for those who are least advantaged. From a pragmatic perspective, "The difference principle, then, seems to be a fair basis on which those better endowed, or more fortunate in their social circumstances, could expect others to collaborate with them when some workable arrangement is a necessary condition of the good of all."[28]

In all fairness, those who have power and authority must provide a seat at the table of decision-making for those who have the least power. Perhaps the most important right of all is participation in the processes that determine policies and structures. Enlarging on Rawls's focus on ideal just structures, Amartya Sen in *The Idea of Justice* emphasizes the importance of the freedom to choose. He says, "The freedom to choose our lives can make a significant contribution to our well-being, but going beyond the perspective of well-being, freedom itself may be seen as important. Being able to reason and choose is a significant aspect of human life."[29]

Creating More Inclusive Organizations

Even when we expand participation in the decision-making process, we often gather voices that are quite similar to our own. This may not be our intention but simply a result of the way our "sight" has developed. I am not making an excuse for being exclusionary; this operating procedure calls for intentional reflection about who is not being heard and the creation of a more inclusive process for decision-making. Laura Sewall in *Sight and Sensibility: The Ecopsychology of Pereception* provides an in-depth analysis of the critical experimentation about how we learn to see. After reporting on the work of Nobel laureates David Hubel and Torsten Wiesel, whose research shows that visual and neural functioning are shaped by experience, she reflects on the larger question of knowing.

> It is no surprise that much of how we perceive is shaped by ongoing experience, by the scripts we follow, by the voices of those around us, by cultural coding. We all share and reinforce the daily assumptions that constitute consensual reality through the language we use, the media we watch, the stories we tell, the science we value, and the methods we use to describe truth.[30]

We see what we are taught to see. We continue to see what we have seen before and we tend not to see patterns and realities that do not fit with our previous seeing. We do not recognize who is at the margins of our society or our organizational culture because we have been privileged by that society or culture, often at the expense of those who are disenfranchised. This operating procedure challenges us to pay attention to our reality as a whole, to seek to understand those perspectives that we don't know we don't know. It requires retraining our eyes, noticing beyond our habitual sight, and sharpening our sense of hearing. This is very difficult work personally and organizationally.

Ultimately, putting this operating procedure into practice requires opening the mind and the heart. On a personal decision-making level, it may require research to get us in touch with perspectives quite different from our own, searching other cultures or countries or disciplines that take us out of our usual way of seeing. On an organizational level, implementing this operating procedure for decision-making requires becoming a truly multicultural organization.

In such an organization, no group is marginalized or disenfranchised. Members from all social and cultural identity groups are invited into the process of decision-making. The organization's mission, vision, values, products, and services then reflect the broad diversity of gifts, talents, and interests that come from the manifold human community. The voices of all are respected and specific listening processes are created to ensure the participation of all organization members. There is regular assessment of the culture and effectiveness of these efforts to hear the diverse voices from throughout the institution or group. Respect for all persons is taken very seriously and all forms of oppression and marginalization are eradicated. Of course, this is an ideal to be sought through constant attention.[31]

There are organizational structures and leadership models that integrate and normalize these operating procedures of enlarging the listening process and creating seats at the table for the marginalized. One such model envisioned by Robert Greenleaf in *The Institution as Servant* is the "council of equals" in which the leader is "first among equals."[32] George SanFacon used this model very effectively when he was director of housing facilities at the University of Michigan. With the cooperation of 250 employees, he was responsible for the maintenance and renewal of a building inventory that encompassed four million square feet of floor space and housed 16,000 residents.[33] The council of equals used consensus decision-making for all significant decisions and an integrated network of overlapping teams to accomplish their work effectively and economically. The teams created an exceptional workplace culture that promoted growth and well-being.

SanFacon's early work experiences propelled him to seek a more human way of working together. "Pretty much wherever I worked, I thought the workplace experience was pretty mediocre, that the way the workplace experience was structured and played out basically turned it into a killing ground of the human spirit," he says.[34] He envisioned a structure where people wouldn't feel a need to constantly protect themselves and be competitive with one another, a structure that would actually nurture the human spirit. The *Facilities Council Handbook* states,

> After considerable research and a few false starts, he finally decided that the best way to accomplish his goals was to abolish the traditional, authoritarian, boss-subordinate management model in favor of one based on shared governance and mutual vulnerability. In so doing, he relinquished his unilateral power and authority over others.[35]

The council of equals model, in which individuals are accountable to the team, nurtures a high level of connectedness and cooperation. People feel included in decision-making and they feel their voice counts. In effect, everyone is responsible to everyone else rather than to one individual who needs to be feared or placated because he or she has power over the others. Since communication is open, talents are recognized, and power is shared, all work collaboratively to make the right decisions and accomplish quality work on time.

CRITERION FOR JUDGMENT 1A: CHOOSE WHAT CONTRIBUTES TO THE COMMON GOOD

If we are genuinely listening to diverse perspectives and there is participation from all stakeholders in the decision-making process, the decisions we make ultimately will be focused on the common good, or what benefits the whole community in the long run rather than only one segment of it or one individual. The concept of the common good has a long, complex history, but I use it here to refer to choosing what upholds the rights of each and the good of all. Only when both individual rights and the good of the community are held in balance can we make wise decisions. Often when fundamental individual rights are arbitrarily limited or denied, the community becomes insular and unhealthy. It fails to adapt and grow because the voices of creativity and difference are silenced. It fails to flourish and thrive because persons lack health, well-being, and fellowship. When decisions respect the critical rights of persons, the community is enriched by the diverse talents of healthy individuals as they contribute to society.

Without attentiveness to the mutual relations between individuals and communities, decision-making tends toward compromising among competing interests. There is the ever present danger that "justice in the world of fish" will prevail, "where a big fish can freely devour a small fish."[36] In *The Idea of Justice*, Sen explains the Indian Sanskrit concept of *nyaya* as a "comprehensive concept of realized justice" where fairness is actualized in concrete actions and decisions.[37] Sen warns that "it is crucial to make sure that the 'justice of fish' is not allowed to invade the world of human beings."[38] He reminds us justice is not simply about institutions and principles. It is about deciding in a way that respects persons and accomplishes good for the community.

The Rights of Each and the Good of All

This criterion to choose what contributes to the common good by being attentive to the rights of each and the good of all is antithetical to the assumption that rational choice requires that I look after my own interests only. The position of ethical egoism is ultimately unfounded, even though there are strong voices in contemporary, market-driven, Western culture that assert doing good for others is against our biological and psychological makeup. At its core is the view that some persons should be treated differently from others, even if they share the same fundamental attributes and needs. As James Rachels succinctly explains in *The Elements of Moral Philosophy,* "Ethical egoism…advocates that each of us divide the world into two categories of people—ourselves and everyone else—and that we regard the interests of those in the first group as more important than the interests of those in the second group."[39]

As with other forms of discrimination that divide persons based on arbitrary differences, ethical egoism violates the basic principle of justice: fair and equal treatment. Since all persons have basic needs, desires, joys, and interests, we are morally obligated to recognize and act so these needs, desires, joys, and interests are fulfilled. Our moral obligation does not require us to bankrupt our own resources, but to share them in a fashion that builds up the community as we value our own lives.

Ethical egoism is a toxic idea because it tends to be a self-fulfilling prophecy. Persons who don't care about others tend to create a society in which there is greater defensiveness, polarization, and alienation. In "Altruism and the Endurance of the Common Good," William Clohesy emphasizes the negative consequences of ethical egoism. He says:

> The more we think of ourselves, our institutions, and our choices solely in terms of individual utility calculations, the harder it becomes for anyone to propose concerted public action based on public deliberation, choices based on principle rather than preference, and the possibility of goods that can be conceived and achieved only by persons thinking and acting together.[40]

Firms of Endearment explores an epochal change in business that puts the common good on a par with other corporate concerns. The authors believe that "an historic *social transformation of capital-*

ism is under way."[41] They point to businesses like Timberland, Southwest Airlines, Trader Joe's, Whole Foods, and others that embrace the welfare of all stakeholders as part of their intentional purpose. Balancing the rights of each and the good of all is translated in this new corporate consciousness to

> an unswerving commitment to do good by all who are touched by their companies. We call their companies *firms of endearment* because they strive through their words and deeds to endear themselves to all their primary stake-holder groups—customers, employees, partners, communities, and shareholders—by aligning the interests of all in such a way that no stakeholder group gains at the expense of other stakeholder groups.[42]

According to the authors, this new development in businesses is based on a broader cultural thirst for meaning, a new attentiveness to transcendence, to that which is beyond the physical and materialistic. Another way to express these concerns is to speak about a triple bottom line. Any responsible organization must be concerned about final results that include economic solvency, employee well-being, and community health and sustainability. We no longer have the luxury of allowing organizations to measure success with one criterion only. It is time to recognize the perennial wisdom to respect all persons, to care about all the stakeholders in our society, and to be attentive to the rights of each and the good of all.

CRITERION FOR JUDGMENT 1B: TAKE INTO ACCOUNT THE POOR AND POWERLESS

The second criterion for wise judgment that comes from the principle of respect for all persons is to give preference to the poor and oppressed, the powerless and marginalized. Robert Greenleaf, the father of servant leadership, expresses this perspective well when he says the best test of a leader's decisions will include the consideration of how the "least privileged in society" are affected; will they benefit from the decision, or, "at least, will they not be further deprived?"[43] Wise decisions must take into account our fundamental responsibility to treat others fairly.

According to Rawls, fairness requires that all persons share basic liberties. It is important to recognize the primary place of personal liberty. Those who are marginalized and disenfranchised often lack the basic requirements for autonomous action. They may experience their lives as devoid of options, controlled by the systems that oppress them. They may lack fundamental information and understanding about possible courses of action. The conditions of their lives may militate against any hope that has a horizon larger than the immediacy of coping with current struggles. The arbitrary limitation of personal freedom also has societal implications. The practice of public reasoning and social evaluation is less than whole when some are denied a voice.

In Rawls's second core principle for justice, any inequalities (for example, more wealth or higher education) must be connected to roles that are truly accessible to all persons through equal opportunity. In addition, these inequalities "must be to the greatest benefit of the least advantaged members of society."[44] Here Rawls draws particular attention to those who are worst off in society. When others have more than enough, very significant sharing of those resources must help to alleviate the deprivation of basic goods and services experienced by the poor.

Perhaps the largest impediment to fairness in decision-making is unconscious bias, the unreflected inclination to act out of our own personal priorities, assumptions, and interests. Rawls's veil of ignorance challenges us to step out of our current reality and to see things impartially. He takes the position that his thought experiment of putting ourselves in an original position in which we have no knowledge of our social or economic status leads to impartial principles for justice. I believe his thought experiment can also help us reflect on our own bias, to see things from a broader perspective. As noted earlier in this chapter, Laurel Sewall in *Sight and Sensibility* provides a fascinating glimpse of the research on perception that shows how difficult it is to achieve an impartial viewpoint. Our attention "selects, enhances, and essentially creates our reality....By selecting what information is perceived with reference to our expectations, immediate needs, and familiarity, attention affirms and perpetuates habitual assumptions, stereotypes, and, quite possibly, a worn-out worldview."[45] Unless we take intentional steps outside of our usual cultural landscape, we will fail to see what others see. It isn't that we are intentionally forcing our limited categories on reality. It is simply the way our brain works.

There are a number of training videos that highlight this point. One of the most popular shows two teams of basketball players, one in white and the other in black uniforms. The viewers are asked to count how many times the white team passes the ball. Often, viewers will give differing results. After a second showing of the video, usually the viewers come closer to consensus on the number of passes made. Sometimes, after the second showing, some viewers will comment on the gorilla that moves through the perceptual field as the teams are playing. It took me three viewings before I even saw the gorilla.

Expanding Our Field of Vision

We need to practice expanding our field of vision if we are ever to make decisions that take into account those who are not regularly part of our everyday experience. How can we become conscious of the fact that we are not seeing what we are not seeing? How do we then learn to see what has before been outside of our view and understanding? One powerful answer to this question comes from the popular spiritual writer Henri Nouwen. In his work *Compassion*, he suggests we voluntarily displace ourselves or move into a place of discomfort.[46] When we put ourselves in places that are unfamiliar, in situations that have less security than we are used to, we begin to experience compassion. We begin to glimpse the suffering of others and to feel it ourselves. We begin to see the concerns of those at the margins and hear their cries for food, medicine, a job, plumbing that works, justice. Only when our personal and organizational decisions take into account the needs of the least among us can we live fairly and wisely.

Wise decisions will begin to address the gaping wounds in our organizations where a mechanistic view of persons and work suppresses spirit and vitality. Wise decisions will take account of the severe tensions that strain at the seams of our country and world because of the increasing accumulation of wealth by a few while nearly one half of the world's population does not have enough food or water. Looking at the world as if it were a village of just one hundred people helps us understand how our social fabric is stretched and torn.

IF THE WORLD WERE 100 PEOPLE

50 would be female, 50 would be male

26 would be children, 74 would be adults,
8 of whom would be 65 and older

There would be:
60 Asians, 11 Europeans, 15 Africans
14 people from the Americas

There would be:
33 Christians, 22 Muslims, 14 Hindus, 7 Buddhists
12 people who practice other religions
12 people who would not be aligned with a religion

12 would speak Chinese
5 would speak Spanish, 5 would speak English
3 would speak Hindi, 3 would speak Arabic
3 would speak Bengali 3 would speak Portuguese
2 would speak Russian, 2 would speak Japanese
62 would speak other languages

83 would be able to read and write, 17 would not

7 would have a college degree
22 would own or share a computer

77 people would have a place to shelter them
from the wind and the rain, but 23 would not

1 would be dying of starvation
15 would be undernourished
21 would be overweight

87 would have access to safe drinking water
13 people would have no clean, safe water to drink[47]

Choosing wisely means asking ourselves the hard questions about fairness and equality, about what each person deserves because of their fundamental human dignity. Wise decision-making will provide places at the table for the disenfranchised. At first they may be unable to speak, but if others listen with full presence, they will find their voice. They may well challenge some of our strongly held assumptions and mental models. If we are open and nonjudgmental, however, we will begin to see reality through a wider lens. To the degree that our decisions take into account the suffering and privation at the margins of our society, our decisions will be wise. Wisdom chooses dignity for all, binds up wounds, and works toward the liberation of the human spirit.

Greater Sensitivity to the Needs of the Poor

What would it look like to make personal decisions with a greater sensitivity to the needs of the poor? How would we invest our time, talents, and treasure to address the suffering of those at the margins? What would it look like for organizations to make corporate decisions with a greater sensitivity to those on the lowest rungs of the social ladder? How might corporations become more responsible citizens in their countries and world? How might they create more learning opportunities for those who are least prepared for promotion? How might they encourage their employees to use their gifts in their communities to alleviate the needs of the poor?

Firms of Endearment offers many examples of businesses that are model citizens and servants. The firms of endearment paid on average a 35 percent tax rate in comparison to tax liabilities of less than 5 percent for approximately 94 percent of U.S. companies in 2000.[48] In contrast to the many corporations that use ambiguous tax shelters or "a 'dual book' system to represent profits differently to the capital markets and tax authorities," the firms of endearment "are generally sticklers for following not just the letter, but also the spirit of the law" in regard to taxation.[49] IKEA is an example of moral global citizenship, requiring "high environmental and safety standards worldwide, even when local regulations are less demanding."[50] New Balance, Patagonia, REI, and Timberland are examples of corporations that have community partnerships, service days, and internships that encourage employee participation in addressing community concerns. For example, New Balance places a priority on community service through their Community Connection Program that offers volunteer opportunities every month for employees.[51] "Patagonia has an Environmental Internship Program that gives employees up to eight weeks of paid leave to volunteer for an environmental organization of their choice."[52] These are only a very few examples of the kinds of decisions that are made when there is a greater sensitivity to the poor and powerless.

Ultimately wise decision-making is both a science and an art. It entails a comprehensive process that researches multiple alternatives and their consequences, that strains to take into account all the aspects of the situation. It is also an art. Over time, the artist develops sensitivity to what fits, what is called for, and what adds to truth and beauty. This first principle of wise decision-making, to respect all persons, requires us to practice noticing each person as a unique story. Life becomes much more interesting when we are open to hearing the amazing stories that surround us. Some of us have covers that are tightly closed. Others have their pages turning constantly. Some of us tell our stories only when we are invited. Others tell their stories very freely. For some, the story is a comedy; at least the opening chapters are full of humor, self-effacement, light, and fun. If we listen long enough and deeply enough, there are also other elements to the story, including common suffering and loss.

As a child, my grandfather was both a comfort and a mystery. He spoke only Dutch and I mostly intuited what he was saying. I spent a good bit of time with him, mostly watching him work, although he would often direct me to get involved in his many chores. He was gruff and tender, demanding and forgiving. I knew he had a complex story, but it only came out in pieces from my parents and aunts and uncles. Here's a piece of the story.

SPLINTERS OF LIGHTNING

He didn't speak English but he could do anything
it seemed to me, especially in his tar-papered
tool shed with its dirt floor so you were always
standing on the earth. White thick hair just long enough
to stand straight and stiff, square jaw, eyebrows

like tumbling whitecaps. He chased the children
out of his plum tree with a hatchet, shouting
at them in Dutch, the sharp blade gleaming.

Every blade was sharp—knife, axe, sickle,
spade tip even; every blade honed to the perfect
edge on his grinding stone. Nothing was more
wondrous to me than the way he sharpened things.
The perfect rhythm of the shuttle, the whir
of the round stone, and the sound of the two
hard worlds, one grinding the other to a useful edge.
The sparks flying off like splinters of lightning.

Every few weeks the blades would have to be set
right again, a slow wearing away of their bodies
so they could do their work. I can remember only
one day when he wouldn't let me in, when I
stood in the cold outside the shed listening
to the wheel turn, the terrible clash of hard worlds.
It was in early January and the day before
we had taken our skates off their hooks in the attic
where they waited to cut a perfect arc in the ice.

Why not let me in to see the playful skates
sharpened to their most graceful edge?
He wouldn't answer but mother told me.
After he came to the new world he had a daughter,
his youngest child, born like a promise in America.
On Christmas day, he gave her fine leather skates
with shining blades like the ones he wore on the canals
in the old country. She never put her feet in them,
she died on a cold, cold day in early January.

We never know the whole story. There is always mystery,
always more. When we listen to the stories, we gain a deeper appreciation for the diversity of experiences. We often wonder at the
resilience and courage of ordinary persons. When we hear the stories
of the poor and oppressed, we are often amazed how difficulties are
transformed into opportunities, how despair is conquered by hope.

Wise decision-making requires that we open our ears and our hearts to the stories of our grandly diverse community. Through deep listening, we hear the connections that bind us each to each, one to all. When we practice listening with sensitivity to our extraordinarily different and common stories, we broaden our scope, enlarge our compassionate brains, and make wiser decisions.

Questions for Reflection

How would you tell the story of your life? What are its desert places and its mountain top places?

Whose story would you like to hear? How might you ask this person to tell it? How can you create the space internally and externally to genuinely listen?

What two concrete actions might you be able to take in your personal or professional life that would lead to deeper listening to yourself and others? How might that deeper listening affect your decision-making processes and outcomes?

An Assessment of Deep Listening

The following assessment may help you understand how well you are listening. As you rate yourself, try to think of concrete examples in the last month of each of the areas that you are rating. If you are unable to recall specific examples of your listening, you may wish to rate yourself on the lower end of the scale. If you are able to articulate for yourself specific instances of listening, you may wish to rate yourself on the higher end of the scale.

I spend enough time listening to my own inner teacher.

High   9   8   7   6   5   4   3   2   Low

I respond easily to my intuition.

High   9   8   7   6   5   4   3   2   Low

I participate in contemplative and reflective practices regularly.

High   9   8   7   6   5   4   3   2   Low

I listen attentively to the words and heart of others.

High   9   8   7   6   5   4   3   2   Low

I nurture dialogue in my relationships and in my organization.

High   9   8   7   6   5   4   3   2   Low

PRINCIPLE TWO

APPRECIATE THE WHOLENESS
OF BEING HUMAN

WISDOM PRINCIPLE	OPERATING PROCEDURES	CRITERIA FOR JUDGMENT CHOOSE WHAT…
Principle 2. Appreciate the wholeness of being human.	OP 2A. Explore all the ways of human knowing. OP 2B. Make room for silence.	C 2A. Values the whole person. C 2B. Brings balance and integration.

*J*ulie signed up for the Authentic Leadership Program because she often felt a great deal of conflict between what her heart was saying and what she was expected to do in her financial management role in a community healthcare system. She was frequently torn between the algorithms of good finance and the needs and desires of the people with whom she worked. She came to the program expecting the experts to tell her what to do and what skills she needed to develop, to give her answers to her dilemmas. Instead of providing answers, in the first Friday night session of our introductory retreat weekend we listened to selections from Antonio Vivaldi's *Four Seasons* and read some brief reflections on the turnings of the year from Parker Palmer's *Let Your Life Speak*.[1] Then we asked the participants to check in with a reflection around the question "What season are you experiencing in your life and in your leadership?" Julie talked about being in a winter place in her job, a lack of light and growth. She didn't speak much during our first evening together but it seemed that something was happening just by the look in her eyes.

On Saturday morning, she showed up in Bugs Bunny pajamas and bunny slippers. She informed us in our check-in circle that these were steel-toed bunny slippers so we shouldn't get any ideas that she was a soft or mushy leader. Throughout our year-long exploration as a close-knit learning community, Julie became a master at using manifold ways of exploring, reflecting, and questioning. She was able to augment her excellent skills in statistics and modeling with ways of intuitive knowing and creative problem-solving. She became very talented at finding music and poems that allowed us to see key dimensions of teamwork and organizational dynamics. She integrated these different ways of calling forth the wisdom of her associates and became adept at developing processes and safe spaces to grapple with their concerns in creative ways. As a result, she engendered a deep sense of respect and shared decision-making even in the context of limited resources and difficult choices. The dilemmas in her workplace didn't go away; but Julie became adept at helping people respond creatively to the challenges.

Appreciation for Human Wholeness in Spiritual Traditions

The second core wisdom principle evident across spiritual traditions is appreciation of the wholeness of human being. This principle is evident in the diversity of Hindu beliefs and practices which are attuned to the diversity of personalities and temperaments and the fullness of our humanity.

HINDUISM

Hinduism offers three traditional paths (*marga*) to salvation: knowledge, devotion, and action. Axel Michaels, author of *Hinduism Past and Present*, identifies its diverse religiosity as "performed in ritualistic (Brahmanism, Tantrism), devotional (Bhakti), spiritual-mystical (asceticism, Yoga, meditation) and heroic modes."[2] In ritual, the religious focus is on prescribed actions and prayers carried out in temples by the priests or in homes by laypersons. Common rituals include washing, breathing, making gestures of respect, and offering incense, rice, or flowers. Those who learn best through kinesthetic engagement, such as formulaic movement, chanting, and determined prayers, are drawn naturally to ritual. The Tantric rituals facilitate the experience of transcendence through sexual ritual that heightens both human intimacy and connection to the divine.[3]

The devotional forms of Hinduism advocate an ardent, dedicated personal relationship with one or several gods and goddesses. One's devotion may be expressed by singing songs, telling stories, recounting core myths, reciting poetry, and dancing. At the core of the devotional aspects of Hinduism is opening the heart, learning to trust, and submitting to the god or goddess.[4] In its mystical or spiritualistic traditions, Hinduism often emphasizes personal liberation. Through study and meditation, the individual can recognize his or her identification with the whole, with what is immortal, to such an extent that there is no longer a knower and the known. Rather, there is only knowledge or enlightenment.[5] Finally, heroic modes of religiosity include doing courageous acts that lead to salvation. Heroic actions may include greatness in battle, participating in difficult pilgrimages, and acting out ritual struggles. There is a long tradition of warrior-ascetics who in the past guarded the streets and trade routes. Today, this heroic religiosity is evident in the martial arts.[6]

BUDDHISM

Various forms of Buddhism also emphasize different aspects of the person and ways to enlightenment. One person might focus on meditation, another on doing good deeds for others, another on worshipping the Buddha.[7] Huston Smith and Philip Novak state: "In Theravada Buddhism, the prime attribute of enlightenment is wisdom (bodhi), meaning profound insight into the nature of reality...."[8] For Mahayana Buddhism, the emphasis is on compassion. Zen Buddhism takes a mystical approach to enlightenment, focusing on radical insight by driving "the mind to a state of agitation wherein it hurls itself against its logical cage with the desperation of a cornered rat. By paradox and non sequiturs, Zen provokes, excites, exasperates, and eventually exhausts the mind..." so that the practitioner is open to the sudden insight of wisdom.[9]

The Buddha's life is often presented as a holistic integration of these different forms. He brings together rigorous reason and a compassionate heart in an exemplary way. He analyzes questions and problems with deep insight, engaging in cool-headed dialogue and calmly unearthing assumptions and ultimate meanings. This acute insightfulness and tender compassion are portrayed in the story of Kisa Gotami, a young mother who is absolutely delighted and ful-filled by her newborn son. When the infant suddenly dies, she is overcome with sorrow and continues to carry her baby as she seeks medicine to cure him. Someone takes pity on her and sends her to the Buddha, who tells her to visit the houses in the town and to bring him a few mustard seeds from every house where they have not expe-rienced death and grief. We can only imagine the interactions she has with her neighbors, how they open their hearts to her as she tells her story over and over, and how she begins to comprehend her own grief as she hears their stories of loss. Smith and Novak conclude their version of this ancient tale as follows:

> At every door in town the reply was the same: "O, Gotami, many have died here!" Finally Kisa Gotami real-ized the nature of the medicine Buddha had dispensed. Her insane grief now replaced by gratitude for the Buddha's compassionate wisdom, she took her son to the cremation grounds.[10]

This integration of wisdom and compassion is at the heart of the Buddhist path to nirvana. That path is called the "Middle Way" because it rejects both the way of extreme asceticism and the way of sensual indulgence. The middle path includes a balance of mental and physical discipline without punishing the body. The Buddha used the example of a lute to explain the kind of balance that is required. If the strings of the lute are too taut or too slack, the sound is awful. If the strings are neither too tightly nor loosely drawn, they have a tuneful sound.[11]

CONFUCIANISM

Balance and harmony are central themes in Confucianism as well. Confucian doctrine can be summed up in the "Three Ways: the Way of Heaven, the Way of Humans and the Way of Harmony. ... It is argued that harmony is not only a central concept, but also the spirit manifesting the life and power of Confucianism; it is both the Confucian reality and the ideal that Confucian believers endeavour to realize."[12] The ideal of harmony includes properly expressing emotions, cultivating moral virtues, and creating and nurturing beneficial relationships within families and throughout society. The concept of harmony applies to right relations in every dimension of reality and everyday life: between mind and body, the divine and the secular, the ruler and the ruled, living beings and inanimate things, heavenly principles and human behavior.

JUDAISM

Jewish wisdom also focuses on the fullness of life and the harmony of its various elements as the ultimate goal of the human person. The Book of Proverbs has countless examples of wise choices that cover the full range of human experience, from friendship to investing, from raising children to treatment of livestock. Walter Brueggemann, in one of the central expositions of the Jewish wisdom tradition, explains this fullness of life as referring "to all the assets—emotional, physical, psychical, social, spiritual—which permit joy and security and wholeness."[13] One comes to wisdom through the engagement of all the ways of knowing. Wisdom isn't comprised only of cognitive understanding, but includes physical security as well as emotional and spiritual wellness.

CHRISTIANITY

Appreciation for the fullness of the person is also foundational to the Christian tradition. The central teaching of Christian theology is the incarnation—that the Word takes flesh in Jesus, that God is embodied in him. In this embodiment not only is God revealed, but the fullness of humanness is revealed. Human personhood reaches its apotheosis. God reveals in Jesus the kind of human life that most fully reflects the image and likeness of God. In the Christian scriptures, Jesus is presented as an integrated, whole person. He has considerable intellectual intelligence and is able to analyze critically the fine points of the law and articulate in creative ways a radical new vision of justice. The Christian scriptures also give us a picture of a Jesus who has broad emotional intelligence, who fully feels the broad spectrum of human affectivity: empathy with the woman taken in adultery, deep sadness with Martha and Mary at the death of their brother Lazarus, profound affection for children and for his disciples, lamentation over Jerusalem, bold anger at the money changers in the temple, joyful participation in banquets and wedding feasts.

Finally, in the gospel portrait of Jesus, we see a person who is well acquainted with silence, who seeks out solitude, who takes his friends off to be alone, who prays well into the night. In Jesus, one finds a person whose spiritual intelligence is profound. The gospels present a whole human being who values the range of human emotion, who exhibits insightful rationality, and whose heart is attentive to the movement of the spirit and the voice of God.

ISLAM

The integration of spiritual consciousness in everyday life is central to Islam. One of the five pillars or essential practices of Islam is to pray five times a day. Muslims face Mecca and perform their prayers wherever they may be at dawn, noon, mid-afternoon, sunset, and evening. The opening verse of the Quran, which recognizes God as creator and compassionate ruler, is repeated in each prayer as Muslims recall God's revelation and guidance for every aspect of their lives. As Muslims pray, they also express their submission to God through prostrations, symbolizing with their bodies their devotion to Allah.

The integration of spiritual, emotional, and intellectual intelligence is evident in the religious exemplars from many religions of the world, from Confucius to Mohammed, from the Buddha to Moses. Following their example, their disciples often created rules and guidelines for living in integrity, harmonizing the powerful dimensions of being fully human. For instance, with the Christian gospels as his guide, Saint Benedict created a community rule that shows a sensitive attentiveness to the whole person. Benedict's rule prescribes a balanced life in which there is time for prayer, physical labor, and intellectual pursuit. This balance is affected by the seasons and is appropriate to the specific abilities of each person. Special attention is given to those who are young, old, weak, or sick. When more physical labor is performed, more food is provided at the table. Benedict presents the image of the ladder by which one is able to ascend to God. He says, "And the ladder thus set up is our life in the world, which the Lord raises up to heaven if our heart is humbled.

For we call our body and soul the sides of the ladder, and into these sides our divine vocation has inserted the different steps of humility and discipline we must climb."[14] For spiritual traditions across the world, wisdom requires the integration of body, mind, and soul.

Principle Two Operating Procedures and Criteria

The spiritual wisdom traditions we have touched on, as well as many others, indicate that wise decision-making must intentionally and artistically integrate modes of consideration and deep reflection, including reason and analysis, intuition and aesthetic knowing, as well as silence. A wise discernment process must combine mind and body, heart and soul, discussion, debate, and argument, as well as reflection on feelings, values, and stories. We must bring the depth of our intellect and reason to bear on any issue or question. We must also identify with others, get a feel for their perspective, and sense their values and assumptions. We must bring to bear the fullness of our heart knowing on any issue or question. Benedict begins his rule with the powerful advice to "incline the ear of your heart."[15]

Two operating procedures for wise decision-making flow from this attention to the fullness of being human: (1) Explore all the ways of human knowing, and (2) make room for silence. In this chapter, I will focus primarily on some of the nontraditional ways of accessing wisdom, since our Western tradition is quite lopsided in its overemphasis on reason. This is not to denigrate the rational processes of clear thinking, quantitative research, and assessment of measurable outcomes that provide important data to inform the decision-making process. On the contrary, human reasoning becomes more fully informed when other avenues for understanding are brought into the conversation.

Critical analysis and creative visioning, reason and imagination, science and art together provide us with a fuller grasp of reality than any one of these pairs alone. We must move beyond the myth of objectivity and the separation of knower and known to participate in the process of deciding with our whole beings. When we use multiple modalities of knowing, the world is experienced as both "out

there" and "in here." We don't sever our "legitimate emotional connections and enduring moral obligations."[16] When we approach our
decisions through a holistic process, we see a fuller range of creative
possibilities and pay attention to potential consequences that are
broader in scope and more long-term. Parker Palmer describes a more
adequate epistemology— "a knowledge that springs from love will
implicate us in the web of life; it will wrap the knower and known in
compassion, in a bond of awesome responsibility as well as transforming joy; it will call us to involvement, mutuality, accountability."[17] When we practice knowing in ways that are attuned to our
whole humanity, our emotions, values, and imaginations keep us
connected to our deepest human needs, our hopes for our children
and grandchildren and generations to come, our diverse neighbors
down the street and around the globe, and our fragile ecosphere.
With the fullness of our knowing, we explore how all these dimensions of our lives are affected by the decisions we make personally
and organizationally. Cold calculations are augmented by warm-
hearted considerations, and we are more likely to make decisions
that recognize our accountability to the larger human and earth community of which we are a part.

OPERATING PROCEDURE 2A:
EXPLORE ALL THE WAYS OF HUMAN KNOWING

The example of Barbara McClintock is one of many that under-
line the importance of the integration of heart and head knowing,
the intuitive and rational modes in deep conversation. McClintock
was the seventh woman to receive a science Nobel Prize and the first
woman to be elected president of the Genetics Society of America.
Her discoveries in the field of genetics were groundbreaking. She
demonstrated genetic recombination, the mechanism for chromoso-
mal information exchange. She showed how certain regions of the
maize chromosome are linked to physical traits and others are critical in conserving genetic information. Her most important discovery
was transposition or "jumping genes," which helped in understanding the mechanisms for mutation.[18] "For six years, McClintock col-
lected evidence, stuffing cards, tables, filing cabinets, and shelves
with data."[19] Her theory was met with skepticism and perplexity by
most of her peers for many years.

Commenting on McClintock's central discovery and how it was initially received in the scientific community, James Shapiro said: "So first they said she's crazy; then they said it's peculiar to maize; then they said it's everywhere but has no significance; and finally they woke up to its significance."[20] McClintock's discovery has helped scientists understand how birth defects are inherited, how antibodies are produced to fight against viruses and bacteria, how bacteria acquire immunities, and how some cancer cells develop.

McClintock's profound scientific genius seemed to come from combining rigorous, detailed, repetitive research and an intuitive identification with her subject. In interviews about her work, McClintock expressed this "unitive" knowing in many ways. She said, "Well, you know, when I look at a cell, I get down in that cell and look around."[21] How is it that Barbara McClintock was able to see more deeply into the complexity of genetics than her fellow scientists? McClintock's biographer provides the answer.

> Over and over again, she tells us one must have the time to look, the patience to "hear what the material has to say to you," the openness to "let it come to you." Above all, one must have "a feeling for the organism."…You need to have a feeling for every individual plant. "I start with the seedling, and I don't want to leave it. I don't feel I really know the story if I don't watch the plant all the way along. So I know every plant in the field. I know them intimately, and I find it a great pleasure to know them."[22]

McClintock's perspective combined exacting analytical reasoning and data gathering with empathy and identification. She seemed to pass through the boundary between observer and object. She entered into the corn and was able to see the intricate beauty and aliveness of her subject. A responsible process of decision-making will not jettison reason but integrate it with heart knowing.

Intuition in the Life of Igor Sikorsky

The story of Igor Sikorsky, inventor of the helicopter and founder of Sikorsky Aircraft, provides another example of combining scientific acuity and sagacious intuition. Judi Neal in *Edgewalkers:*

People and Organizations that Take Risks, Build Bridges, and Break New Ground explores Sikorsky's life as a paradigm of edgewalking—being able to walk in two different worlds and combine their wisdom. At age twelve, Igor "read a book by Jules Verne titled *The Clipper of the Clouds*, published in 1887, about a flying machine with propellers on the top."[23] At this young age, he started envisioning the helicopter and experimenting with sticks and rubber bands to make whirling propellers. At age nineteen, Igor began working in aviation and tried to design a helicopter. Others in the aviation industry convinced Igor that he should stop attempting the impossible. Igor refocused his efforts and designed fixed-wing aircraft, gaining great success and wealth, but he never gave up his vision of the helicopter that could rescue persons from the most difficult situations.[24] Neal quotes a letter of condolence from Charles Lindbergh to Sikorsky's widow: "His scientific designs gained from his spiritual awareness just as his spiritual awareness was enhanced by his scientific knowledge, and he understood as few men do the essential relationships involved."[25]

One of the many stories of Igor's insightful intuition is about an aircraft that he designed and was scheduled to test fly. The night before the test flight, Igor walked around the airplane and had a very uneasy feeling about the tail of the plane. Even though it was built to exacting design specifications and everything looked fine, Igor decided not to test it. That night he put a sign on the aircraft—"Test flight cancelled." The next day he went to work redesigning the tail and two weeks later had a successful test flight. A year later, he saw a "badly smashed French airplane that had a tail design just like the original one that he had rejected. When he asked what had happened, he was told that the pilot was killed on the first flight because of a flaw in the tail design that no one had foreseen."[26]

The examples of Barbara McClintock and Igor Sikorsky emphasize the importance of paying attention to all our ways of knowing. Intuition itself is being understood more fully as research on the topic continues to grow. Marta Sinclair explains three distinct kinds of intuition: intuitive expertise, intuitive creation, and intuitive foresight.[27] From her perspective, the McClintock and Sikorsky examples would be termed intuitive expertise, instances of unconsciously drawing upon a large fund of knowledge accumulated through professional experience. Sinclair says, "In other words, we match our stored patterns with the current situation, with a specific goal in mind."[28]

Intuitive creation seems to be a process that integrates experience more broadly, bringing together expertise in a particular field with experiences from other disciplines and from ordinary life to envision a new possibility. Intuitive foresight may be related to intuitive expertise or intuitive creation. If one's intuitive foresight is the result of entrepreneurial success in the past, such as seeing patterns of possibility that have been productive previously, the intuition is related to expertise. If the intuitive foresight is the result of a more holistic integration of clues across the broad range of experience, the intuition is related to creation. In general, intuition in the workplace tends to increase with higher levels of expertise and authority as leaders with extensive knowledge within their organizations and professions face new issues and problems that don't have precedents or clear protocols. Whether the situation is personal or organizational, intuition should be seen as an important source of data or knowledge that needs to go into the mix of a well-considered decision. One's gut reaction should be placed in dialogue with other ways of knowing so that a decision is made with the benefit of our whole human knowing.

A thorough discernment process will intentionally examine philosophical arguments, scientific data, empirical observations, personal stories, case studies, values reflections, and songs or visual images that connect us to the experiences of those who may be affected by the decision. Accessing all the ways of our human knowing can be facilitated by inviting participants in the decision-making process to share feelings as well as ideas, to talk about their values as well as the environmental impacts and economic results that help to understand the reality considered. The decision-making process might include time for personal journaling, taking a walk, listening to a piece of music, or interviewing three persons who will be affected by the decision.

Music and Poetry as Sparks to the Imagination

In facilitating leadership conferences and workshops and strategic planning retreats, I often use music and poetry as a way to spark the imagination and open a heart space for sharing. I find songs, stories, and poems promote deeper conversations, closer listening, and a connection to people's values and hopes. For two major learning events, I had the pleasure of working with Creative Leaps International, a group of learning specialists and performing artists who are known throughout the world for their engaging "Concerts of Ideas." Their founder, John Cimino, is passionate about using the arts to jump-start creative thinking and courageous visioning, create the climate for heartfelt dialogue, and stimulate the intellect as well as the soul. For more than thirty years, Cimino has used his broad education in physics, learning theory, and music to create arts events for engaged learning at the White House, the Center for Creative Leadership, the Center for Excellence in Municipal Management in Washington, DC, and leadership training programs of dozens of Fortune 500 companies, universities, and professional organizations. He believes innovative arts programming can open deep and respect-ful dialogue, facilitate innovative, bold problem-solving, and nurture the dreams and spirits of people.

One of the greatest tests of his belief came in the wake of Hurricane Katrina, which decimated New Orleans in 2005, and became one of the largest and costliest natural disasters ever experi-enced in the United States, killing more than a thousand people and displacing over a million.[29] One of the most important and most effective responders to this tragedy was the Southeast Louisiana chapter (SELA) of the American Red Cross. Staff and volunteers worked tirelessly not only in the immediate days and weeks follow-ing the hurricane, but month after month. They pushed themselves again and again to the limits of physical and psychological endurance. After two years of providing truly heroic assistance, SELA was drained, frazzled, and on the verge of organizational col-lapse. The American Red Cross knew they had to help the local organization because there was still so much work to do, and so many fragmented lives left to heal. Somehow SELA had to be reinvigo-rated not just with new communication structures or a strategic plan, but with the long-term ability to cope with tragedy and to believe in possibility.

The American Red Cross called on George Washington University's Institute of Crisis, Disaster, and Risk Management to shape a recovery and revitalization process. The Institute found the problems to be severe. Relationships were strained, persons felt they were not appreciated, and communication was ineffective. People weren't listening to one another. "Misunderstandings abounded at every turn, documentation of basic needs had slipped out of control, and constructive discussion was nearly nonexistent."[30] Into this organizational quagmire, Carol Pearson brought her tools from literature and psychology. Drawing on the concept of archetypes, she helped the participants to see how they were making sense out of living in this context of a shattered city, how they had taken upon themselves ancient, universal human roles. The large majority of the staff identified with one of three archetypal roles: (1) "Servant/Helper: someone completely dedicated, but lost without leadership, (2) Leader: a person playing an essential role, but who may try to exert too much control when faced with disorder, or (3) Hero: a person who continues against all odds, even without leadership."[31]

The reflection process took them beyond identifying external behaviors that were getting in the way of their work together; they were challenged to go inside, to understand how they were feeling, to recognize their own reactions, hopes, and values. People began to feel hopeful again, to believe they could face the destruction and mammoth needs with a positive attitude again. However, Creelman said that some important relational and organizational aspects of SELA were not "quite jelling. They needed to bring the recovery process to a close with some sort of capstone experience. The Red Cross called on Creative Leaps International to … create a two-day Resilience and Renewal Retreat for the staff and volunteers, about eighty-five people."[32]

The retreat began with a "Concert of Ideas" focused on themes of courage, compassion, and leadership. Aaron Copland's inspiring "Fanfare for the Common Man" was the first number. Then the Creative Leaps team, mixed in among the audience, started singing the traditional Shaker hymn "Simple Gifts":

> 'Tis the gift to be simple, 'tis the gift to be free.
> 'Tis the gift to come down where we ought to be,
> And when we find ourselves in the place just right,
> 'Twill be in the valley of love and delight.
> When true simplicity is gained
> To bow and to bend, we shan't be ashamed.

To turn, turn, will be our delight
'Till by turning, turning, we come 'round right.

Although a few of the SELA participants were hesitant at first, the ninety minutes of music, poetry, and stories brought smiles, laughter, and tears. After the performance, participants gathered in small groups to share thoughts and impressions. Following an hour in their small conversation circles, the entire group was summoned back to the auditorium to report on their discussions. The large auditorium grew silent, and no one was "quite ready to say publicly what had been held inside for so long."[33]

> Then, suddenly, one fellow stood up and moved quickly to the front of the room. He was a young man and physically by far the largest person in the group, someone it was revealed later, who against orders had repeatedly led heroic rescues house to house into the night in his boat when the flood waters were still raging. He looked out at the group—everyone knew who he was—and he just started to talk. He spoke plainly from his heart about what he and everyone else had seen, of the pain and isolation each of them had felt. He never mentioned the word courage or hope, but they were in his eyes for all to see. He did say something about determination and healing up and moving on because it was in them to regain their strength and get back to work for the people and the city they loved....Other speakers followed, each one heartfelt and brave, some speaking in quiet voices, some tearful, others nearly raising the roof with their voices, but to a person, each speaking his and her truth and pledging their willingness to rise from their pain.[34]

It is probable that a series of PowerPoint slides would not have achieved the same result. Strategic plans are very important, communication training and information distribution protocols are essential to building trust and common investment, but music, poetry, and stories have the ability to reach the heart and the values that motivate us. If we are intent on making wise decisions, we will consider how best to use all the ways of human knowing. We will make more room in our meeting agendas and planning retreats for accessing our creative, visionary, and feeling selves.

Daniel Pink in *A Whole New Mind* suggests that these aspects of human knowing will become exceedingly important as we move from the Information Age to the Conceptual Age, which he describes as follows:

> It is animated by a different form of thinking and a new approach to life—one that prizes aptitudes that I call "high concept" and "high touch." High concept involves the capacity to detect patterns and opportunities, to create artistic and emotional beauty, to craft a satisfying narrative, and to combine seemingly unrelated ideas into something new. High touch involves the ability to empathize with others, to understand the subtleties of human interaction, to find joy in one's self and to elicit it in others, and to stretch beyond the quotidian in pursuit of purpose and meaning.[35]

He is not advocating that we jettison logical, rational, or linear abilities; but he is asserting that these skills must be paired with artistic, empathic and big-picture ways of knowing.

Accessing Wisdom Through Visualization

Another way of accessing the inner wisdom resources for good decision-making is through imaginative visualization or drawing. In other words, don't just talk about what you want to see happen but picture it in your mind and sketch it. When we engage the creative arts and our imaginative capabilities, we use our whole brain. Images, memories, and metaphors jump into our consciousness; a larger and more open space for seeing the possibilities is created. A richer and more creative consideration of viable alternatives comes to light. When we are faced with a difficult leadership decision at work or at home, exploring our metaphor for leadership can be very helpful. Is leadership a process of gardening—planting the seeds, watering the seedlings with care, shining the light on the green shoots of possibility, pulling the weeds that can get in the way of growth? Is leadership guiding a strenuous climbing expedition—mapping out the route clearly, ensuring that all the right resources are available, keeping people roped together to ensure the success of the climb, timing the various aspects of the journey? If we walk around in our chosen metaphor, we often discover aspects of our unconscious understanding that can help us make better decisions about the challenge that confronts us in the moment.

Sometimes when we are faced with a decision, we need to take a step back from the current, individual concern to gain perspective. Faced with a particular customer complaint, we may need to ask the customer service team to create a mental image of the kind of service they want to give and then consider the complaint from that perspective. Faced with the strategic question of developing a new product or new service, we may need to take a "Fast Forward Break" in which we try to imagine how our customers might be different ten years from now and how our organization might respond. Faced with an individual choice about a new job or moving to a new community, we might try to imagine what we would like our family life or community interactions to look like in ten years. When we imagine or sketch things out or create a symbol, we often see things from a broader perspective.

Although I have used many of these techniques repeatedly in both consulting and training, the importance of "having a picture" was brought home to me forcefully when I volunteered as an ally in a Circle of Support program. A Circle of Support consists of two or three volunteers called allies who are matched for eighteen months with a participant, either an individual or family, who wishes to take steps to move out of poverty. Poverty is understood not only in terms of economic need but also in terms of the needs for social support and a meaningful life. In the Circle of Support, the participant is in the driver's seat; allies help in ways that the participant determines could be supportive in his or her journey out of poverty.

I was teamed up with Tamara (not her real name), a courageous single mother of six children, who was struggling to meet their needs and build new skills to start a small business out of her home. One of the important dimensions of the Circle of Support program is regular meetings among the participant and allies to identify goals and reflect on progress. For the first several months we met, Tamara's goals kept changing. There was so much she wanted to work on and so many barriers that she wanted to push out of the way. She wanted to grow a garden and learn to cook healthier meals for her kids. She wanted to learn how to create a business plan so she could develop a small sewing business out of her home. She wanted to clean out the boxes and boxes of saved clothes and toys and other things that cluttered every room of the house. She wanted to learn computer skills so she could help her kids with school projects and stay connected with friends. She wanted to build a patio and landscape her yard so the family could enjoy their home more fully.

Meeting after meeting, Tamara vacillated from one goal to another. One week she would ask for help to learn technology, the next week she would call her allies to help her start on the patio, the next week she would arrange for a room-cleaning party. After three months, the Circle of Support staff recommended that Tamara might take some time to visualize her priorities as a way of focusing her attention and the efforts of her allies.

The whole group met with an artist who had hung a huge piece of newsprint on one wall of the meeting room. When asked what she would most like to see change in her life, Tamara began talking about her home and what it meant to her, how she wanted it to be warm and clean, how she wanted a room for her sewing machine. As the artist began to draw, asking Tamara about colors and rooms and where the sewing room could be and what would be in it, Tamara's spirit caught fire. She glowed as she spoke about the sewing room and the book shelves in the living room and a clean kitchen where everyone could gather around the table. She talked and the artist drew for thirty minutes straight without a pause. The process of putting a picture on Tamara's dream was deeply insightful for her. Her goals became crystal clear. The rest of our eighteen months together were largely devoted to removing many boxes of stored clothes and broken toys, rearranging rooms, and planning the remodeling of her kitchen. Tamara's home became much more organized, functional, and homey. More importantly, these first steps on the journey out of poverty allowed her to regain her sense of self-esteem and the power of her own dreams. But without "the picture," it might never have happened.

Integrating Knowledge from Body, Mind, and Spirit

Our Western culture has focused almost exclusively on rational knowing and the mind as the instrument of knowledge. Only recently have we begun to value the Eastern traditions that holistically integrate knowledge that comes from body, mind, and spirit. Laura Sewall in *Sight and Sensibility* emphasizes the narrow limitations of our Western cultural perspective. She says:

> Looked at from the conditioned perspective of our dominant culture, the dreaminess of the imagination, the erratic qualities of the ever-responding body, and the irritating, nonspecific nature of intuition are all problematic. They are generally not considered to be legitimate ways of knowing and are thus not consulted in the context of any serious question or consideration.[36]

We are slowly learning the importance of a more integrative knowing for wise decision-making, and heart knowing is based in contemporary science. The heart doesn't only pump blood, it knows things. Terms such as "heartache" or "heartthrob" hint at the kind of knowing the heart does in constant connection with the brain and the rest of the body. Recent research reveals the brain is really a distributed web of neurons throughout the body. Sometimes we can actually feel the knowing that comes from the nervous system and surrounds our stomachs when we have a gut reaction to an event or a story.[37] Imaginative knowing through metaphor "is the root of relatedness, the linking of things, events, and constellations of experience....Metaphor is a way of being informed by the other, recognizing and acknowledging the likeness with language."[38]

Accessing our multiple ways of human knowing requires we create a safe container and climate of openness in which sharing these different modalities is encouraged and appreciated, whether we are doing this with a friend or a team of colleagues. Shifting to a more holistic decision-making process, considering how values apply to the question at hand, or how metaphors might open up new perspectives about a situation, is something we may feel uncomfortable with at first. With time and practice, however, people begin to see more and know more.

OPERATING PROCEDURE 2B:
MAKE ROOM FOR SILENCE

A second operating procedure that encourages us to get to the heart of our humanness in the decision-making process is to make room for silence. The lack of comfort (dis-ease) with silence in our Western culture must be addressed with patience and persistence. In most social situations, my unscientific testing suggests no more than seven or eight seconds of silence is allowed. After five seconds of silence, some people start feeling anxiety and at eight seconds almost always someone feels compelled to speak. Many in our contemporary Western culture have an aversion to silence and reflection. In *Leading from Within*, Parker Palmer reminds us that reflection is not something that our contemporary Western society values.

> Those of us who readily embrace leadership, especially public leadership, tend toward extroversion, which often means ignoring what is happening inside ourselves. If we have any sort of inner life, we "compartmentalize" it, walling it off from our public work....Leaders need not only the technical skills to manage the external world but also the spiritual skills to journey inward toward the source of both shadow and light.[39]

Inviting silence into the decision-making process involves working against the grain of our culture, swimming upstream against the current of our comfortableness. Reflective decision-making requires we check our old habits of automatically turning on the radio, TV, CD player, iPod, or computer rather than listening to the voice within. It demands we schedule time to be alone, to retreat, to check in with our own feelings, and to consider how our actions fit with our values and vision. Giving priority time to silent reflection is not an easy adjustment. Even those convinced of the need for silence to listen to the inner teacher find it difficult to do.

Our present American culture, including our educational systems, training agendas, and leadership workshops, are clearly focused on externals. Reflection is neither prized nor taught. We tend to fill up any empty moment with auditory and visual stimulation. We seem to be running away from our uniqueness, denying the essence of who we are as human beings. What differentiates us from all the other animals is our unique ability for self-reflection. We have the capacity to ask probing questions of ourselves, to search for new meanings, and to dream new visions for ourselves and our world.

When we stop listening to our inner voice, we stop being human. We stop taking our unique place in the universe. When we stop creating space and time to hear the longings of our hearts and the creative imaginings of our spirits, we stop doing what we alone can do. One day, after looking everywhere, I found my daughter, Rebecca, sitting in the dark on the stairway to the basement. When I opened the door, there she was crouching in the silent darkness with her head in her hands. I thought something must be wrong. Had she gotten into a fight with one of her friends? Did I say something that hurt her feelings? Was she facing some difficult challenge? When I asked what was wrong, her response startled me. She said, "Dad, I'm just thinking about my mind thinking." She was four years old. The fact is reflection is part of our hard wiring. Silence can be an awesome place for discovery.

The Spaciousness of Silence

David Whyte, poet and organizational creativity consultant to many Fortune 500 companies, emphasizes the importance of silence in dealing with critical personal or organizational questions. He calls silence "a place of spaciousness in our lives that awaits us everyday in the midst of whatever besieging circumstances we feel we're a part of."[40] Often, we need to step out of the direct conversation about the issue at hand to get a broader perspective, to see it in relation to the central priorities and heart knowing of our best selves. Whyte says,

> Sometimes in your great questions about your work or your career, you actually can't begin the conversation in the subject itself. You go to a place where you can see a landscape, you listen to a piece of music, you spend time in silence, you turn the lights off and sit in the kitchen in the dark. And you go to another place that's some form of invisible, untouchable foundation for everything you want to build.[41]

Through the practice of silence, we stay in touch with our own heart knowing, and our deepest values and truest priorities. I have spoken with many people who are dedicated to some kind of contemplative practice. The common theme I hear from them is the silence allows them to be grounded, to have a sense of inner calm, and to be aware of their own bodily sensations, emotions, and mental models. It is often in the silence the still small voice of one's inner teacher can be heard. When we have a practice of silence, it becomes more difficult to evade the central urgings of our hearts. Palmer tells a powerful story about a retreat of twenty elected officials who were struggling with the dissonance between their values and the political nature of their work, the compromises they were often asked to make. One of the officials had been a farmer for twenty-five years and was now working for the Department of Agriculture. He talked about a proposal regarding the preservation of Midwestern topsoil that was on his desk at the moment. Palmer says:

> His "farmer's heart," he kept saying, knew how the proposal should be handled. But his political instincts warned him that following his heart would result in serious trouble, not least with his immediate superior.
>
> On the last morning of our gathering, the man from Agriculture, looking bleary-eyed, told us that it had become clear to him during a sleepless night that he needed to return to his office and follow his farmer's heart.
>
> After a thoughtful silence, someone asked him, "How will you deal with your boss, given his opposition to what you intend to do?"
>
> "It won't be easy," replied this farmer-turned-bureaucrat. "But during this retreat, I've remembered something important: I don't report to my boss. I report to the land."[42]

Silence gives us the opportunity to remember what is most important, to stay in touch with our authentic selves. Palmer, who has used the Quaker method of the clearness committee with thousands of persons discerning their direction in life, suggests humble discernment requires attention to inner and outer voices.

We have much to learn from within, but it is easy to get lost in the labyrinth of the inner life. We have much to learn from others but it is easy to get lost in the confusion of the crowd. So we need solitude and community simultaneously: what we learn in one mode can check and balance what we learn in the other. Together, they make us whole, like breathing in and breathing out.[43]

He recommends that persons who are serious about wise decision-making find a circle of trust, a small community of people who will help them access their own deep wisdom. In such a circle, persons help the individual in the decision-making process by asking open-ended questions that facilitate reflection and listening to the inner teacher. With compassion and patience, without judgment or assumptions, they surround the decision-maker with unconditional love and acceptance, a force field that provides the safe space in which one can bring the wisdom of the soul into the light.[44] Throughout A Hidden Wholeness: The Journey Toward an Undivided Life, Palmer emphasizes the importance of going slowly, of letting the soul take its own time to reveal itself. Humility requires that we admit that we do not know so we can allow the soul to speak its truth, the deeper knowledge that only comes through sustained silence and loving conversation.

Depending upon our personality and upbringing, silence may be more or less comfortable. Introverts tend to welcome silence more easily than extroverts. Whenever I am facilitating group processes, I try to remember to create space for those who process information and feelings externally and internally. Since my partner is a strong extrovert and I am solidly introverted, I have learned to understand that not everything he says is a conclusion. Early in our relationship, I often presumed that when he made a statement about something, he had come to a decision about it. I would be surprised when a few hours or days later, he would be talking about another option or alternative. I have learned to check if he is still in the processing phase. I have learned not to buy the tickets the first time he mentions going to the concert.

My colleague Bob Hartl tells another story of a healthcare team of thirty managers and senior leaders that struggled with this issue of personality style. He was originally asked to consult with the group on leadership development. As he often does, he used a dialogue process to try to understand the needs of the team. He started with very general questions so the group could share their concerns and experiences. Initially they raised a number of the usual problems that small hospitals have: trying to meet the financial bottom line, persuading patients they don't need to travel to the larger systems in the city to get good care, and so forth.

About midway through the dialogue, someone said words to the effect, "It would be great if we could get greater participation in this group. A few of us are always doing the talking." After a long silence, someone responded, "You've said that many times in our meetings. I can't give snap responses; I need to think awhile, and when I feel pressure, it makes it very difficult to make meaningful contributions. I can give an answer, but it's not going to be my best response." Then other people started sharing similar issues; it became apparent that this was an ongoing issue and the senior leaders wanted operating level managers to take a more active role in speaking up at meetings. At least one or two at the leadership level were putting pressure on the managers and that was creating some resistance. Hartl continues the story.

> So they started talking openly about this phenomenon that had been plaguing them for a long time, at least a couple of years. And someone said "You know, my learning style is such that I have to reflect too and I think there are several of us in this group who do. And I'm wondering if there isn't a way to structure our decision-making differently so that for those of us who need that time, we can get it." There was a long pause. And someone said, "Oh, I am so sorry. I have been putting pressure on you to speak up and I have been trying to be true to myself in doing that because that is what I felt needed to occur. But I just realized that I am causing you not to be true to yourself. I am so sorry." It was a very powerful moment that occurred in the dialogue. Once we left the dialogue and started doing concrete action planning, it was as if the floodgates were opened and suddenly they were talking openly about

this mechanism. So you know what each other thinks and you understand this dynamic. And they came up with an excellent plan how to do it, and from what I can tell they're using it.[45]

When we don't make room for silence, we are often short-circuiting the decision-making process. We are excluding from the process those who need time to reflect and consider, those who do not process material externally. This is another reason why silence is an important operating procedure that flows from the recognition of the wholeness of persons. In short, the operating principles for wise decision-making implicit in this fullness of the human person invite and nurture all the ways of knowing: body, mind, and heart. Integrated whole persons who intentionally consider the options in a difficult situation using intellectual, emotional, and spiritual intelligence will likely make a wise choice.

CRITERION FOR JUDGMENT 2A: CHOOSE WHAT VALUES THE WHOLE PERSON

There are two criteria for judgment that are evoked by this focus on human wholeness. The first criterion is to choose what values the whole person, whether we are making a decision that will affect us individually or others in our families, workplaces, and communities. When we choose what values the whole person, we are attentive to the conversation that needs to happen constantly among the various dimensions of our individual and organizational lives.

There are four key areas of responsibility for each of us as whole persons. Literally, we have the ability to respond, to take into account the fullness of our lives through our decisions. First, I am called to live in tune with my own values, talents, gifts, and urgings. I am challenged to continue to develop the abilities I have been given and to explore the interests and passions that make me come alive. When I am living and growing out of my authentic self, my contributions to the world produce energy and vitality rather than a feeling of depletion. When I am regularly challenging myself with new information and new processes for learning, the world keeps getting bigger and more interesting.

Second, I am responsible to live in loving and faithful relationships with others, which may include a spouse or family or friends. These are the persons who have a special place in my life without whom I would be diminished, intimate relationships that constantly provide opportunities for growth. In whatever decisions I make, these persons are always part of the picture. My unique relationship of care with them must color all of my choices.

Third, I am called to be fully present and invested in the work that I do, committed to making a meaningful contribution to the world. Quality of service and quality of craft are key aspects of this responsibility to do my work with ethical sensitivity and passion. Clearly, this aspect of valuing the whole self is closely related to how I understand my own strengths and yearnings. If I am attempting to do work that is not allied with my authentic self, it is probable I will not be able to give myself to the work in a way that brings life for myself or quality products or services for others.

Fourth, I am responsible for my society. I am called to participate in the systemic transformation of institutions, policies, and culture so our world becomes a more humane and beautiful place. Because I live inextricably related with others, I must do my part to create a world of equal opportunity and compassion.

When making a decision, I must turn to each of these four responsibilities and consider how I live as a whole person—self in relationship with self, self in relationship with intimate family and friends, self in relationship with work, and self in relationship with the larger community. In each of these relationships, I must pay attention to the physical, emotional, mental, and spiritual aspects of myself and others. Wise decision-making values each and all of these dimensions of the person and considers how they will be affected.

The good decision is not necessarily the one that gives equal weight to each of these dimensions; in many circumstances that is not possible. Rather, we must be attentive to the four dimensions of the person within the particularity of the current situation. Who I am physically, emotionally, mentally, and spiritually must be considered in making a wise decision about the current question I face. What impact a decision will have on the physical, emotional, mental, or spiritual aspects of others must be considered if that decision is to be wise. How a decision affects my or another's relationship to self, to family and friends, to work, and to society must be taken into account if we are to make wise choices. A few simple examples might help concretize this criterion. If I have been yearning for years to deepen and broaden my education, I may choose to enroll in a program that takes significant time away from my usual family commitment because I recognize that my own advanced learning has become a central concern for my continued well-being. Within an organization, if the employees are experiencing a steep learning curve related to new processes, it would be ill-advised to initiate a cross-training program at the same time that might exacerbate the difficulties people are feeling. In less stressful circumstances, it might be a very wise decision. The particularity of the situation and the particularity of how persons are experiencing the dimensions of wholeness will point the way to a wise decision.

CRITERION FOR JUDGMENT 2B: CHOOSE BALANCE AND INTEGRATION

In *The Three Marriages*, David Whyte focuses on the first three of the relationships listed above—self, spouse, and work. He contends our relationship to each of these is a marriage that requires a full, intimate, and engaging commitment. His remarks help to understand what I mean by choosing what brings balance and integration. Whyte says:

> The current understanding of work-life balance is too simplistic. People find it hard to balance work with family, family with self, because it might not be a question of balance. Some other dynamic is in play, something to do with a very human attempt at happiness that does not quantify different parts of life and then set them against one another. ... These hidden human dynamics of integration are more of a conversation, more of a synthesis and more of an almost religious and sometimes almost delirious quest for meaning than a simple attempt at daily ease and contentment.[46]

The balancing and integration implicit in the principle of paying attention to human wholeness are a complex dialogue about how to stay faithful to the vows we make with self, family and friends, work or vocation, and community in the context of the unique situation that calls for a decision. I am thinking of balance not as some sort of static state but as a process that includes all of the large and small adjustments that must continually be made from micro-second to micro-second to facilitate optimum life. When I do the yoga tree posture, standing on one leg with my arms outstretched on either side of me, I am aware of the constant adaptations that my foot, leg, back, and arm muscles are making to keep me very temporarily in this pose. Integration refers to the complexity of the interplay among these responsibilities, to the conversation that must continually go on from decision to decision about how to live a life of meaning, purpose, joy, satisfaction, and excitement. In wise decision-making, we balance and integrate the dimensions of our human wholeness, our various commitments, and vows that are at the center of our lives in an effort to pay attention to all of the aspects of the conversation. This is why wise decision-making is often called an art. Art deals with the sensitivity required to see what is appropriate in the specific situation to keep the conversation going, choosing just the right word to move the dialogue forward.

This criterion of wise decision-making also includes the integration of self and others as physical, emotional, intellectual, and spiritual beings. The Eastern models of wellness are much more explicit about the harmony of the whole person. "A Body-Mind-Spirit Model in Health: An Eastern Approach" explains that health in Eastern traditions "…is perceived as a harmonious equilibrium that exists between the interplay of 'yin' and 'yang': the five internal elements (metal, wood, water, fire, and earth), the six environmental conditions (dry, wet, hot, cold, wind, and flame), other external sources of harm (physical injury, insect bites, poison, overeat and overwork), and the seven emotions (joy, sorrow, anger, worry, panic, anxiety, and fear)."[47]

Whether we are speaking of the integration of aspects of the person or the integration of our relationships, wise decisions are made with integrity. Integrity and integration share the same root, pointing to wholeness, soundness, and trueness. Wise decisions fit with the soul of who you are, and bring together the elements of your being and the dimensions of your life in a harmonious way.

Parker Palmer in *A Hidden Wholeness* says, "When we understand integrity for what it is, we stop obsessing over codes of conduct and embark on the more demanding journey toward being whole."[48] That journey, Palmer explains, means joining role and soul, what one does with who one is, being the same person on the outside as on the inside. He provides this prescription for wise decision-making within organizations:

> In fact, when we live by the soul's imperatives, we gain the courage to serve institutions more faithfully, to help them resist their tendency to default on their own missions.... As adults, we must achieve a complex integration that spans the contradictions between inner and outer reality, that supports both personal integrity and the common good.[49]

Wise decision-making requires the scientific and artistic fitting together of the diverse dimensions of our persons and our relationships. Exemplars from the religions of the world portray this integration of body, mind, and spirit; their teachings repeatedly draw attention to the importance of living in integrity, being whole and healthy persons. In making personal and organizational decisions, we cannot forget the needs of the body and the essential foundation it provides for all of our human activities. If we fail to take account of the physical needs of ourselves and others, we soon reap the whirlwind of our neglect in mistakes and disease and battered relationships. Good decisions will recognize the mental needs we have to continue to learn and to be challenged. We must consider our emotional needs for belonging and purposefulness in life. We need to pay attention to the spiritual dimension that connects us to the demands of justice and the wonders of compassion.

Wise decisions depend on a deep consideration of our whole humanness, a kind of appraisal and reckoning that often takes us into silence. In silence we are able to listen to the teacher within and to the voices of need without. We need to find that sanctuary space and time where we can open our whole being to deep consideration, a bright clearing in the decision-making process where we listen with the ear of the heart to the vows we have made with self, with our intimate others, with our work and our community. We need to tune in to where our heart knowing and our head knowing concur in a deeper comprehension of reality and the choice that is wise.

Questions for Reflection

In what aspect of your life are you the healthiest? In what aspect of your life are you least healthy? How can you continue to strengthen your healthiest area and begin to address your least healthy area?

What aspects of your life are most difficult to integrate or keep in balance? What is at the root of this difficulty?

What two concrete actions might you be able to take in your personal or professional life that would lead to greater integration and balance in your life? How might that integration affect your decision-making processes and outcomes?

An Assessment of Integration

The following assessment may help you understand how well you are integrating the dimensions of yourself and your relationships and commitments. As you rate yourself, try to think of concrete examples in the last month of each of the areas that you are rating. If you are unable to recall specific examples of your integrating, you may wish to rate yourself on the lower end of the scale. If you are able to articulate for yourself specific instances of integration, you may wish to rate yourself on the higher end of the scale.

I feel that the various aspects of my life are connected and balanced.

High   9   8   7   6   5   4   3   2   Low

I regularly consult my feelings and intuitions when making decisions.

High   9   8   7   6   5   4   3   2   Low

My decisions reflect a deep consideration of the many aspects of persons.

High   9   8   7   6   5   4   3   2   Low

I am comfortable showing and sharing my feelings.

High   9   8   7   6   5   4   3   2   Low

I focus on the greatest possible good for others and for my organization.

High   9   8   7   6   5   4   3   2   Low

PRINCIPLE THREE

RECOGNIZE THE INTERCONNECTEDNESS OF ALL REALITY

WISDOM PRINCIPLE	OPERATING PROCEDURES	CRITERIA FOR JUDGMENT CHOOSE WHAT…
Principle 3. Recognize the interconnectedness of all reality.	OP 3A. Consider how systems will be impacted. OP 3B. Research effects on community and environment.	C 3A. Responds to the needs of the whole community. C 3B. Attends to the long term health of the earth.

$\mathcal{M}$ost of my childhood summers were spent on Uncle Bill's farm. I learned to appreciate the immense wisdom of nature as I witnessed calves and kittens being born, milked the cows, plowed and planted the fields, and watched the oats turn golden under the July sun. I learned that everything was connected to everything else. The amount of rain and sun would determine the yield and quality of alfalfa, oats, and corn. The amount and quality of alfalfa, oats, and corn fed to the cows would determine the yield and quality of milk. The yield and quality of milk would determine how much Uncle Bill had to invest in livestock and seed and a new used truck. Although there were plenty of small lectures from Uncle Bill about these things, I can remember learning the interconnectedness of things in a cellular way one day after we had finished dragging a field to make the soil fine and ready for the seeding of oats.

PREPARING THE SOIL

I don't know how old I was but I can hear
    the labor of the old Farmall
pulling the drag over the clumps and clods
    of red clay, taste the oily heat
coming off the engine as I sit beside my
    favorite uncle, see the long

wide acres stretching under a rolling, roiling sky.
    I wasn't old enough
to drive but I could watch for rocks where
    we would make our next pass
over the land, big rocks that would break
    the teeth or bend a bar, rocks

that kept rising up out of the earth year
    after year. Above us the clouds
were moving on this spring day, arranging
    and rearranging themselves
into mounds and mountains with the blue
    thunder gathering in their bellies,

the thunder we were racing against to get
    the seed planted before the rain.
When we had passed over the field twice,
    first running north to south,
then east to west, we stopped on the edge
    of the field and my uncle

got down off the tractor and I followed
    without knowing why. I thought
we would be rushing to get the grain drill
    and start the planting.
He settled into a knee bend and took
    a scoop of soil with both hands,

bringing his hands together under the dirt
    to lift the soil like an offering

or a prayer. I crouched beside him and he told
    me to feel the soil.
He said, "It's ready now, fine, warm, ready."
    Then he opened his fingers

just a little and let the dirt sift slowly
    through them. And there on the edge
of the field with the dirt in my hands
    it all connected, the ashes
from Ash Wednesday a few weeks before
    pressed onto my forehead,

the drone of the priest, "thou art dust,"
    the grit falling onto my eyelashes
and my nose, what gives us life and takes
    our life at the end. The whole
immense rhythm rising out of the earth,
    I knew everything was moving,

even the earth was shifting, rising, breathing,
    everything was moving
in waves, music, birth, some immense rhythm
    moving in the guts of all things.

I wrote this poem decades after the event, but I already had a deep and felt sense of the interconnectedness of all reality. My Christian background included the religious ritual of being "signed with ashes" on Ash Wednesday, which initiated the penitential season of Lent. Many religious traditions include rituals and seasons devoted to self-reflection that encourage participants to recognize their own faults and shortcomings, meditate on their mortality, and participate in practices of turning the heart more closely to the love of God and neighbor. That day in the field, with the rumble of thunder in the sky, somehow the dust of the ashes connected with the dirt in the field, the rhythm of the external and internal seasons meshed, and I had a gut-level feeling of a zillion threads woven, pieced, knotted into one big, round, pulsing universe.

A fundamental perception and clear recognition of the interrelatedness of all reality is required to make wise decisions. Wise decisions refuse short-term profits that bring with them long-term harm of persons, organizations, and environments. Wise decisions take into account the big picture, not only the problem or issue that is close at hand. They consider the consequences of actions not only for those who have a voice in the matter but for those without a voice and those in future generations. Wise decisions accept responsibility for the inextricably interrelated world that is alive with ingenuity and vitality as surely as we human beings are alive.

I witnessed my uncle's clear respect for the earth and its rhythms. He believed there were laws of nature that couldn't be circumvented, patterns and cycles of the web of life that were persistent and true. He assured me repeatedly that if we worked in tune with nature, we would know abiding satisfaction and joy.

The Interconnectedness of All in Spiritual Traditions

The Lakota writer Luther Standing Bear provides one example of the understanding and sense of relationships that many indigenous peoples have with other animals and aspects of nature. He says:

> Kinship with all creatures of the earth, sky and water was a real and active principle. For the animal and bird world there existed a brotherly feeling that kept the Lakota safe among them....The old Lakota was wise. He knew that man's heart away from nature becomes hard; he knew that lack of respect for growing, living things soon led to lack of respect for humans too. So he kept his youth close to its softening influence.[1]

Kinship connotes reciprocal relationships of care for each other. Not only does nature provide food and tools for humans, but humans are responsible for living in harmony and good relationship with nature. Without romanticizing their struggle for survival or oversimplifying the complexity of diverse perspectives held by indigenous peoples around the world, I wish to explicate briefly two common elements that are evident across many different cultures and traditions. These common attitudes show a deep realization of the interconnectedness of reality.

First, indigenous peoples tend to live in intentional and respectful relationship with their local community, which, for them, includes the landscape, plants, animals, regional weather, and fellow human beings. For instance, the Maori of New Zealand call themselves "people of the land," not in the sense they simply live in a particular geographical region but in the more profound sense that they come from the land, are tied to the land as with an umbilical cord, and identify with the land as their source of existence and ongoing wellspring of energy and wisdom.[2] For many tribal peoples, particular animals or spirits can impart insights or special abilities. Particular places may "express community identity, make present ancestors, and evoke oral narratives....Along with kinship, spatial, and biographical relationships with places, another key feature of indigenous lifeways is traditional environmental knowledge...."[3] One's life may be transformed by the use of certain plants for healing or the washing in certain pools, wells, or streams.

Second, evident in many indigenous practices and understandings is the realization that wisdom and maturity are grounded in close relationships with the interconnected web of reality. Many indigenous cultures throughout the world provide some sort of vision quest experience as a rite of passage from childhood to adulthood. Young persons who are ready to take on adult responsibilities are separated from the community and go into the wilderness to receive their unique call. Alone in the wild, listening intently to the messages from the animals and trees and wind, they may be visited by an animal spirit or receive a vision indicating their particular purpose in the community. Later in life, at critical decision points, an indigenous person might return to the wilderness or to the place of the original quest as a means for renewing their vision. Robert Wolff expresses the fundamental wisdom that he experienced with the Sng'oi people of Malaysia as "being *part* of All-That-Is."[4] That deep knowing brings with it recognition of the basic rhythms of life, an attentiveness to the ways, qualities, and properties of animals, plants, and particular places, and a sensitivity to what fits with the inextricably interconnected web of life.

HINDUISM AND BUDDHISM

This interlinked network of life is expressed in the diverse Hindu faiths and traditions as the interplay of the five elements: earth, water, fire, air, and space. Christopher Chapple in "Hinduism and Deep Ecology" quotes from the *Mahabharata* epic:

> The Lord, the sustainer of all beings, revealed the sky.
> From space came water and, from water, fire and the winds.
> From the mixture of the essence of fire and wind
>   arose the earth.
> Mountains are his bones, earth his flesh, the ocean his blood.
> The sky is his abdomen, air his breath, fire his heat,
>   rivers his nerves.
> The sun and moon, which are called Agni and Soma, are the
>   eyes of Brahman. The upper
> part of the sky is his head. The earth is his feet and the
>   directions are his hands.[5]

The human being, divinity, and the cosmos are inseparable. Ultimately, the Hindu religions deny duality. All is one, one is all. Axel Michaels expresses the "voice of India" as a call to recognize "that the new is also the old, that the future is also the past, that man and animal are one, that god is also man, but man is also god, that the part, the singular, the individual, is the whole, that This World is the Next World and the Next World is This World."[6] In this context, yoga and other religious practices cultivate a habit of peacefulness and nonharming that leads to freedom from attachment and, ultimately, liberation. Meditative practices result ideally in full immediate presence and the recognition that we are one with all.

For the Buddhist, all persons are interconnected and all reality is interdependent. When we touch anything, we touch everything. Separation or isolation is an illusion. Given this deep recognition of connection, the heart of Buddhism is compassion—truly seeing, feeling, and hearing the other. The realization of oneness extends to all reality. As humans, we survive by breathing the oxygen from the trees. Our lives are dependent on the web of life and the interactions of elements. In turn, we must act from the fundamental Buddhist insight that there is no separation between humans and nature or humans and humans. We must act with compassion. We are ultimately one. Jack Kornfield tells of his teacher's instruction to do a daily contemplation of interdependence, recognizing that each breath gives and receives "carbon dioxide and oxygen with the maple and oak, the dogwood and redwood trees of our biosphere. Our daily nourishment joins us with the rhythms of bees, caterpillars, and rhizomes; it connects our body with the collaborative dance of myriad species of plants and animals. Nothing is separate."[7]

The whole of reality and its individual parts are equally valuable. Although we can separate them mentally, they cannot be separated in reality. There are many images or metaphors that can be used to understand this holistic and interrelated perspective of Buddhism, but they all fall short when they are expressed in the subject-object language of English. Two metaphors might be helpful in attempting to move us beyond the paradigm embedded in our very speech. David Barnhill explains the Huayan Buddhist philosophy of relational holism by using the metaphor of waves in the ocean.

> The waves are seen as acting in interdependent harmony, each one affected by and affecting all the others, each one an integral part of the whole ocean. In fact, each wave *is* the ocean. But in order for a single wave to be the ocean, each wave "includes" (works in conjunction with) all the other waves.[8]

In a similar way, an electromagnetic or gravity field is one complete whole and yet it is possible to talk about points or locations within the field as distinct or unique. As with the waves and the ocean or points within an energy field, every being is part of the whole and makes up the whole. In the totality of relationships with all other beings, we come into being and pass away. Diversity and oneness are simply different ways of seeing the one multiple and totally interrelated and integrated reality.

CONFUCIANISM

Confucianism, as well, affirms the essential relationality not only among humans but also between humans and the natural world. Human beings and their immediate relations within family and society are lived out in the larger community of bounteous nature. The harmonious rhythms of nature sustain all life. Humans are part of nature, not dominant over it; they participate in the same fundamental organic continuum as the rest of reality. Mary Evelyn Tucker in her essay on "Confucianism and Deep Ecology" says,

> Within this world view of nature, human culture is created and expressed in harmony with the vast movements of nature....This need to consciously connect the patterns of nature with the rhythms of human society is very ancient in Confucian culture. It is at the basis of the anthropocosmic world view where humans are seen as working together with heaven and earth in correlative relationships to create harmonious societies....In this context, nature is primary and humans realize themselves by forming a triad with nature.[9]

Nature provides the boundaries and laws within which a prosperous human life can be lived in tune with the seasons and patterns embedded in all reality.

As referenced in the last chapter, Confucianism sees an inextricable relationship among the great triad of heaven, earth, and humans. Thus, humans only achieve the fullness of their being as they develop right relationships with earth and heaven. The integral realization of the self and the proper actualization of social relations within the family or the larger society can only be affected through harmonious participation with earth and heaven. Again, our English language seems inept at expressing the interrelatedness of humans, earth, and heaven. Relationship here must be understood in terms of "the mutual presence of heaven, earth and humans."[10] The Confucian worldview is one of continuity and interpenetration, of harmony woven in the fabric of reality.

JUDAISM, CHRISTIANITY, ISLAM

In the Abrahamic traditions of Judaism, Christianity, and Islam, this theme of interconnectedness is deeply evident in their common emphasis on creation. Human beings and all of nature are the result of God's loving, creative power and, therefore, have intrinsic value. All of creation reflects the image and goodness of God. This does not make nature sacred. Only God is divine and has absolute value. However, all of nature reveals God's glory. The Jewish and Christian scriptures repeatedly affirm that God establishes creation forever, and all creation praises God and fulfills God's word (Gen 1–4; Pss 104, 148; Job; Isa 55). In the Quran, Muslims recognize that "whithersoever you turn there is the Face of God" (11:115) and "there is not an animal [that lives] on earth. Nor a being that flies on its wings, but [forms a part] of a community like you" (6:38)[11] Human beings, animals, plants, sun and moon, all reality comes from God's abundance. Humans are part of the one community of all creation which reflects God's power and praises God's name. The Abrahamic traditions are consistent in seeing creation as an interrelated whole.

In the second chapter of Genesis of the Hebrew scriptures, God creates Adam from *adamah*, which in Hebrew means clay. Humans do not stand apart from the earth; rather, they are part of it and have a special responsibility to tend the garden of creation. In the Islamic tradition, all creation is created from the same element of water. Nawal Amar refers to two verses from the Quran to emphasize this point of the underlying unity of all creation—"We made from water every living thing" (12:30)—and continues in another verse by stating, "And God has created every animal from water; of them there are some that creep on their bellies; some that walk on two legs; and some that walk on four....It is he who has created humans from water" (24:45).[12]

There are particular insights and examples from each of the Abrahamic traditions that are worth exploring to see the broad basis for this theme of interconnectivity. In Judaism, the understanding of Sabbath rest applies not only to human beings but also to one's livestock (Exod 20:10, Deut 5:14). Jews are required by law to be compassionate toward their animals and other aspects of nature. Eric Katz refers to the principle of "*bal tashchit*" or "do not destroy," which prohibits "the wanton destruction of natural entities, living beings (plants and animals) and even human artifacts."[13] Similarly, the law commands the land itself must be allowed to rest (Lev 25). These examples emphasize the moral responsibility humans have toward nature.

In the Christian tradition, this respect for nature is grounded in the many examples of Jesus' teaching in which he uses nature as his authority. To speak of God's lavish care, he refers to the lilies, which neither toil nor spin but are arrayed in glory greater than King Solomon. He emphasizes the importance of acting in tune with one's words with the example of the good tree that bears good fruit. Similarly, the seed sown in good soil produces a hundredfold and the house built on a strong foundation endures. In the teaching of Jesus, nature is a source of God's revelation. We can learn fundamental truths by reading the rhythms and seasons and examples of the whole interconnected web of life.

Muslims point to the words of the Prophet Mohammed and the continuing tradition to emphasize the centrality of the oneness of all creation for Islam. Nawal Amar states, "Hence, the Prophet in his last Sermon stated, 'People: your God is one, you all belong to Adam and Adam to earth…the most honored is the most pious and there is no difference between an Arab and a foreigner.'"[14] There are numerous examples of the Caliphs doing good deeds that respect creation. "Hence, it is reported that the first Muslim Caliph ordered his army 'not to cut down trees, not to abuse a river, not to harm animals and be always kind and gentle to God's creation, even to your enemies.'"[15] In their various ways, the Abrahamic traditions see the universe as interconnected and interdependent. Linked to the one creator of all, nature in its abounding multiplicity is to be respected. God chooses to live in relationship to the whole world, engendering the universe out of love. In response to this recognition, human beings are called to live in harmonious relationship with all created reality.

Principle Three Operating Procedures and Criteria

This principle of interconnectivity in the religions of the world challenges us to be attentive to the organic integration of all reality as we make decisions. We cannot touch the world in one place without sending ripples out in all directions. We cannot change one aspect of an organization, one program, or one policy without having an impact on its many interrelated systems. Removing or adding one member of a team has an impact on all of the relationships among team members. In the mechanical model, we often thought of the system as simply a series of discreet pieces operating in a controlled fashion. When one piece of the machine wore out we could replace it with another piece made with the exact same mold. We now recognize that the mechanistic model does not reflect the dynamism, unpredictability, and coalescence of systems.

Given the inextricable interdependence of reality, we are challenged to investigate the systems of our families, businesses, teams, supply chains, churches, and other human endeavors as we contemplate decisions. Every action we take has an impact on others and on the earth, and has been affected by others and the eco-community to which we belong. We always start in the middle of things, recognizing how our own upbringing, experiences, values, mentors, colleagues, family, and previous decisions affect our present way of seeing a situation that calls for our decision.

Our decisions will have rippling effects on the complex interwoven fabric of natural and human systems, often taking years to play out in long-term consequences that are difficult to envision in the present. Yet, that is our challenge as we make decisions: to see the possible systemic effects of our actions. Peter Senge alludes to the great difficulty of this work when he says, "Since we are part of that lacework ourselves, it's doubly hard to see the whole pattern of change. Instead, we tend to focus on snapshots of isolated parts of the system, and wonder why our deepest problems never seem to get solved."[16] The operating procedures for decision-making and the criteria for judgment that emanate from this principle of interconnectivity offer concrete ways of enlarging our vision, broadening our horizon, and getting to the root of our questions and problems.

OPERATING PROCEDURE 3A:
CONSIDER HOW SYSTEMS WILL BE IMPACTED

In 2005, I set out on a solo backpacking trip and vision quest, a silent time to contemplate my past story and listen for a call that might give me direction for the future. The preparations included several months of journaling and spiritual preparation. Bill Plotkin's *Soulcraft: Crossing into the Mysteries of Nature and Psyche* was an important guide as I planned my interior and exterior journey.[17] For the exterior journey, I chose Isle Royale, a remote island wilderness in Lake Superior and also a natural laboratory for the world's longest continuous study of the relationship between one predator and one prey, the wolf and moose. Since the island does not allow hunting or vehicular traffic, the impact of humans is negligible. Because there are no elk or deer on the island, the relationship between the wolf and a singular prey can be studied. Finally, the cold waters of Lake Superior provide a kind of natural fence that limits the movement of the population in and out of the study area.

Since 1958, wildlife biologists have attempted to understand the relationships between the wolf and moose populations. They use all of the obvious ways of observing these creatures. They count them. They measure predation rates by counting the total number of moose that a wolf pack kills divided by the pack size divided by the number of days the pack is observed. They collect moose bones and teeth to identify age and diseases. They measure the growth of plants that moose eat and the depth of snow that has an impact on the availability of food and the mobility of moose calves. Moose fecal and urine samples are also taken from the snow to help determine pregnancy, diet, and nutritional status.[18] These measurements are done year after year in an attempt to reveal a pattern in the relationship between island wolves and moose.

What are the key factors in the rise and fall of the populations of predator and prey? Can we know all the variables? Rolf Peterson, one of the main researchers on Isle Royale, tells many surprising stories about the unexpected disappearance of an alpha female wolf, the wondrous resiliency in one wolf pack when, after two years of zero reproduction, four new pups show up to continue the line, the female wolf who acquires her sister's pups and becomes the alpha female of the pack while her sister is banished.[19] Peterson concludes his latest commentary on the long Isle Royale study with sobering words about the complexity of the world and how tentative our conclusions must be:

> ...when it comes to the dynamics of predator and prey, we don't know as much as we once thought....We don't put much stock in predictions anymore, even on Isle Royale, where so much is known about the wolves and the moose. A bit of humility is in order, for scientists as well as politi-

cians.…Finally, on an optimistic note, the world is a fascinating and resilient place…[20]

There is a squiggly dotted line that connects my days of fasting, hiking, and listening on Isle Royale to your reading this book. Of the five days of my vision quest, the first two were full of sunshine. The last three brought drenching cold rains and constant winds more than 30 miles an hour and gusts to 50. I learned a great deal about listening to the voice within and about letting go of expectations. In five days, I hadn't seen a moose or heard the call of wolves. I wanted some deep and transformative message that would set me on a new course with clear direction. It wasn't until I gave up all hope of receiving such a message that I could genuinely listen with unguarded vulnerability. On what I thought would be my final night on the island, I sat in my tiny tent pelted by rain and buffeted by the wind. In the midst of one of the blackest nights of my life, there was indeed the spark of insight, the voice of wisdom.

When I arrived at the visitor center the following day, tired and ready to go home, the park ranger informed me that the ferry, which almost never canceled a trip, was not running because of the stormy conditions. Clearly, I was not in control. During my last, unscheduled night on the island, in the cold and silent darkness, I heard the howls of wolves, a song of the wild interconnectedness of things that still resonates in my soul and in my work. The next day, just before the ferry left the island, I spotted a moose and her calf. My time on Isle Royale gave me a deeper sense of the interwoven web of life and the importance of bringing the ancient and universal wisdom of the spiritual traditions into our personal and organizational lives.

When I returned to Isle Royale during the summer of 2011 for five days of backpacking with my partner, I read an exhibit in the Windigo visitor center that reported on Leah Vucetich's determination to find new ways to observe moose. She simply wrote down everything she saw as she visited one of the swamps where moose regularly came to feed. The placard noted that Leah's observations led to the systematic monitoring of the annual tick infestations on moose. Using note cards with the profile of a moose, observers indicate "how much hair moose have lost to ticks—an indicator of tick loads."[21] Study of these observations indicates that there may be a correlation between high tick loads, which weaken moose, and the rates of wolf predation. I was struck that it took more than forty years to come to the realization that this small insect may be a big player in the complex story of predation and survival.

Be Attentive to Interconnections in the System

What is very clear from the Isle Royale experiment and from observing organizations of every kind is the importance of taking into account the interactions within the system. To make wise decisions, we must be attentive to the interconnecting factors that are involved, the patterns of behaviors, and the multiple influences that impact a situation. Fred Kofman in *Conscious Business* gives an example from the building trade. Substitute your organization's product or service for Brazilian pink granite and the example may sound very familiar.

> Brazilian pink granite, in slabs two feet square, sliced to face onto twenty-four-foot precast concrete columns. The granite should be half flamed and half polished. The joints have to be perfect so the columns look like solid granite. We need thirty columns, by the end of April at the latest. Can you do it?[22]

The sales manager promised the order on time without consulting the production supervisor or the granite supplier in Brazil, without seriously considering the present production backlog, the level of inventory, the possibility of shipping delays, or many of the other major factors that may impact the ability to deliver this order. He focused instead on the opportunity to get a major new customer. The final result included failing to meet the deadline, angering the new customer, whose repeat business is doubtful, further stressing a workforce already working significant overtime, and failing to meet a commitment made to a longtime customer whose order was put on hold.

Systems-thinking requires more attention to the intersections of the diverse factors required to deliver the order on time. Even more, it requires a long-range vision that considers the consequences of not fulfilling one's promises. Devoid of systems-thinking, the sales manager may well put the blame on one of the players in this scenario—the production supervisor or the supplier—without understanding the role he played in it and the complexity of the interactions among all the players. Systems-thinking helps us see the decisions considered will often have significant consequences many years down the road. These consequences are obvious when we think about investment in research and development, creation of new facilities, and the hiring of key personnel. In such situations, it is critical to consider long-term consequences by raising difficult questions about the complexity of the future organization. This is very difficult to do in organizational cultures in which there is pressure to have the answers and always to look competent. The most competent organizations will intentionally explore the unknown and look beyond their own assumptions and mental models through rigorous inquiry.

Systems-thinking is critically important in our personal decision-making as well. Wise parenting requires us to pay attention to the interactions among our family members, developmental processes of growth, diverse relationships with friends, and the talents, passions, and aversions of our children. It requires a long-range perspective that attempts to see the consequences of decisions well into the future as we help to shape the character of our children.

One of my most difficult parenting decisions was taking away driving rights for six months from my youngest son. He had gotten into some significant trouble, although it was obvious he wasn't the only one to blame. Yet, I wanted the punishment to clearly reflect the gravity of his inappropriate behavior. At the same time, I didn't want the punishment to be so onerous that it would impact his positive and buoyant perspective on life. Taking away the car was a very big deal and he made sure that I understood this. After a month, he sat down and spoke with me about the situation. He expressed his regret for getting into trouble. It would have been easy to back down on the punishment; it also would have decreased the hours spent driving him to many practices and events. I decided not to decrease the punishment, not after the first month or the second or the fifth, although each month he repeated his request. Now that he is an adult, he has more than once told me how important that lesson was and how much he learned about keeping one's word.

Going back to school, taking a different job, moving to a new home, and volunteering on a non-profit board are all decisions that can have major impacts on the physical, psychological, and spiritual aspects of individuals and their friends, family, and coworkers. Faced with these or similar decisions, we must attempt to consider how our decision will affect all of these dimensions of our lives and how interdependent interactions may also have an influence on the situation. For instance, the age of children in the family may be a significant factor in deciding about a possible move to a different city. There are times in a young adolescent's life when friendships begin to play a larger role than family as children shape their identity. However, we must extend our thought process to consider the interactions among the child's developmental process, psychological health, relationships with friends, relationships with teachers, quality of education in the new location, children in the neighborhood of the new home, and so forth.

See the Whole Picture

Systems-thinking challenges us to see things as wholly as possible. Seeing the whole picture requires we look beyond individual events to patterns of behavior, look beyond patterns of behavior to the structures, policies, procedures, and unwritten laws that impact those patterns, and, finally, look beyond structures to the underlying ways of thinking, assumptions, and mental models that created the structures. Pegasus Communications, a major provider of systems-thinking materials, newsletters, and conferences, provides an example that clarifies these different ways of seeing:

> ...suppose a fire breaks out in your town. This is an *event*. If you respond to it simply by putting the fire out, you're reacting. (That is, you have done nothing to prevent new fires.) If you respond by putting out the fire and studying where fires tend to break out in your town, you'd be paying attention to *patterns*. For example, you might notice that certain neighborhoods seem to suffer more fires than others. If you locate more fire stations in those areas, you're adapting. (You still haven't done anything to prevent new fires.) Now suppose you look for the *systems*— such as smoke-detector distribution and building materials used—that influence the patterns of neighbor-

hood-fire outbreaks. If you build new fire-alarm systems and establish fire and safety codes, you're creating change. Finally, you're doing something to prevent new fires![23]

Although the importance of systems-thinking seems obvious when looking at this example, our decisions are often a response to singular events. Sometimes, we intentionally explore patterns of behavior in our decision-making. Unfortunately, only a minority of individuals and organizations regularly explore systems and mental models in the decision-making process. When there is an increase in crime, it is not unusual for a city to hire more police or locate a police station in the distressed area.

The police department in Carrollton, Texas, offers a systems approach motivated by a servant leadership philosophy. Carrollton is a suburb of about 115,000 citizens in Northwest Dallas; it has more than 160 sworn personnel. After many years of command-and-control hierarchy and focusing attention on urgent matters and routine operations without getting around to solving chronic problems, an inspired and empowered group of officers who were introduced to servant leadership created a Community Problem-Oriented Policing (CPOP) unit. They volunteered to be part of the group and were determined to "tackle a tough problem and show the effectiveness of this kind of voluntary servant leadership."[24]

They decided to tackle one of their biggest headaches—vehicle break-ins. When it was first suggested, most of the officers thought it was preposterous. Why attempt the impossible? The department was spending thirty hours for each investigation of a vehicle break-in; the problem was a tremendous drain on their time, energy, and morale. The CPOP decided to take a holistic approach to the problem, one that included attention to lighting, reasons for break-ins, education of citizens, and reinforcement of learning.

> ...they communicated with neighbors...by going door to door, leaving fliers when people were not at home. The night shifts reported areas where street lights were out. Street signs were put up advertising the "H.E.A.T." (help end auto theft) effort. Officers created a report card which they left on car windshields as they walked or biked the

beat. The car got a passing grade if it was locked and no valuables were visible within. Conversely, a failing grade was given (and the reason for it) if the car was unlocked or there were valuables visible.[25]

Local media gave the program major free publicity and the results were astounding. The total number of vehicle break-ins reported dropped by 94 percent in the first eight months. When we look holistically at a problem or situation, our decisions respond to root causes rather than react to symptoms.

For those serious about systems-thinking, a study of system archetypes, links, and loops can be very helpful. Even without significant study, there are some rules of thumb that help to engage a systems-thinking approach. First, ask "why" at least five or six times. This will help to get to the root cause of the problem, to the root reason of one's own motivation, or to the root understanding of what another is really thinking. Sometimes asking "why" several times allows me to see that I am emotionally reacting to a situation and that some of my fears are unsubstantiated. Second, as far as possible, broaden the conversation so that different perspectives are taken into account as options are considered. Everyone's perspective and understanding of a situation that calls for a decision can be expanded through respectful listening to others (even those who disagree) and investigation of diverse views. Finally, whenever possible, take the time to see things from a mega-temporal vantage point. Look at past experience and trends as well as future viable options and probable consequences for all of the stakeholders related to the decision.

The leaders of the highly successful firms of endearment to which I have referred in previous chapters "tend to think in unitive fashion, approaching their tasks with holistic vision in which no player in the game of commerce is *a priori* more important than any other player, all are connected."[26] They see their various stakeholders as "part of a complex network of interests that function in a matrix of interdependencies."[27] To be effective leaders of our own lives and families and communities, we need the same kind of expansive approach that looks at systems and assumptions in the wise decision-making process.

OPERATING PROCEDURE 3B:
RESEARCH EFFECTS ON COMMUNITY
AND ENVIRONMENT

The Western notion of the individual person who strives for independence and self-actualization is only one way of seeing ourselves. A different outlook acknowledges that we are fundamentally communal. Our biological life arises from the union of our parents. It is only in relationship we learn to speak and love. Our mental and emotional well-being is bound to the larger story of a family, a people, a country, a species. We are connected to earth and orbit, breathing stardust and taking our nourishment from the soil. If we attempt to separate ourselves from our sustaining planet, we soon die of thirst. We are undeniably part of a human community that is dependent upon the earth. To make wise decisions, we must seriously reflect on our inextricable relationships with one another and our planet, lest we risk our own health and our very existence.

Although much has been done in the past forty years to help developing countries, more than a quarter of the population of the world still lives on less than $1.25 per day and doesn't have access to clean water, sufficient food, or adequate sanitation.[28] The United Nations 2011 Human Development Report shows that sustainability is inextricably linked to basic questions of equity, fairness, social justice, and a better quality of life. Those most affected by environmental degradation are the poor.[29] Each change in the environment, climate, or quality of air or water has consequences for the seven billion people who presently populate the earth and for the billions of future generations.

Human Development Threatened
by Ecological Degradation

The UN report makes a powerful statement about the interlinking of continuing human development and our ecological challenges. Those who are in dire poverty "are more vulnerable to the wider effects of environmental degradation…Forecasts suggest that continuing failure to reduce the grave environmental risks and deepening social inequalities threatens to slow decades of sustained progress by the world's poor majority—and even to reverse the global convergence in human development."[30] After decades of rising indicators and remarkable progress in the quality of life for the poorest of the poor, water pollution, air pollution, deforestation, and global warming threaten the progress that has been made. The findings of the UN report are not new; similar research results were affirmed at the 1972 Stockholm Conference on the Human Environment, the 1992 Rio de Janeiro conference on Environment and Development, and the 2002 Johannesburg World Summit on Sustainable Development. If the world community resolutely addresses the environmental concerns that we face, the UN report provides a hopeful vision.

> If we deal decisively with these challenges, we could be on the cusp of an era of historic opportunities for expanded choices and freedoms. But if we fail to act, future generations may remember the early 21st century as the time when the doors to a better future closed for most of the world's people. We care about environmental sustainability because of the fundamental injustice of one generation living at the expense of others. People born today should not have a greater claim on Earth's resources than those born a hundred or a thousand years from now. We can do much to ensure that our use of the world's resources does not damage future opportunities—and we should.[31]

We are beginning to realize how deeply in trouble we are as a global community and as a planetary ecosystem. An attitude of arrogant scientism and unbridled consumerism in developed countries has deeply harmed our human community and our planet. It is time to take a more humble stance toward the natural world, to admit "that there are gaps in our knowledge large enough for the future of the planet to fall through."[32] It is time to recognize the bonds of human affection that link us as sisters and brothers around the globe. It is time to ask ourselves, with every decision we make, how our actions will impact the lives of others and the environment that sustains us. We must err on the side of preservation, conservation, simplicity, and respect.

Perhaps the element of air most clearly represents our fundamental dependence on the environment and our interdependence as a species. We cannot intentionally stop breathing. In less than thirty seconds, our bodies scream for air, heart and head pound to get our attention. If we don't listen, the body turns off the conscious mind and takes over to ensure that this most basic process of inspiration happens. As we breathe, we "absorb atoms that were once part of Joan of Arc and Jesus Christ, of Neanderthal people and woolly mammoths. As we have breathed in our forebears, so our grandchildren and their grandchildren will take us in with their breath."[33]

We become painfully aware of our interconnectedness as air-breathers when radioisotopes or lethal chemicals are released into the air and blown over a community or a large geographical area. The results are deadly, as with the chemical leak at a pesticide plant in Bhopal, India, in 1984 that immediately killed at least 3,800 people and caused significant morbidity and premature death for many thousands more."[34] In 1986, an explosion and fire at the Chernobyl nuclear plant in the Ukraine released significant quantities of radioactive contamination that were first detected in Sweden and brought to the attention of the world. The food supply and farming of much of Europe were affected. For instance, radioactive caesium in the upland soil and grass in Britain was ingested by sheep. It has taken twenty-five years for the radioactivity to decrease to a safe level so the testing of lambs from originally 9,800 sheep farms may be discontinued in 2012.[35]

Lest we think these are issues of the past, the Fukushima Daiichai nuclear disaster that occurred as a result of the earthquake and tsunami on March 11, 2011 has been categorized as level 7 on the Nuclear Event Scale, the highest possible level, with significant ramifications on water and food supply. Air is a shared resource. It has no national boundaries. Our common bond as a human family is very real.

Interdependent Flourishing

In our interconnected community, we human beings have an immense responsibility. As individuals and organizations, our actions reverberate beyond the present moment and we have the reflective awareness to make decisions that take into account the hoped-for future, our dreams for generations to come. With our innovative and curious minds, we have investigated the depths below us and the heights above through science and technology. We have created a broad web of shared information with computers and telecommunications. Our present challenge is to use our knowledge and creativity "to rediscover our connections to time and space, our place in the biosphere...search for a new understanding of the world, regain a sense of its fecundity, its generosity and its welcome for the errant species we've become."[36] At the same time, we must reaffirm our connections to each other and the importance of all our diverse voices and unique perspectives as we attempt to understand what is true and good.

When we consider the effects our actions may have on our local and global community and on our environment, we make decisions that support our continuing interdependent flourishing. That flourishing includes not only economic or material well-being but also the health of our spirit. *Firms of Endearment* investigates businesses that transcend "the narrower perspectives of most companies in the past, rising to embrace the common welfare in its concerns."[37] This sea change of social responsibility and community orientation is happening not because of some consummate business strategy based on broad interacting variables or some new calculus to accumulate personal wealth. More and more individuals, including CEOs, are concerned with making a difference in the world. When a 2002 Conference Board survey asked seven hundred executives "why their companies engaged in social or citizenship initiatives...84 percent said they were driven by motivations such as improving society, company traditions, or their personal values."[38]

Perhaps the economic and social effects of greed and rampant self-interest in every facet of our society over the past several decades have awakened our sense of responsibility. Perhaps we are finally recognizing how our wild rush to accumulate material goods has brought our planet to the brink of systems failure. Whatever the cause, there is broad evidence of a renewed moral sensibility that acknowledges our inextricable interdependence. In 2004, Jeff Immelt, CEO of General Electric, told two hundred of his top executives that "GE needed to do four things to remain a leader. Three of the four were laudable but predictable: execution, growth, and hiring good people. But at the top of the list was virtue."[39] He based his remarks on his perception that people want to work for an organization that is making a contribution in the world and cares about people. The authors of *Firms of Endearment* identify one key characteristic at the core of all the highly successful businesses they researched—"they possess a humanistic soul.…These companies are imbued with the joy of service—to the community, to society, to the environment, to customers, to colleagues."[40]

Certainly there is much evidence that indicates that a great deal needs to be done by many more organizations and individuals in order to turn the tide of environmental degradation or to begin to address the wide gap between the wealthy and poor that has continued to widen over the past several decades.[41] However, organizations are no longer motivated to go green only by environmental regulations or fines and penalties. "Why Companies Go Green: A Model of Ecological Responsiveness" indicates many firms believe that their long-range competitiveness depends on ecological responsiveness that may include energy and waste reduction and the development of green products.[42] Some authors argue that sustainability is the key competitive advantage in the present environmental context.[43] It is even more important to note that many firms are involved in significant environmental efforts because they are committed to greater ecological responsibility. "A salient feature of this motivation was a concern for the social good. The ethical aspects of ecological responsibility, rather than the pragmatic, were emphasized…Firms acted out of a sense of obligation, responsibility, or philanthropy rather than out of self-interest."[44]

Along with increased ecological responsibility, many companies are recognizing they have an obligation to society and to the community of which they are a part. They "encourage and reward employees for volunteering time and talents to support initiatives that benefit the local communities in which they operate."[45] *Firms of Endearment* provides commendable examples from REI, Harley-Davidson, Honda, New Balance, Patagonia, and others. From creating foundations that focus on local needs to investing in the infrastructure of their communities, businesses are making decisions that keep the community in mind as one of the key stakeholders.

Most of the examples in this section have been from businesses, but what we do as individuals can have a tremendous impact on the environment and on our local and global community. When we buy a hybrid car, refrain from using bottled water, ride our bike to work, or shop at the local farmer's market, our decisions decrease fossil fuel consumption and pollution. Greenchoices.org says 72 percent of our car trips are less than five miles and 50 percent are under two miles.

If we made those trips on foot or by bicycle, car mileage could be cut by one-sixth.[46] Most of us could use the extra exercise and we might even slow down our lifestyle a little. We are making a positive difference when we eat at a restaurant that buys local organic food, volunteer at a non-profit organization that provides job training for the poor, mentor a struggling student, or contribute to the local food shelf. Our individual actions joined with the decisions of our fellow citizens can impact the environment and bring about real change in the lives of many in our communities.

If we are serious about being part of the solution, action is required on three levels. First, we need to continue to learn and grow in our understanding of the issues and concerns in our local and global community. In a sense this is interior work, developing our knowledge and our sensitivity. Second, we must do what we can to address the issues at hand. The examples in the last paragraph are all things that we can do ourselves to address environmental and community concerns. This is the level of personal involvement—making a difference by our individual actions and decisions. The third level of action relates to the structures, policies, and institutions of society. Most major changes at this level only come about because significant groups of people are working for change together. Each of these levels of involvement is important. Only when we continue our own personal development and education do we recognize the important issues that face us. With this knowledge, we realize we must become personally involved, using our own time, energy, and resources to make a difference in a way that fits with our skills and interests. We also recognize that larger systemic innovations often require being a part of an organization that advocates for changes in company policies, governmental regulations, laws, educational programs, institutions, and the like.

CRITERIA FOR JUDGMENT 3A:
RESPOND TO NEEDS OF THE WHOLE COMMUNITY

When we recognize the interconnectedness of things, we also realize our concerns as individuals and organizations must be focused on the interactions and relationships that make up the whole community, the whole web of life within which we live and work. We do not have the luxury of being one-issue persons or organizations. Profit or wealth accumulation cannot be our only concern or our only measure of success. What firms of endearment and many other good-citizen businesses are teaching us is that balancing the values and needs of all stakeholders leads to a sustainable and productive organization. Healthy families, unions, churches, and social organizations are similarly involved in the careful balancing of multiple perspectives and needs.

Whole Foods formalizes this recognition in its Declaration of Interdependence, which states:

> One of the most important responsibilities of Whole Food Market's leadership is to make sure the interests, desires, and needs of our various stakeholders are kept in balance. It requires participation and communication by all our stakeholders. It requires listening compassionately, thinking carefully, and acting with integrity. Any conflicts must be mediated and win-win solutions found. Creating and nurturing this community of stakeholders is critical to the long-term success of our company.[47]

This increasing recognition by businesses of the value of multiple stakeholders is concretely translated into actions that have far-reaching effects in the lives of communities, employees, suppliers, shareholders, and inhabitants of the planet. Here are a few examples:

- Patagonia gives one percent of sales or ten percent of profits, whichever is greater, to earth-related concerns.[48]
- Starbucks helps to preserve small family coffee bean farms.[49]
- New Balance manufactures 30 percent of its shoes in the United States, using well paid workers who are ten times more productive than its Asia workers.[50]
- Wegmans pays well above average wages (15 to 17 percent of sales compared to the typical 12 percent of sales) to keep knowledgeable employees who provide exceptional service to customers.[51]
- UPS in two years helped 20,000 part-time employees attend college, spending more than $9 million on tuition, fees, and books in the first year of the program.[52]
- Costco employees earn more than twice as much as Wal-Mart employees but generate three times the revenue.[53]

One of the most promising models of an organization that is responding to the needs of the community and creating green jobs at the same time is the Evergreen Cooperative "in Cleveland's Greater University Circle community, where the unemployment rate exceeds 25 percent and the median household income is less than $18,500."[54] A series of cooperatives owned by workers supply the needs of anchor institutions— Case Western Reserve, the Cleveland Clinic, and University Hospitals—with laundry services, solar power, and fresh lettuce and herbs. Each of the cooperatives is green to the maximum. Evergreen Laundry uses considerably less water and energy than its competitors. Ohio Cooperative Solar installs solar panels on the rooftops of the anchor institutions and sells them the solar energy. Green City Growers uses robust water and energy-saving technology in its hydroponic greenhouse.

This is an amazing story of hope—transforming lives, creating good jobs for those in poverty, rebuilding a community, providing exceptional service and products for the anchor institutions, and doing all of it in a way that respects the planet.[55] When decisions truly take into account the needs of a community and the environment, creative solutions can create value for all stakeholders.

When we make choices in our individual lives to become active in our local and global community, we often create relationships across economic, cultural, and racial divides that broaden our vision and our empathy. Our lives are enriched as we engage in events and activities that bring together a diverse community of concerned, involved citizens. We keep learning and expanding our understanding of the complex dynamics of our political systems, our governmental agencies, our business community, and our nonprofit organizations. When we sow our talents and gifts in the community, we often reap a deeper sense of hope. We are encouraged by the dedication of others and the stories of success. The word *encourage* comes from the French word for *heart*. Our hearts get bigger when we serve an important cause or reach out to others in need.

Choosing what responds to the needs of the whole community requires that we see the complexity of its interactions. Without an awareness of the interrelated systems at work, often we are not able to bring about substantial change. The difficulty of effecting reform in the U.S. public education system is an instructive example where major funders like the Annenberg Foundation, Ford Foundation, and Pew Charitable Trusts abandoned major efforts because of lack of progress. In contrast, a powerful success story is emerging in Cincinnati and northern Kentucky. "In four years since the group was launched, Strive partners have improved student success in dozens of key areas across three large public school districts."[56] What sets this effort apart from so many other attempts at reform is the intentionally close collaboration among diverse agencies. They are succeeding where others have failed because more than three hundred concerned community leaders from corporate foundations, city government, three public school districts, eight universities and community colleges, and hundreds of education-related nonprofit groups gave up their individual agendas to work collectively toward a set of agreed-upon student achievement goals.

> These leaders realized that fixing one point on the educational continuum—such as better after-school programs —wouldn't make much difference unless all parts of the continuum improved at the same time. No single organization, however innovative or powerful, could accomplish this alone. Instead, their ambitious mission became to coordinate improvements at *every* stage of a young persons' life, from "cradle to career."[57]

When we recognize the interrelationships within our community, we are more able to choose what responds to the needs of the whole. No individual or organization can do everything, but we can do something. Some persons and organizations will address immediate needs, while others work at collaborative efforts that address significant issues at a systemic level. Whatever role we choose to play, we must attempt to recognize the needs of the whole community and choose that which brings about benefit for the greater common good.

CRITERIA FOR JUDGMENT 3B: ATTEND TO THE LONG TERM HEALTH OF THE EARTH

When we view the needs of the whole community from the broadest possible perspective, we recognize the foundational importance of the ecosystem of the earth. We depend upon the earth and we are shaped by it. It is the all-encompassing context that affects every organic function of our bodies and every mental construct of our minds every moment of our existence. Although we can reroute rivers, engineer new hybrid crops, lower our cholesterol and blood pressure with pharmaceuticals, and predict, quite inaccurately, volcanic eruptions and earthquakes, still our every breath is taken within the precious envelope of the atmosphere of earth. David Abram in *Becoming Animal* offers a stunning recital of the earth's influence on every iota of our existence.

> ...we could say that the brain itself is an introjection of the earth, an analogue or avatar of the planet happily riding atop our spine....the large-scale structures of the brain (the cerebral tissues and organs found across persons and even across species) have formed themselves in response to the most stable structures of the perceptual field, to the openness of the horizon and the density of the ground on a planet with this specific gravity, to the chill nourishment of rain and the steady singing of birds.[58]

From Abram's perspective, the attainment of our full humanity depends on a deep identification with and respect for the earth and all its creatures. It depends on our "interbeing with the earth" which "swells within and unfolds all around us."[59] He calls for a renewed empathy with soil and trees, sky and birds, rivers and fish, forests and four-legged creatures. This is an immense challenge since our instinctive sensitivity to the earth has been stunted by seeing ourselves as divinely mandated to tame the wild. We have failed to imagine the consequences of our greedy gobbling up of the earth's resources to fulfill our every wish and whim.

I will not attempt to catalog the degradation we have done to our planet or the present fragile state of our ecosystem. I hope it will be enough to hear the consensus of "more than sixteen hundred senior scientists from seventy-one countries, including over half of all Nobel Prize winners" who released a document entitled "World Scientists' Warning to Humanity" on November 18, 1992.[60]

> Human beings and the natural world are on a collision course. Human activities inflict harsh and often irreversible damage on the environment and on critical resources. If not

checked, many of our current practices put at serious risk the future that we wish for human society and the plant and animal kingdoms, and may so alter the living world that we will be unable to sustain life in the manner that we know....No more than one or a few decades remain before the chance to avert the threats we now confront will be lost and the prospects for humanity immeasurably diminished.[61]

In this context, we must carefully consider the consequences of our individual and organizational decisions on the health of the planet, not only for the short-term but for long-range sustainability. Whether we are buying a refrigerator, building a home, designing a new product or its packaging, or engineering a manufacturing process, we must ask ourselves how we can be most responsible in our stewardship of the earth. We must study and try to imagine the consequences of our choices on an already deeply compromised ecosystem.

This criterion for wise decision-making not only stems from a review of the spiritual traditions of the world; it is also part of the best practices of strong organizations. For instance, on the Deloitte Web site, a major player in providing business consulting, risk management, and audit services, there are several documents on water stewardship. The following quotation by William Sarni, director and practice leader, Enterprise Water Strategy, for Deloitte Consulting LLP, provides clear, general advice:

> ...it is essential for companies to develop a holistic strategy and plan for reducing water usage, protecting and preserving the water supply and developing contingency plans to ensure business continuity in the event of a severe shortage. In this day and age, smart companies wouldn't dream of operating without a risk management strategy for critical resources such as information systems and energy. It's time to think of water in the same way.[62]

Thankfully, there are many firms leading the way in responsible use of resources. IKEA puts strong demands on its suppliers to use timber only "from responsibly managed forests certified by the Forest Stewardship Council."[63] BMW's plant in Greer, South Carolina, is recognized by state and federal environmental agencies as "holding one of the most stringent environmental certifications in the business" and uses "methane from a local landfill to generate 25 percent of the electricity of the plant," which "earned it the Environmental Protection Agency's Green Power Leadership Award of 2003."[64] Patagonia's "Reno, Nevada, service center was constructed with only recycled or reclaimed materials" and it uses only organic cotton in its entire sportswear line.[65] In 2005, "Timberland offered $3,000 to each of its 6,000 employees to help fund the purchase of new hybrid electric vehicles." It has long been a leader in reducing the use of solvents and toxic chemicals in its production of footwear.[66]

If the long-term health of the earth is to be a key criterion in our decision-making, we must find ways to give voice to the planet. This may seem like a strange idea, but Paula Underwood's classic story *Who Speaks for Wolf* has been a tremendously formative tale for me. The story tells of one person in the tribe who learns the way of the wolf, becomes brother to wolf, and speaks for wolf when important decisions are made. Similarly, the decision-making process includes listening to other experts, the one who understands the flow of waters, the one who is adept at Long House construction, the one who knows the storms of winter, and the one who is most wise about the three sisters—corn, beans, and squash—and the soil and climate that is best for them. On one occasion, when the people were deciding on a new place to relocate the growing tribe, the one who speaks for wolf was gone. Wolf's concerns were not heard before the decision was made. So the people moved to a place that was a center place for wolf. The relations between the people and wolf were very difficult. The people attempted to defend themselves against wolf but wolf was too shrewd. They attempted to feed wolf but wolf soon began to consume too much of their time and food supply. Finally, the people considered killing wolf. Here is a bit of Paula Underwood's story:

> They saw, too
>> That such a task would change the People:
>>> they would become Wolf Killers
> A People who took life only to sustain their own
>> would become a People who took life
>>> rather than move a little

It did not seem to them
   That they wanted to become such a People[67]

Sensitivity to the voice of the planet in our decision-making confronts us with that ultimate question: Who are we now and who do we want to become? Perhaps every one of us is being called to speak for the earth. If we befriend one small piece of the earth, one tree we daily greet outside our window, a stretch of river we hike along once a year, a few acres of prairie we walk through occasionally, we will learn to listen to its voice. We will develop a close relationship with one small part of the body of the beloved earth, observe its rhythms, feast at its table, listen to its songs, and learn to speak for earth. If we dare speak the language of earth at our decision-making tables, we could dream of our grandchildren's grandchildren down to the seventh generation.

On Uncle Bill's farm, I learned that every action has consequences. In giving voice to the earth in our decision-making, we consider perhaps the most important consequence of all—the quality of life for us and our fellow dwellers on the planet. The consequences are sometimes very clear, as in my experience of promising to fill the water tank.

WORD

I spent most of my growing summers on my uncle's green farm.
He worked nights in the factory, days in the fields, and knew
the ache and joy of a dream. So every hand was welcome
and something cellular in me longed for the farm's rituals,
its stretching horizon, its lessons simple as seed.

Cutting alfalfa in the shiver of an early morning, oily warmth
coming off the tractor's engine, sweet perfume rising
from the severed stalks, then, a feast of breakfast and milk
full of cream from last night's milking. All gathered in the warm
kitchen, everyone's role in the day ahead laid out like dance
   steps.

I remember the day I promised to fill the water tank
before the lumbering cows, each with a name, came

home from pasture. Cows don't give milk unless
they drink water. And I forgot. My uncle took me aside:
"Your word must mean something." No lecture, no
long examples. That evening, he told me to carry carefully
the pails after each cow was milked, pail after pail half empty.

And still I name my deepest longing a word that means
something, a word made flesh, no difference between
the promise and the act. When war is waged
   on less than truth
and language slick as Minnesota sleet fills laws and speeches,
Word, true as milk and bread, light the stars again
and let me not forget to be what I have spoken.

In many of our decisions, the consequences are certainly not as obvious as in the poem above, but that doesn't let us off the hook. Our challenge in the decision-making process is to recognize the interconnectedness of the elements within systems and the systems themselves that are impacted by our choices. Without seeking certainty, we must err on the side of compassion and harmony. We must take into account the poor and disenfranchised in our communities. We must listen to the earth itself, groaning under the heavy burden of our misuse. We are part of the interconnected web of life. What we do to the earth, its soil, water, and atmosphere, we ultimately do to ourselves.

Questions for Reflection

What are two of your strengths and two weaknesses in ecological sensitivity and responsiveness personally or as an organization? How can you continue to enhance your areas of strength and begin to address your areas of weakness?

What are the two most important concerns or needs in your local community? What are you or your organization doing about these concerns? Are you involved enough or could you do more?

What two concrete actions might you be able to take in your personal or professional life that would lead to deeper consideration of the needs of the community and environment in your personal or organizational decision-making?

An Assessment of Community Awareness and Involvement

The following assessment may help you understand how well you are attending to the needs of your local community. As you rate yourself, try to think of concrete examples in the last month of each of the areas that you are rating. If you are unable to recall specific examples of your involvement, you may wish to rate yourself on the lower end of the scale. If you are able to articulate for yourself specific instances of involvement, you may wish to rate yourself on the higher end of the scale.

I am informed about the key issues and concerns in my community.

High   9   8   7   6   5   4   3   2   Low

I regularly take into account the concerns within my community when making decisions.

High   9   8   7   6   5   4   3   2   Low

My decisions reflect a deep consideration of the poor and marginalized.

High   9   8   7   6   5   4   3   2   Low

I am a contributing and involved member of my community.

High   9   8   7   6   5   4   3   2   Low

I bring people together to collaborate on needs in my community.

High   9   8   7   6   5   4   3   2   Low

VALUE INNER WISDOM AND PERSONAL EXPERIENCE

WISDOM PRINCIPLE	OPERATING PROCEDURES	CRITERIA FOR JUDGMENT CHOOSE WHAT...
Principle 4: Value inner wisdom and personal experience.	OP 4A. Reflect on experience deeply and broadly. OP 4B. Appreciatively inquire into values, vision and best practices.	C 4A. Addresses the full reality of the present experience. C 4B. Is most constructive to life.

*I*t is often easier to take the outer journey than the inner one, easier to ask for advice, hire a consultant, interrogate another expert, gather additional data, hold another meeting, brainstorm more options, read another book, or research another benchmark. Although all of this external wisdom can be helpful and important, it cannot substitute for the wisdom that comes from within. To make wise decisions, we must consult the deep knowing that arises out of our own experience and core values, the call that resonates at the heart of our authentic self.

One of my teachers about this interior wisdom has been Virginia "Ginny" Gilmore. I was vice president for academic affairs at Marian University when I first met Gilmore. She arrived at my office one late summer day with a request. At least that's what she called it; in reality, it was a proposal delivered with passion and conviction. She wanted to complete her bachelor's degree by studying servant leadership and spirituality. And she wanted her first course to be a self-directed, two-month sabbatical experience in the woods during which she would read, journal, and reflect on her calling. I remember saying to myself, "This lady is clearly determined and this is a much more constructive response to a midlife crisis than buying a red convertible."

Since I had spent several years as dean of lifelong learning, creating and managing degree and certificate programs for non-traditional learners, I could assure her we had a process for self-designing a major and enough courses in leadership and spirituality that she could craft something that would fit her vision. I also had a wonderful colleague in the theology department who could work with her on creating her very personal first course. Gilmore proceeded to tell me her story and to ask me to share mine in return. In the course of a few months, she had experienced three major changes in her life: her youngest daughter graduated from high school and was enrolled in college half way across the country; she was separated from her second husband, who soon started divorce proceedings; and she left her position as vice president of customer service in a family business that she co-owned and worked in for seventeen years.

Gilmore wrote a seventy-three page final report on her soul-searching in the woods, consulting her experience and listening to her heart, which she entitled "The Heroine's Journey." In the prologue of this document she writes:

> So there I was: no children at home, no husband and no job! Besides that, I was about to celebrate my fiftieth birthday.…I planned a two-month sabbatical for September and October in a setting that reminded me of sacred time, my childhood. I was ready for a new journey of silence and solitude. I could no longer find excuses to wait. I had come face to face with my own heart. It was time to meet my soul.[1]

She called her journey of listening to her inner wisdom and personal experience "time to meet my soul." The spiritual traditions have their own names for the soul: the core, the interior spirit, the authentic self, or the essential character of a person. Parker Palmer refers to some of these diverse names for the soul in *A Hidden Wholeness*. He says, "Thomas Merton called it true self. Buddhists call it original nature or big self. Quakers call it the inner teacher or the inner light. Hasidic Jews call it a spark of the divine. Humanists call it identity and integrity."[2] Whatever tradition we consult or whatever name we use, a common realization exists across cultures and religions that there is a center in a person where we are called to be responsible for our own life. This core is constantly in formation and development, taking in new data and experience. The soul can be enlarged consciously or unconsciously through openness to new ideas, interesting persons, art of all kinds, reflective or meditative practices, and deep listening to others' stories. Even though everyone has such a core, accessing it or meeting one's soul often doesn't happen at will or upon request. The soul is a shy and wild thing. It often requires silence, solitude, and patience.

Although Ginny's time in the woods included many difficult experiences of feeling alone and abandoned, of doubt and exhaustion, she slowly began to experience a deep sense of new direction and purpose in her life. She wrote:

> Movement toward self-acceptance and self-forgiveness is evolving. By last night, I was really comfortable being on my own with my God. It has been so long since I felt I could try to look straight at my God, and I am doing that now. I think I feel the heart of God often. It is there for me, and I know I truly want to serve that Love with my life.[3]

It would take a few years and several experiments for Gilmore to find the right form for her vision of service. During her two months in the woods, however, she began a process of deep interior reflection that continues to keep her connected to her soul. As she finished her retreat in the woods, she wrote, "I became quite clear that I didn't know what was ahead for me, but I was more comfortable that I would get the direction I needed if I continued to listen to that Inner Voice."[4]

Gilmore finished her degree with a focus on servant leadership. In addition, she cofounded the Center for Spirituality and Leadership at Marian University, designed a stimulating eighteen-month process to explore servant leadership for several colleagues and community leaders, and created a family foundation which she named after the wisdom she continually seeks—Sophia Foundation. She continues to live out her realization that "solitude is the key to balance. I must have enough time to pray, commune with nature and listen. I am more and more willing to let go of the past and accept a new future....I want to continue to move my life more and more toward my home in my heart where I will again feel the alignment of my existence with all of creation!"[5]

If we do not consult the soul, we never know what we really believe or who we really want to become. Without accessing our inner knowing, we follow the crowd or listen to the loudest voice or shape our lives to someone else's expectation. When we do not take the time to listen to the inner teacher, we end up living a life that is not really our own. We are split in two; our outside decisions and actions are never really in tune with our interior, authentic self. Palmer's writings are helpful in understanding the negative effects of persons who are not authentic, whose actions aren't attuned with their words. We often experience such persons as untrustworthy and distant. When we are in a relationship with someone who seems to be without integrity, "we hunker down in a psychological foxhole and withhold the investment of our energy, commitment, and gifts. Students refuse to take the risks involved in learning, employees do not put their hearts into their work, patients cannot partner with physicians in their own healing, and citizens disengage from the political process."[6] It is not surprising, then, that spiritual traditions across the world emphasize the importance of interior wisdom and living in tune with the spirit within.

The Value of Inner Wisdom and Personal Experience in Spiritual Traditions

Karen Armstrong provides an extensive argument based on painstaking, detailed evidence that a fundamental shift in human consciousness took place during the period of approximately 900-200 BCE. Along with the great philosopher Karl Jaspers and other noted historians, she refers to this critical period as the Axial Age. She traces the rise of interior spiritual reflection in the religions of Hinduism, Jainism, Buddhism, Confucianism, and Judaism. The Axial Age brings about a basic reorientation of the human spirit toward the within, a new way of being human and a new way of being spiritual that focuses on interior wisdom. She says in *The Great Transformation*,

> From about 900 to 200 BCE, in four distinct regions, the
> great world traditions that have continued to nourish
> humanity came into being…During this period of intense
> creativity, spiritual and philosophical geniuses pioneered
> an entirely new kind of human experience.…The Axial
> Age was one of the most seminal periods of intellectual,
> psychological, philosophical, and religious change in
> recorded history; there would be nothing comparable
> until the Great Western Transformation, which created
> our own scientific and technological modernity.[7]

The radical shift in consciousness that occurred in each of these
great spiritual traditions is a turn away from bloody sacrifice and
external ritual as effective in itself and a turn toward an interior spiritual attitude that emanates in altruistic behavior. These new religions brought the crucial realization that enlightenment, wisdom,
and the true way could be known and experienced by entering into
one's center, hearing the call to compassion in one's heart and living
it out. The prophets and teachers of these religions didn't impose this
understanding or craft new legal codes, but rather asked people to
experience the wisdom at their core, the deep peace and freedom
that could come from interior knowing. Consistent with the turn
toward interiority, they told their followers that, "It was essential to
question everything and to test any teaching empirically, against
your personal experience."[8]

HINDUISM, JAINISM, BUDDHISM

This shift in consciousness is first seen in India in the ninth
century, when ritual experts made a sweeping change to the ritual
system, removing "competitions, chariot races, mock battles, or
raids"[9] and replacing them with songs and gestures that required
practitioners to consciously connect their symbolic words and
actions with the ancient myths. Fully conscious practitioners offered
not some bloody sacrifice but themselves, conquered death by swal-
lowing it up symbolically, breathed in the fire of life itself from the
sacred fire, and became immortal themselves, just like the gods.
Whereas the old rites were focused on appeasing the external reality

of the gods, the reformers focused instead on the interior world and "the creation of the atman, the self."[10]

Over the next few centuries, the focus of the various religious traditions that are today lumped together with the term *Hinduism* would become more and more emphatically the self. Soon no ritual would be required to achieve immortality. The practitioner could use solitary meditation to enter the state of the gods. Wisdom would be found not in some external sacrifice or published law but in the heart of every person. In the eighth and seventh centuries, the early "renouncers" appeared on the scene—men who left the safety and comfort of their homes to live a life of begging and wandering focused on the spiritual quest, the interior fire, and enlightenment. These wandering ascetics would continue to deepen the practices of yoga and heightened consciousness. Yoga refers to the process of yoking or connecting the cart to the beast. In the case of the renouncers, they would connect the self to the very "power that held the universe together."[11] The renouncer or monk became the hero of the Axial Age, devoted to nonviolence and "determined to discover the absolute by becoming aware of the core of his being."[12]

By the fifth century, major upheavals in the structures of Indian society were brought about by increased agriculture and trade, new forms of monarchical government existing alongside smaller states run by elders of the old clans, and the rise of a merchant class. There was rampant greed, increased tension between people in the cities and the country, biting competition between bankers, merchants, and artisans. For many, there was wealth and excitement; for many others, there was great suffering and the loss of connection to the old rites and values. The growing number of schools of renouncers and communities of hermits seemed to agree on one thing—life was full of suffering and loss. Their teachings focused on practical ways to attain liberation and enlightenment. In this context, two new spiritual traditions arose with similar emphases. The Jains focused on a radical form of nonviolence, an empathic recognition of the life-force in every other creature and every element of creation. Some of the Jains took their *ahimsa* vow to extremes, refusing to move during the night lest they step on the smallest animal or plant. Twice each day, they would ask forgiveness for any slight distress they may have caused to seeds on the ground, the cobwebs of spiders, or the earth itself as they walked upon it as carefully as possible.[13]

In the latter part of the fifth century, another man would begin his search for liberation. After Siddhatta Gotama found that the teachings and practices of other great teachers and ascetics did not lead to release or bliss, he developed his own method, an eightfold path to nirvana that included ethical conduct, meditation, and mental development and wisdom. He came to his own insights about finding release from the constant disappointment of life, all of its little and big sufferings, and encouraged his followers to test every method and teaching against their own experience. Armstrong emphasizes that this focus on individual insight and experience became "one of the central tenets of his spiritual method. He constantly told his disciples that they must not accept anybody's teachings, no matter how august, if those teachings did not tally with their own experience."[14] He was called the Buddha by those who followed him, the one who had awakened.

The way to enlightenment was not some rare wisdom but an innate tendency within all persons, a state of disinterested compassion, a sense of loving-kindness for all beings. All of the mental and physical desires could be observed and recognized for what they were, simply passing states of yearning that ultimately resulted in further desires and disappointments. Beyond this practice of eliminating desire, Gotama meditated deeply on his oneness with all reality, becoming friends with all, seeing all reality as equal and united; he opened his entire being in equanimity and love of all, going beyond his own ego in genuine compassion. Thus, he became "the Tathagata (*gone*), implying that 'he' was no longer there" and "had achieved the state of complete selflessness."[15]

Ultimately, the inward turn practiced by the Indian sages of the Axial Age would lead to the realization that the spark of the divine resides in the core of every human, the same fire that gives life to the cosmos. Armstrong emphasizes the tremendous importance of this realization.

> This was a discovery of immense importance and it would become a central insight in every major religious tradition. The ultimate reality was an immanent presence in

every single human being....By disciplined introspection, the sages of the Axial Age were awakening to the vast reaches of selfhood that lay beneath the surface of their minds. They were becoming fully "self-conscious."[16]

CONFUCIANISM

In China, the story of awakening the inner self includes similar challenges and developments. As the monarchy declined in the eighth century, a new sense of moderation developed as the aristocrats dealt with dwindling resources. The minor nobility began to compile the classics and "to codify the ceremonial and customal practices of the noble families....These rituals (*ru*) made the principles of the noble life accessible and clear to everybody."[17] In past centuries, the king was understood as the son of heaven and ruled with divine authority. There were stories of the ancient kings controlling the floods and fighting dragons with magical powers. Only the king was allowed "to sacrifice to the High God," only the capital "was allowed to hold the prestigious royal rites in honor of the deceased kings of China..."[18] The king performed the lavish sacred ceremonies and hosted huge sacrificial banquets which preserved the natural order of things, uniting the Way of Heaven with the Way of Earth.

In the eighth and seventh centuries, however, new stories were emphasized. "Yao and Shun, the sage kings of remote antiquity," were raised up as models of another kind of power.[19] They were humble and insightful, truly respected the people, and were focused on their needs.

In this story, the wise and kind decisions of the kings were recognized as their ultimate power rather than the power of might. In Armstrong's words, "the royal potency was beginning to change. Instead of a purely magical efficacy, it was becoming an ethical power that brought spiritual benefit to the people."[20] A new ideal was being articulated, not only for the king but for all people.[21] For a time ritual, restraint, and civility permeated every facet of life, even the battlefield, until new aggressors without and within toppled the old structure of ruling families. Through painful upheaval, "a more egalitarian polity that would undermine the hitherto

unchallenged rule of the hereditary princes" was beginning to permeate Chinese society.[22]

In this context, toward the end of the sixth century, Confucius
became a charismatic, wandering teacher, determined to restore
some semblance of the old rites that had been the source of harmony
and peace. He was also an innovator. He taught that everyone, not
only the aristocrat, could be a fully developed human being—a *junzi*.

He insisted "that anybody who studied the Way enthusiasti-
cally could become a 'gentleman,' a mature or profound person."[23]
However, it wasn't the rites alone that were important. Confucius
ushered in the Axial Age in China by focusing on intention and
reflection, on the interior spirit that must permeate the ritual. When
the ritual was done with the right intention, it "helped people get
beyond the limitations of egotism…, cut out the old obsession with
status" and created a community where respect and human dignity
were practiced.[24] For Confucius, the rites could be practiced by all.
One's role, position, or status did not matter. All could become fully
human by following the true spiritual way, which required empathy
for all persons and treating each person as you wished to be treated.

JUDAISM

For Israel, the Axial Age and the turn inward began in the
eighth and seventh centuries with the prophets Amos, Hosea, Isaiah,
Jeremiah, and Ezekiel, who demanded the people go beyond a formulaic following of rituals. They spoke in the name of Yahweh and
exhorted the people to understand that true religion was not focused
on feasts, sacrifices, and festivals, but on feeling the plight of the poor
and the widow, the orphan and the outcast (e.g., Amos 2:6-8, Hos
4:1-3, Isa 1:1-17, Jer 7:8-15, Ezek 22:1-31). The prophets proclaimed
the people didn't know God. They lacked "yada," knowledge in the
deepest sense of intimacy and relationship with the divine. Like the
ritual reformers in India, the prophets were inviting their people to
understand God at the depths of their being, to enter into God's
empathy, "urging the Israelites to examine their inner lives, analyze
their feelings, and develop a deeper vision based on introspection."[25]

Jeremiah was prophet during the most difficult period of
Babylonian exile. Large numbers of Israelites had been deported to
this foreign land where they were disenfranchised and disoriented.

They had lost everything, not the least of which was their sense of identity as Yahweh's people. Their capital of Jerusalem and its beautiful temple had been utterly destroyed. Yet, in these dire circumstances, Jeremiah proclaims a new covenant in the future, not based on temples or sacrifices but written on the hearts of the people, God's new law planted within each individual (Jer 31: 33-34). This vision of God's presence and message in the heart of the person was shared by the prophet Ezekiel as well, who proclaimed:

> I will give them a new heart and put a new spirit within them; I will remove the stony heart from their bodies, and replace it with a natural heart, so that they will live according to my statutes, and observe and carry out my ordinances, thus they shall be my people and I will be their God. (Ezek 11:19-21)

However, it will be up to the individual to live out that internal call of the divine. The old proverb about the children reaping what the fathers have sowed is no longer valid. Each person is responsible for his or her own actions. Ezekiel is adamant that all lives belong to God: "the life of the father is like the life of the son, both are mine; only the one who sins shall die" (Ezek 18:1-3).

Out of the radical displacement and suffering of the Babylonian exile, a new version of Israel's story was created by the Priestly school of writing, which, like the prophets, focused on personal responsibility and the dignity of all persons. Most biblical scholars agree there are several retellings of Israelite history in fragments or developed documents written from various perspectives and historical periods. The latest version comes from the Priestly school and focuses on laws and codes of holiness. Even the creation story is revised to reflect the ritual of Sabbath observance. The days of the week are used as the structuring principle of creation so that on the Sabbath God rests and sets the expectation for weekly human rest and a day devoted to gratitude and prayer. One recognizes how radical the Priestly creation account is when it is compared with the Babylonian myth of Marduk and Tiamat, two opposing forces of good and evil warring against each other. According to the Babylonian account, the heavens and earth are made out of violence and combat.

The Priestly school proclaims that Israel's benevolent God is without compare, has no cosmic competitors, and creates all things good. All persons bear the image of God, even the Babylonians. The holiness laws provide the Israelites with challenging codes of conduct but also with a demanding ethical imperative. They must treat even the stranger with respect. In effect, the Priestly writers help to initiate the Axial Age by proclaiming the importance of divine and human empathy in their story. The suffering and chaos of exile must not harden the hearts of the people but must enlarge their hearts to feel the suffering of all. Karen Armstrong writes that "the great achievement of the exilic priests and prophets had been the avoidance of a religion based on resentment and revenge, and the creation of a spirituality that affirmed the holiness of all life."[26]

Beyond the prophetic and historical writings, there is another important tradition in the Hebrew scriptures called "wisdom literature," which clearly focuses on interior sagacity, personal experience, and hearing the ethical imperative within. Although some biblical scholars have confined wisdom literature to the specific books of Proverbs, Job, Ecclesiastes, Sirach, and the Wisdom of Solomon, most hold that the wisdom tradition is more largely distributed throughout the Hebrew scriptures.[27] However, the Book of Proverbs is a good place to begin to see the distinct focus on the natural, ordinary wisdom that resides in the heart and experience of all persons.

Proverbs offer maxims of common sense, understandable to anyone who stops to observe everyday life. For example: "In the sin of his lips the evil man is ensnared, but the just comes free of trouble" (Prov 12:13). Numerous childhood fables and sayings portray the troubles that come from lies and untruths. The honest person doesn't have to worry about remembering the excuse he gave or whether or not an accomplice will tell the same story. It is often the case that dishonest persons get caught by their own inconsistencies. Here's another example: "The fool immediately shows his anger, but the shrewd man passes over an insult" (Prov 12:16). The wise person knows an angry response to an affront often escalates the situation, whereas a measured response that focuses on identifying one's own feelings often helps the offending person see how certain actions were experienced as hurtful. Proverbs are very different from prophetic sayings or messages from an oracle. They do not rely on some transcendent or omniscient authority; rather, they express what humans know from their experience and from simply paying attention to what is happening in the world. Wisdom comes from reflection on common human experience, not as some supernatural revelation to an elect few. Behind the wisdom tradition is a fundamental confidence in our human ability to access the truth through reflection on our own experience, by listening to the empathic pull in our own hearts.

One of the most powerful wisdom stories comes at the beginning of the Book of Exodus. The Hebrews have become a threat to the Egyptians and, even though they are enslaved and forced to do endless manual labor, their numbers continue to grow. The story says the Pharaoh, who rules with divine authority, meets with the midwives Shiphrah and Puah and gives them the direct order to kill the Hebrew newborn boys. Instead, they act on their own wisdom as midwives; knowing the preciousness of life, they refuse to follow the dictates of the external authority. They don't have to consult the law or the priests. They know from their common human experience that newborn babies are meant for life, and they are willing to stand up to the highest authority in the land with their certain wisdom. Some commentators propose that these midwives were Egyptians themselves and still they refused to follow their leader. They protect the lives of the newborn Hebrew boys even though they have been told these children will grow to be a threat to their own existence. The midwives act in harmony with the natural process of life itself, with the fundamental wisdom that resides in reality and can be accessed by anyone who is willing to observe and reflect.

The wisdom traditions in the Hebrew scriptures say that all persons have their own authority because each person has knowledge of what is right and good through intuition, observation, and good reasoning. All persons have the authority to decide for themselves because they have the capability to figure out what is the wise thing to do. Authority for right action comes not from some external power but from interior wisdom.

CHRISTIANITY

In the Christian scriptures, this wisdom from common human experience is seen in the parables of Jesus. When one lights a lamp one doesn't put it under a basket (Matt 5:15, Luke 11:33, Mark 4:21).

When something very valuable is lost, one sweeps the whole house to find it or searches everywhere for the lost sheep (Luke 15: 3-10, Matt 18:12-14). Seed that falls on good ground produces a hundred-fold (Mark 4:8, Luke 8:8, Matt 13:8). When another human being is found beaten alongside the road, a responsible person doesn't pass by (Luke 10:25-37). The simple wisdom of soil, sheep, seeds, and neighbors is at the heart of the message of Jesus. Wisdom comes from close observation and clear thinking, recognizing the common, natural consequences of one's words and actions.

As with the other wisdom teachers, Jesus emphasizes the freedom and responsibility of human beings. He forgives prostitutes, tax collectors, and sinners of all kinds and calls them to turn from their ways. Jesus is optimistic about humans. They can change and choose their way of life. They can recognize one another as brothers and sisters and choose to act with compassion. An important aspect of the Christian tradition is the understanding that the Spirit of God inhabits the followers of Jesus after he is no longer physically present among them. The Pentecost experience is described in the Christian scriptures in the Acts of the Apostles as follows: "Tongues as of fire appeared, which parted and came to rest on each of them. All were filled with the Holy Spirit. They began to express themselves in foreign tongues and make bold proclamation as the Spirit prompted them" (Acts 2:3-4). With the spark of the divine within them, they are moved from the core of the self to live in community, share what they have in common, heal the sick, and do good works for the well-being of all (Acts 2:42-47). As in the Hindu and Buddhist traditions, there is an expanded sense of the self, not as ego but as oneness with the transcendent.

ISLAM

For the Muslim, wisdom is fundamentally contained in the law. Islam means to surrender to this law, to submit to God's will. Although human reason is helpful in understanding how the law applies to new questions and circumstances, it is not seen by most Muslims as a complement to revelation, and certainly not an equal source of guidance. The complex developmental process leading up to this standardization of the law certainly involved debate and dialogue among a diversity of perspectives, input from reason, theology, and philosophy, and borrowing from local customs and traditions. Respected Muslim scholar John Esposito says:

> By the tenth century most Sunni jurists had come to believe that since the guidelines for individual and community were established, personal interpretation (ijtihad) was no longer necessary or permitted....Thus, tradition was effectively standardized and sanctified by grounding it in revelation and sacred law.[28]

Lest one conclude that there is absolute unanimity within Islam, it is important to note there are four major schools or ways of interpretation in Sunni Islam: "the Hanafi, Hanbali, Maliki, and Shafii.... Today, they are dominant in different parts of the Islamic world.... Shii Islam has generated its own schools, the most important of which is the Jafari..."[29]

The law, however, does not necessarily provide a clear indication for personal decision-making. In regard to individual ethical decisions, it is often the case that the decision would be left up to the individual or family. Since God alone knows what is right and wrong in the individual ethical case, the "individual conscience is considered a better guide for action, since it is ultimately the individual who will have to answer to God on the day of judgment."[30] Individuals are left to consult the Quran in their own faithfulness, to consider the stories and sayings of Muhammad, and, perhaps, even to find advice in contemporary *fatwas*—"legal opinions pronounced by well-known religious jurists (*muftis*)" and often "published in daily newspapers, periodicals, booklets and compiled volumes, and/or broadcast on radio and television in most Arab and Islamic countries."[31] However, *fatwas*, which are the most current application of *sharia* (Muslim law), sometimes contradict one another or take quite different approaches to an ethical question.

Since the focus is on specific cases, Islam doesn't attempt to delineate particular rules related to contemporary ethical issues. "It considers cases, and in its normative pronouncements leaves space for the particulars of a situation to be inserted, and perhaps to modify the finding."[32] Thus, individual Muslims are faced with making important decisions with an informed conscience, in faithfulness to their own understanding of God's will.

For a minority of Muslims, the practices of Sufism focus more specifically on the path inward. Sujezana Akpinar in "The Ethics of Islam" describes this path as leading "individuals toward the center of their being," which includes "the cultivation and education of the self, the *nafs*, an Arabic word that denotes both soul and breath."[33] The many Sufi schools provide practices and disciplines to purify the inner being, to know God, and to experience directly the ultimate reality. Rather than focusing on the external law, the Sufi concentrates on annihilating the inner small self so the divine that dwells within all persons may be realized.[34] Many of the ascetic practices focus on detaching from the material world so the Sufi can "become aware of the divine, which was always present but ordinarily hidden from view...."[35] As in Hinduism and Buddhism, the cares and distractions of the little ego are dissolved so the fullness of being at the center of the true self can be experienced. The Sufi's devotion to and oneness with God are expressed in the moral life of compassion and kindness to all.

This brief overview of the place of inner wisdom in some of the major religions of the world shows the universality and centrality that there is a deep well of knowing at the core of the true self and that reflection on personal experience is the final test of wisdom. Tradition has it that as the Buddha was dying, he advised his dear disciple Ananda: "each of you should make himself his island, make himself and no one else his refuge...."[36] The Buddha taught repeatedly that his disciples had to rely on their own wisdom, they had to test every teaching and every teacher by their own experience. They had to find their own truth.[37] This reliance on inner wisdom is voiced in divergent ways in many religions of the world. Now we turn to the task of incorporating this central insight in our decision-making processes and criteria for judgment.

Principle Four Operating Procedures and Criteria

Listening to the inner teacher, or paying attention to the inner voice, is not an easy way to wisdom. Rather, it challenges us to deepen our reflection and our attentiveness. The profound wisdom traditions sampled above are not saying we don't have to listen to experts or authorities, to consult principles or research. However, the messages from external sources are only the beginning of wisdom. They must be reflected upon and considered in relationship to our deepest interior knowing. Often this kind of interior wisdom is called knowledge of the heart. We must also give close consideration to what has happened and what is happening in our own lives. This keen attention is called mindfulness in the Eastern traditions, being fully present and fully receptive to what is taking place in our experience.

OPERATING PROCEDURE 4A:
REFLECT ON EXPERIENCE DEEPLY AND BROADLY

The principle of valuing inner wisdom requires that we seriously consider how our past experience applies to our current situation, and how our reservoir of previous learning might provide cues and clues to making our present decision. There are many processes that can help us deeply investigate our own experience. I will briefly consider three of them: (1) journaling, (2) clearness circle, and (3) wisdom teacher conversation. Not every process or technique works for everyone. Of course, you won't know what works until you try them. Then you can use the methods that work best for you to reflect on your experience individually or as a team or organization.

Journaling

The process of journaling is an exceptional tool for exploring our own experience. Journaling is free writing, allowing our inner thoughts and feelings to simply pour onto the page without judgment or editing. It doesn't have to be pretty, just real—following wherever our mind and heart take us. Sometimes it takes the form of phrases or lists. Sometimes it connects us to past experiences in our childhood. Sometimes it takes us into recalling the details and specifics of a situation. Sometimes patterns in our experience will jump out at us. Sometimes nothing will come and we will simply write that nothing is coming to us.

There are no rules, no rights, and no wrongs in journaling. The important thing is to jot down whatever comes to mind: the silly, the weird, the stories, the feelings, the insights, the petty thoughts, the grievances, the affirmations, all of it, whatever comes. Turn off the censor—that little voice that wants things to look good and sound right, that wants correct spelling and punctuation. The censor is not allowed into your journaling sessions. Your journal writing doesn't have to be logical. It doesn't even have to make sense. Journal writing often allows us to see our experience from a new viewpoint or to see aspects of our experience we didn't see before. Sometimes our journaling will simply reaffirm what we already know; sometimes it may lead to new insights. One thing is for sure: free-form journaling lets the inside come out so we can consider it.

At the police department in Carrollton, Texas, they have used journaling to help officers intentionally grow their emotional intelligence as a central component of their new Officer Leadership Development Program.[38] The program focuses on five aspects of emotional intelligence—self-awareness, self-regulation, self-motivation, empathy, and social competence. After assessing their strengths and weaknesses in these areas, the officers were asked to journal about one area they decided to develop as they reflected on their work experiences throughout the week. As you might guess, there was some discomfort about this process at first. Reflecting on his initial experience with journaling, one of the officers said, "I wondered where the pink bow and locket was."[39] Once he got beyond that initial uneasiness, he found the journaling to be life-changing for himself and his team members. Ann McGee Cooper, who has worked with a number of organizations in Texas to develop servant leadership competencies, reported this story from a servant leadership learning community.

> For example, one officer was low on social competence. Through journaling he could write about his commitment to grow that competency. He could log examples from the day where he met his goals and where he felt he came up short. He worked with his mentor who invited him to do small exercises—like going into a local convenience store and getting to know something about the cashier as a way to develop relationship. That officer grew from a recruit who wouldn't have made it on the Force, to one of the best, most exemplary, officers.[40]

Through journaling, we may be able to see patterns in our experience that help us see the way forward in our present decision. Often journaling allows insights from the unconscious to come forward into consciousness, perspectives or ways of seeing that may have been sent underground by other pressures or the voices of experts or those in authority.

The Clearness Circle

Another method for exploring personal experience and the inner teacher is often called the clearness committee, clearness process, or clearness circle.[41] Parker Palmer has been instrumental in popularizing this effective process for discernment that comes from the Quaker religious community. He explains the dilemma we often experience as we face a significant decision or issue in our lives:

> On the one hand, we know that the issue is ours alone to resolve and that we have the inner resources to resolve it, but access to our own resources is often blocked by layers of inner "stuff"—confusion, habitual thinking, fear, despair. On the other hand, we know that friends might help us uncover our inner resources and find our way, but by exposing our problem to others, we run the risk of being invaded and overwhelmed by their assumptions, judgments, and advice—a common and alienating experience. As a result, we often privatize these vital questions in our lives: at the very moment when we need all the help we can get, we find ourselves cut off from both our inner resources and the support of community.[42]

The process of the clearness circle is simple and challenging. Anywhere from one to a few persons gather to support a focus person who brings a concern or question to explore in the group. The group participants have one fundamental goal—to help the focus person access his or her own inner wisdom by providing open-ended questions. They are not to give advice, reflect on their own experience, or suggest resources or readings for the focus person. The circle participants attempt to ask questions that help the focus person investigate her own inner resources for finding her own answer, to listen to her own voice of truth and guidance within. Since we are so used to giving advice and offering our own perspective, this process of only asking helpful questions is quite difficult. Even our questions are often disguised recommendations that reflect our own assumptions and judgments.

The participants may be friends, family, or coworkers of the focus person, or fellow-seekers on a retreat or in a workshop. Four basics are required of participants: (1) hold the focus person in unconditional care, (2) respect the focus person's inner wisdom, (3) only ask open-ended questions, and (4) maintain confidentiality about the focus person's question or issue and any responses they made in the clearness circle. Palmer characterizes the relationships in a clearness circle in the following way.

> A circle of trust consists of relationships that are neither invasive nor evasive. In this space, we neither invade the mystery of another's true self nor evade another's struggles. We stay present to each other without wavering, while stifling any impulse to fix each other up. We offer each other support in going where each needs to go, and learning what each needs to learn, at each one's pace and depth.[43]

One of the participants, other than the focus person, should be the time keeper and facilitator. This person's role is to gently keep time according to the timetable that was agreed upon by the group and to remind persons of the "questions only rule" and the "confidentiality rule." The facilitator's role is not an easy one. I highly recommend reading A Hidden Wholeness or participating in a facilitation program from the Center for Courage and Renewal.[44] An in-depth clearness circle should last about two hours.

The focus person should come with a brief statement, either written out or thought out, so they can introduce their issue or question to the participants. The focus person might give a bit of history about this issue or question in their lives, how the concern has affected them, and what sort of hints or directions they have been considering. This introduction may last from ten to twenty minutes. When the focus person is finished, the facilitator will remind the participants that only open-ended questions are welcome in the clearness process; no advice-giving or fixing will be allowed. For the next sixty to ninety minutes, the participants ask questions to which they do not know the answers. They attempt to articulate questions that might be helpful for the focus person to consider, that might take the focus person more deeply into their own inner knowing. The focus person may provide answers to some or all of the questions or may simply take some or all of the questions into their interior space without providing answers verbally. Participants need to be sensitive to the flow of the experience so the focus person doesn't feel barraged by questions and there is room for silence and adequate reflection by the focus person. If there is a lull in the questioning, allow the silence to deepen the work of the focus person and the participants. Stay in silence until additional questions arise.

After sixty to ninety minutes of questioning, the facilitator should remind the participants of the confidentiality rule. The rule that is recommended by Palmer is "double confidentiality." This means two things: first, nothing that has been said in the clearness process will ever be shared by anyone, and second, no participant will ever approach the focus person with comments or questions about the process or their issue. If the focus person brings up the issue with one of the participants outside of the clearness process at some future date, it is a separate invitation to consider the issue they raised. The clearness circle ends with celebration, allowing whoever wishes to provide expressions of gratitude for the process.

In the many clearness circles that I have facilitated and several in which I have been the focus person, I have always been amazed by what I learn. As a focus person, the questions of others have consistently taken me into a deeper reflection process than I thought possible. Often what I thought was the issue or question that needed exploration, opened up into other more important areas of my life with the aid of questions from the participants. As a participant in clearness circles, I have often come face to face with important questions for myself. The focus person's courage opens something in me that needs investigation, areas in which I am called to listen to my own wisdom teacher. As with any process in which we are vulnerable, the clearness process takes courage. We become more comfortable and more skilled at it as we experience it repeatedly. It is a powerful way to explore our own experience and our own inner wisdom.

The Wisdom Teacher Conversation

A final method for investigating personal experience is called the wisdom teacher conversation, a dialogue between yourself and your own inner teacher or the imagined wisdom of a mentor or sage in your life. Although this can take many forms, I suggest using two pens or pencils of different colors. Choose one color for your own questions and the other color for the responses from your wisdom teacher. The first step is to identify your wisdom teacher within. Take a few minutes of silence to find the wisdom teacher within you, at the heart of who you are. Find the place within you where you know you are loved completely and unconditionally. Perhaps your wisdom teacher speaks from your heart or from the center of your forehead or from your gut. This may be a place where the wisdom of other important persons in your life also flows into you—a beloved aunt who was always there for you, a mentor who guided you to important insights, a trusted friend who knows your gifts and foibles and loves you for them all.

The second step is to begin the conversation between you and your wisdom teacher with a question. Use the color you chose for your own questions and reflections to begin the process. Then listen deeply to your own inner wisdom and use the other color to respond to the question. As you reflect on the response to your initial question, allow another question to arise. Continue the process, alternating between questions and the responses from your wisdom teacher within, until you have asked at least five questions. Don't edit or censor your questions, allow them to arise freely in the process.

Many people find that this process brings up interesting questions and surprising responses. As with the journaling process, the unconscious may be allowed to speak and the answers to your questions may go beyond your usual, rational viewpoint. The key to any of these deep listening processes is to be as open as possible, to pay attention to the small voices within, and to observe sensations in your body and emotions that may be connected to particular questions or responses. When I use this process, I often find something new opening up for me at about the fourth or fifth question. I recall things I haven't remembered for a long time or a pattern in my life shows itself.

In the scriptural Book of Proverbs, wisdom is personified as a wise woman who "cries aloud in the street, in the open squares she raises her voice…" (Prov 1:20). She is called Sophia in several Greek myths and other mystical traditions. These many representations share the common theme that wisdom is incarnate, lives within this earthy reality, and calls to us in our daily experiences. Often our negative experiences will be teachers as much as, if not more than, our positive experiences.

Ginny Gilmore, whose story opens this chapter, was drawn to servant leadership in large part from her negative experiences of command-and-control and hierarchical styles of leading. She longed to experience more respectful ways of working together where the voices of all would be heard and cherished. Gilmore's deep listening to her own experience motivated her to investigate dialogue, compassionate listening practices, and the council of equals model of shared leadership. After much deliberation and reflection on her own journey, she started the Sophia Foundation, which focuses on creating a more caring community in Fond du Lac, Wisconsin. The Sophia Foundation provides development opportunities in servant leadership and engages community partners in important conversations about social concerns. From the inception of the Foundation, Gilmore ensured that the Sophia board of directors embodies the principles and practices of seeking wisdom together. Every meeting involves reflection on an inspirational text, a check-in and check-out process to ensure that everyone's voice is heard, and often some extended dialogue or inquiry practice to explore a significant emerging question.[45]

Wisdom speaks to us through the highs and lows of our experiences. We need to listen to both as we confront whatever change is in front of us. In the following poem, Sophia speaks to us; she calls us to bring all the moments of our past and everything we have learned to make a decision in the present that is as fully informed and as wise as possible. Paradoxically, as we reflect on our particular experience, we come to understand that we are wondrously unique and at the same time share a common, fundamental humanity that connects us surely to every other person in the world.

SOPHIA

I come from the silent desert
and the singing river

from the dry desperation of failure and betrayal,
from the ecstasy of connection.

I know the alchemy
of metamorphosis and macrophage,
the seed, the seasons, the heart.

I call to you now from every doorway
from the precipice of every hope.

Step into the river where everything
is flowing, brave the undercurrent
sucking at your ankles and scoop
the silver syllables to your face.

Drink it in, open your body, remember
the common code swimming
inside the helix of your marrow, muscle, blood.

And the light that leaps from you then
could be a word, a covenant, a bridge to peace.

The importance of valuing inner wisdom becomes clearer when we recognize the unique particularity of each one of us. As the ethicist Daniel Maguire reminds us, "No two persons and no two situations are identical. Even physiologically, the very structure of our brain suggests the unrepeatable uniqueness of every individual member of the species."[46] Responsible decision-making requires that we consider our own unique experience and perspective and refuse to give up our authority to the group or organization. Often decision-making is done in situations where there is a good deal of pressure to think like everybody else thinks, to simply accept the expectations and assumptions of the organization or religion or culture to which we belong. Mature decision-making requires living in the tension between the community and the individual, the wisdom of "we" and the wisdom of "I." When we listen deeply both to the voices of others and to the voice of our own experience, we have a better chance of making effective, wise decisions.

OPERATING PROCEDURE 4B: APPRECIATIVELY INQUIRE INTO VALUES, VISION AND BEST PRACTICES

This operating procedure for wise decision-making challenges us to explore our own values, vision, and best practices as organizations, teams, or individuals so our decisions will be congruent with our central priorities and directions. David Cooperrider, the guru of the organizational change process called Appreciative Inquiry, advises organizations to truly understand their "positive core."[47] That positive core for both organizations and individuals includes our achievements, strengths, innovations, assets, competencies, vision, life-giving traditions, social capital, partnerships, and values.[48] In essence, the positive core is what makes us positively unique. Wise decision-making requires that we are conscious of what is at the center of who we are individually or organizationally.

In an organizational context, the process of appreciative inquiry related to decision-making would include interviewing "organization members and stakeholders using questions related to: highpoint experiences, valuing, and what gives life to the organization at its best."[49] People would be asked to reflect on how their experiences of truly living out the organization's values in the past might apply to the current situation. In a personal appreciative inquiry process, one might spend time reflecting on previous positive experiences of deep meaning or satisfaction. Individuals may recall how they have lived out their values in the past and what that has meant for them. One could even create an image or symbol or word picture of the core of one's authentic self. The present situation is then approached from the perspective of this newly recognized core self. One might ask, "What is the boldest possibility for my life in this situation as I recognize who I am and the talents and gifts that I embody?" The organization might ask, "How can we fully embrace our highest values and vision and continue to strengthen our best practices in relation to the situation that confronts us in this decision?"

Ultimately, good decision-making is a process of bringing the inside and outside into alignment. Cooperrider says, "The single most important action a group can take to liberate the human spirit and consciously construct a better future is to make the positive core the common and explicit property of all."[50] It is critically important for both groups and individuals to be clear about their core values, vision, and best practices. Values are what truly motivate us and are most important in our lives. Vision names the mental image of successful accomplishment of one's purpose as an individual or organization. In essence, vision is what the full realization of one's mission would look like in the world. When we investigate our best practices, we recognize our strengths, competencies, talents, and uniqueness as an individual or organization. When we intentionally reflect on our values, vision, and best practices in the decision-making process, we ask what specific actions will keep us on track, moving in the right direction, playing to our strengths, and true to our identity. This is the key question of congruence. What decision in the present circumstance fits with the positive core of who we are? I am not suggesting we need to launch a comprehensive appreciative inquiry process every time we make a decision, but simply that we must intentionally bring to mind our positive core to shed light on the current situation.

The Concept of Congruence

This concept of congruence is often referred to as "fit." We look for new employees who will fit with the organization's culture. We hire consultants based on the fit between our needs and their skills and experience. We consider whether a job announcement fits with our past experience and skills. But there is a deeper kind of fit that wise decision-makers explore. It is the fit between the inner geography and the outer geography. Is my outer life congruent with my most deeply held values and vision? Lack of congruence is experienced in many different ways—a nagging, intuitive hunch that my life just isn't working, sleepless nights struggling with issues that won't go away, an upset stomach over decisions I wish I could reconsider, a deep desire to want to stop everything and simply go away somewhere to think. All of these feelings are indicators that something is not congruent.

Congruence can be analyzed on three different levels. The first level is the fit between what I know about myself and my dreams and what I have articulated to myself or, even better, written down. In other words, am I clear with myself about my deepest values? Although this level may seem simplistic, many of us are not clear about what our hearts and souls are saying to us. It's easy to get caught up in cultural expectations and consumer distractions. Sometimes we reach middle age before we stop and ask, "Is that really what I want; is that really what makes my heart sing?" Congruence, then, requires that I be as clear as possible about the values and priorities at the core of my person. I recommend these central values be written down in a few phrases or sentences and regularly used in making decisions.

The second level of congruence involves the match between my values and my thoughts, words, and actions. Do my behaviors fit with my priorities? We all know persons who are able to articulate a set of values very well, but when it comes to living those values, they fall far short of the mark. This kind of dissonance in a person's life can be both personally and organizationally destructive. Persons who recognize the inconsistency between their words and actions often experience significant interior conflict and personal stress. There may be a nagging feeling of dissatisfaction in their lives, a sense of being stuck or even paralyzed.

The recognition of dissonance between values and actions may result in a process of personal transformation into greater integrity or a process of disillusionment and jettisoning one's values. Living in a state of significant dissonance or incongruity is difficult and consumes a great deal of energy. For some, the energy is spent on rationalization or making internal excuses. For others, such dissonance floods their lives with depression and anxiety. For healthy persons, the dissonance is not significant. There is energy, sometimes real joy, and always heartfelt satisfaction in doing what is congruent with our values. The minor incongruities are greeted as personal challenges. As the level of congruence between values and actions increases, we experience more satisfaction and a deeper sense of meaning.

The third level of congruence is the fit between my values and the policies, structures, and culture of the organization where I work. Can I be myself where I work? Do I have to change my usual way of dealing with people when I walk into the plant? Do I find my attitude changing as I approach the building entrance? When there is a fit between my values and my workplace, I experience my place of employment as a supportive and nurturing environment. It becomes an avenue for becoming the person I want to be, for living out my birthright gifts in the world, for putting my passion into practice.

Work, with all of its difficulties and challenges, becomes deeply satisfying. I feel like I'm doing what I ought to be doing.

Not all workplaces, however, nurture individual gifts, talents and values. Some workplaces can be toxic to our spirit. In such situations, we try to change what we can. At times, we can be courageous and advocate for ways of doing things that are both more human and productive. At times, our only recourse is to set clear boundaries so we are not sucked into activities that sap our energy and vitality. If possible, we try to find an organizational context that fits our values.

I experience a strong sense of "fit" in my life when there is congruence between my deepest values and my own goals, between my values and my actions and decisions, between my values and the core principles in my workplace. This kind of congruence at the level of values provides for real fitness, not just on the physical level but on the level of spirit and heart. When there is a fit between my values and the various dimensions of my life, I feel well as a whole being. When I'm living congruently, I smile more, am clearer in my focus and less distracted by all of the competing voices defining success in the world's terms. For all of us, there is some dissonance between our values and our decisions, between our vision and our current reality. We don't always do it right. But if we keep our focus on our core values, we learn to take a step back from the situation and reflect more deeply. Congruence between our inner core and our outer decisions and actions is an ongoing process that requires many years and a constant struggle. Above all, being values-based requires reflection. The integration of values cannot happen without taking the time to be aware of those values and facing the question of congruence.

Reflection on Core Values

To live with congruence between my values and my life and work, I must constantly ask deep questions. What is the foundation for my decisions and actions? How do I live my personal values and the core values of the organization? One helpful way to facilitate reflection on core values is to ask people to choose an object from their home, from their prized personal possessions, that represents or symbolizes in some way one of their core values. It is a very simple activity but one that often results in the telling of powerful, moving stories. The magic of this activity is that people usually don't feel uncomfortable because they are speaking about an object. Since the object doesn't clearly state the value, they must explain what the object means to them. Most often, the object is connected to a significant experience or event. Through the explanation, persons go beyond simply stating their values. They tell how they came to this value. Often they reveal how important persons in their lives have influenced them to be dedicated to a particular value.

Let me share one powerful story that came out of this activity. I was asked to give a series of presentations to an adult education group on creating more inspired and respectful workplaces. We spent a good bit of time discussing our core values and how we tried to live those values at work. It was a diverse group. Many discussed the struggles and incongruence they felt between their own values and the values of their organizations. Others were happy to share their experience of feeling a real sense of fit between their values and the culture of their organizations. Because the group jelled quite well in the first two sessions, I asked them to bring to the third session an object that symbolized or represented one of their core values. One of the most involved participants in the first two sessions was Bob. He had strong opinions and he wasn't afraid to voice them. His demeanor was open but a bit gruff. Bob was pretty skeptical of anything "touchy-feely."

As I introduced the activity at the beginning of session three, I asked simply, "Tell us the story of the object you brought with you today. How does it represent one of your core values?" Bob leaned forward in this chair and volunteered to go first. I was hoping someone would start who could take the group to an even deeper level than our earlier discussions and I wasn't sure Bob was up for it. As he slowly took off his watch and dangled it in front of our faces, I thought to myself, "I've heard this one many times before—the symbol of time, the value of time." Bob surprised me. "This is my grandfather's watch," he said, "and it means everything to me." Bob told the story of his grandfather who was a hard worker. He sold insurance and his days often extended late into the evening, making as many calls as he could. As hard as he worked, his family just had enough. Nothing fancy, nothing luxurious. There was always enough food on the table, always enough clothes for each of the kids, always enough to pay the light bills, but nothing more. It seemed his long hours and dedication could only pay the bills and provide for their basic needs. Here's how Bob continued the story:

> When grandpa died, we learned that he was the top sales-person in the Midwest. He sold more insurance than every other agent in the area, more than two or three of them combined some years. So, where was all the money going? What did he do with all of the wages that never made it home, that never bought the larger house, the newer car, the fancy clothes?[51]

With tears in his eyes, Bob told us that grandpa was buying "passage" for people from the old country. Month after month, year after year, he would set aside a significant portion of his earnings so others could come to the land of the free, just as someone had sponsored him to come to America. He finished his story this way, "And my mother always wondered why, if her father was working so hard, she didn't have new dresses or live in a bigger house. Why they didn't have more to show for all his effort. She didn't know grandpa was living his values, investing in human lives." Bob's grandpa is a hero for him and has helped him shape his own values. His concrete, regular practice of actualizing his core values is certainly an example to emulate. However, we might ask how things may have been different if he had shared his deep commitment openly with his family, if he had made "the positive core the common and explicit property of all."[52]

Whenever I think of making decisions consistent with one's positive core, I am reminded of my friend Judi Neal, director of the Tyson Center for Faith and Spirituality in the Workplace at the University of Arkansas. Early in her career, she worked for Honeywell as the manager of organizational development and training at the Joliet Army Ammunition Plant. She was there for about two years when her boss asked her to work with the ballistics team because they were experiencing low morale and a number of them had asked to transfer to other jobs within the company. Ballistics tested ammunition that was to be used by the U.S. Army, Navy, and Air Force. Since positions in the ballistics area were very well paid, her boss was troubled by these transfer requests.

When Neal began interviewing team members, it became clear people were being told by management to alter test results. They were being directed to report that the ammunition met all of the government specifications when, in fact, it was faulty. There were significant production and design problems with the ammunition. Each person she spoke to was devastated by having to lie in order to keep their jobs, having to do something that their own code of ethics didn't support. When she was able to gather enough evidence to absolutely prove there was wrongdoing, she called the company's ethics hotline and reported the situation. When I asked her if she agonized about her decision, this was her response:

> In terms of the agonizing, once I was really clear that they were altering the ammunition data, I knew that was against the law, that's fraud, there was just no question that I had to do something because of the consequences. If we're selling faulty ammunition to the Army, the Navy and Air Force, we are putting our own servicemen in danger. If there was faulty ammunition it could back up in the gun, it could explode, the gunner is going to get killed. If the gunner is in a plane, the whole plane is gonna go down. People's lives were in danger. So, there's just no question. I couldn't live with myself if I didn't do something. That's what it came down to….So the spiritual part of it is how do I live with myself. I could just keep it hush hush, but God would know. That's the bottom line for me, God would know, my soul would know and I couldn't live with myself. Part of me would die if I didn't do something, if I didn't do the right thing.[53]

In very difficult situations, the call to congruence, to living in alignment with our values, is often experienced as "I couldn't live with myself." If we are not in the habit of listening to our inner teacher, it is possible to quiet this small voice or to let it be drowned out by voices of authority or our own survival needs. If we build intentional reflection on our core values, vision and best practices into our decision-making process, we will be more apt to choose what is truly congruent with our positive core.

The spiritual principle to value inner wisdom and personal experience needs to inform not only our decision-making process, but also the criteria or standards upon which we base our decisions. When we explore the implications of this principle, we recognize we must make a decision that is responsive to the totality of the present experience and constructive to life itself. These two criteria for judgment are foundational benchmarks for making good decisions.

CRITERIA FOR JUDGMENT 4A: CHOOSE WHAT ADDRESSES THE FULL REALITY OF THE PRESENT EXPERIENCE

Respecting the wisdom that comes from experience, the wisest decision will respond to the fullness of our reality and take into account the diverse dimensions of the present decision-making context. It is easy for us to become narrowly focused on one or two dimensions of the reality that confronts us. In our Western culture, we are particularly prone to dualisms, to breaking things down into two competing choices. We tend to have an "either/or consciousness" that "translates into a form of flatland, devoid of texture or nuance."[54] We live in a landscape that has been flattened and tamed, "where topography has been bulldozed out of our experience . . . The drive-through meal is now an American norm, convenience an American ideal, and money is the nearly singular measure of value."[55] Our perception of depth and complexity has been stultified by our regular diet of sameness. We can eat exactly the same burger or sub sandwich or chicken meal in any large or small city we happen to be in at the time. For a few years, I directed a program for students to spend a semester studying near Grantham, England, about an hour north of London. I was always amazed that when the students traveled to London, they regularly ate at McDonald's. Our perceptual field in the West has literally become more narrow and superficial, and our conceptual field has been diminished as well.

It takes significant focused attention and creative energy to perceive depth and complexity and to hold the fullness of experience in front of us as we consider our choices. It requires practice to juggle the pieces of reality that need to be seen in their multiple relationships with one another. The spiritual principles and operating procedures discussed in chapters two through four help to broaden our consideration of the diversity of experience and plurality of view-points. When we invite the voices of all stakeholders to be heard at the decision-making table, we cannot help but see the context for the decision more fully. When we use all of our ways of human knowing, we recognize aspects of our reality that we did not notice previously. We tune in to values and feelings through deep listening and accessing our intuitive and affective powers. When we seriously consider the interconnectedness of reality, we see the larger systems within which we live and work. We begin to notice how the concern or question in front of us is entangled with larger processes or systemic issues. Criterion 4A, to choose what addresses the full reality of our experience, asks us to consider how our decision is intentionally responsive to the multiplicity and complexity of the inputs into the decision-making process. A good way to check on this responsiveness to the whole is to review the reality that confronts us with a set of basic questions.

Questions to Reveal Reality

Daniel Maguire's moral wheel model for ethical decision-making includes a set of questions at the hub of the wheel that reveals or discloses aspects of reality. According to his method, these are questions that must be asked and fully answered before the moral evaluation process can even begin. The questions immerse us in the particularity of the situation that is calling for our decision. The questions are simple and profound: What?, Why?, How?, Who?, When?, Where?, Foreseeable Effects, and Viable Alternatives.[56] Each of these questions opens up essential aspects of the reality that confronts us. The wisest decision is responsive to the whole reality. We begin with the simplest and most difficult question, *What?*. If we lack clarity and completeness in answering this question, it will plague us throughout our decision-making process. If we oversimplify the what, we set ourselves up for major disappointments, disillusionments, and readjustments after the decision has been made. If our understanding of what is in front of us fails to recognize the interconnectedness with other aspects of our lives or organizations, our decision will have major unforeseen impacts. Some of the most egregious errors in decision-making are made by not having a clear picture of the what, the full reality.

The *why* question asks us to be clear and honest about our intention, what is motivating the decision. What is the desired outcome? Why are we doing this? Will our decision realistically lead to the desired result? This is an area that requires the recognition of our shadow because our ego can sometimes get in the way of the common good. Sometimes the stated reason for a decision may sound altruistic and well-intentioned when underneath it is motivated by a self-serving goal. We must analyze the situation to determine whether the motivation is really centered on the good of the whole. The *how* question asks us to review the possible means or ways to the desired goal. The benefit of the goal does not give us free reign to use whatever means we wish. The means or method must meet the same standards as the end. The *who* question takes us back to the recognition of all the stakeholders that will be affected by the decision. It also requires we ask questions about the competencies and skills of the persons who will be charged with carrying out the decision. In both personal and organizational contexts, we must ask if the decision takes into account in a realistic way the particular persons involved, their abilities, talents, weaknesses, existing workload, psychological preparedness, and so forth. Decisions are carried out by real individuals. When we recognize that fact in making the decision, we pave the way for success.

Depending on the decision, the questions *when* and *where* may be critical as well. If we are determining the location for a new plant or a new home, the *where* question may require a great deal of study and consideration. If we are considering bringing a child into the world or making a significant shift in organizational leadership, the *when* question may be paramount. Wise decisions take into account situations when these considerations are particularly important.

The last two reality-revealing questions require major imaginal skills: the ability to imagine possibilities and to consider the unknown. The best decisions are based on the comprehensive and close consideration of the *viable alternatives* in a situation. Have we considered all the real options? Have we been creative in imagining options that bring together constellations of what we value the most and what reflects our best practices and talents? Again, we are faced with the daunting task of seeing more broadly, of creatively envisioning new ways of being and doing. One of the major questions to be asked of each creative option is: "What are the *foreseeable effects?*" The wisest decision will examine the various scenarios of alternatives and their projected outcomes. The diversity of stakeholders can bring important insights to this imaginal work of thinking about how persons and processes will be affected by a decision.

The brevity of this section on revelatory questions doesn't represent the importance of each of the inquiries in helping to determine a wise decision. A comprehensive study of these questions to whatever extent possible will facilitate a more informed decision. All good decisions are situational, and they depend on a clear analysis of the specifics of the reality facing us. The wisest decisions will be responsive to the fullness of that reality: the What?, Why?, How?, Who?, When?, Where?, Foreseeable Effects, and Viable Alternatives that we are confronting in the present context of this particular decision.

CRITERIA FOR JUDGMENT 4B:
CHOOSE WHAT IS MOST CONSTRUCTIVE TO LIFE

The second criterion for judgment that comes to light by reflecting on this central principle of the importance of human experience can be stated as follows: Do what is constructive to life. A key test of a decision is to ask if it builds up the human person, the human community, and the universe that supports life. This is the broadest and most important single criterion for discerning wise decisions. Wise decision-making must bring about new ways of thinking and acting that will support the ultimate value of human life and its sustaining environment.

This criterion reflects the foundation for all ethical choice and determination of the good. When we are pressed to identify the source of our understanding of the good and the right, we most often share our experiences of the inestimable value of persons. We say things like, "People deserve respect," or "We ought to treat people like we want to be treated," or "People have dignity and the right to freedom and equality." Where do we get these notions about human beings? I haven't found a more direct and clear answer to this question than the one provided by Daniel Maguire:

> The foundational moral experience is the experience of the value of persons and their earthly home in this uni-

verse. This profound value-experience is the distinctively human and humanizing experience and the gateway to personhood. It is this experience that marks us as human. It is the primordial "Wow!" from which all moral theory and all healthy law, politics, and religion derive. This experience is the seed of civilization, the root of culture, and the badge of unique human consciousness.[57]

This experience of the unconditional value of life itself is the ground or ultimate basis of wisdom, the final benchmark to determine if something is wise or foolish, right or wrong, good or bad. Of course, having a criterion doesn't solve the issues of application. It is very clear from our experience that we have conflicting positions on nearly every important issue in our society. We often experience significant emotional attachment to our deeply-held positions precisely because they are consciously or unconsciously our interpretation of what the value of life requires.

All people in every culture have some experience of the value of life itself and the value of persons in particular. The good news is we can intentionally develop our sensitivity and openness to these experiences of wonder and awe at the preciousness of life. Some experience this preciousness when a child is born. I don't think it is possible to witness birth without experiencing a sense of the absolute value of the human being. Some experience the profound value of persons when they are loved unconditionally by a parent, friend, or spouse. Some are struck with this realization when someone they love dies. Sometimes, we experience this absolute value of persons by witnessing atrocities and having a gut reaction that something is not right, not human.

In making wise choices, we must reflect on this fundamental basis of all wisdom, no matter how we have experienced the value of life itself. We must ask ourselves what action will respond to the dignity of persons. What decision will benefit life? What choice is most respectful of people? Another way of articulating this criterion is to ask what love requires, not a sentimental or romantic love, but the unconditional care that every person is due simply because they are a person. This is the touchstone of wisdom.

Questions for Reflection

What are three of your key values? Identify one way in which you can live out each of these values more clearly and strongly. What concrete steps can you take within the next three months to live with greater congruence with these values?

What are two of the key values of the organization for which you work or volunteer? Identify one way in which the organization could live out each of these values more clearly and strongly. What concrete steps can you take within the next three months to live with greater congruence with these values?

Identify two activities that might allow you to experience more deeply the value of life itself and the dignity of persons. Plan the practical steps required to heighten your own sense of the absolute value of persons as persons.

An Assessment of Congruence with Core Values

The following assessment may help you understand how well you are living in congruence with your core values. As you rate yourself, try to think of concrete examples in the last month of each of the areas that you are rating. If you are unable to recall specific examples, you may wish to rate yourself on the lower end of the scale. If you are able to articulate for yourself several specific instances, you may wish to rate yourself on the higher end of the scale.

I regularly reflect on my core values and vision for my life.

High   9   8   7   6   5   4   3   2   Low

In my work experience, I regularly reflect on the core values, vision, and best practices of my organization as I make decisions.

High   9   8   7   6   5   4   3   2   Low

I regularly ask myself the hard questions about how my decisions and actions fit with my values.

High   9   8   7   6   5   4   3   2   Low

I have a clear sense that I am living my life in harmony with my deepest values.

High   9   8   7   6   5   4   3   2   Low

I regularly ask others in my family, community, and workplace how our most important values can be enacted in our decisions.

High   9   8   7   6   5   4   3   2   Low

ATTEND TO PRESERVATION AND TRANSFORMATION

WISDOM PRINCIPLE	OPERATING PROCEDURES	CRITERIA FOR JUDGMENT CHOOSE WHAT...
Principle 5. Attend to preservation and transformation.	OP 5A. Be attentive to origins and foundations. OP 5B. Practice radical creativity.	C 5A. Preserves the core focus and vision. C 5B. Moves toward the boldest possibility.

*W*e live at the intersection of the past and future. Every present decision is grounded in a significant history of past events that have brought us to the present. In making a wise decision, we rely on the resources and experiences of the past. We create the future using memories, dreams, values, principles, promises, and the wounds and betrayals of the past. However, we are not determined by our history. We have the opportunity in each moment to create something new, to respond to the lure of imagination and possibility. With the signing of its constitution by Nelson Mandela on December 10, 1996, the Republic of South Africa formed a radically new society out of the fierce fires of hatred, separation, and discrimination. Even more than these negative experiences, the dream of a radically transformed country arose out of the incomprehensible immensity of human forgiveness and connection.

In that particular intersection of the past and future, when South Africa envisioned a new possibility, people remembered the bombings, massacres, shootings, and disappearances, and the everyday exclusion and poverty related to apartheid. They knew they could not forget about their past. Desmond Tutu, chairman of the Truth and Reconciliation Commission (TRC), says in *No Future Without Forgiveness* that there wasn't "any controversy about whether we should deal effectively with our past if we were going to be making the transition to a new dispensation. No, the debate was not on *whether* but on *how* we might deal with this only too real past."[1]

Many envisioned something like the Nuremberg Trials that prosecuted the major war criminals of a defeated Nazi Germany at the end of World War II. Others simply wanted a blanket amnesty or a truth commission that would meet behind closed doors without exposing atrocities to the bright light of a public process. Beyond harsh judgment and artificial amnesia, South Africa chose a third, courageous possibility—the Truth and Reconciliation process. Tutu explains that this third way "was granting amnesty to individuals in exchange for a full disclosure relating to the crime for which amnesty was being sought."[2] In this process, those who had been silenced and marginalized would recognize their own dignity and personhood. "Now they would be able to tell their stories, they would remember, and in remembering would be acknowledged to be persons with an inalienable personhood."[3]

The Preservation of *Ubuntu* and *Inimba*

Tutu suggests that the Truth and Reconciliation process was successful because one of the fundamental and core principles of the African worldview was preserved in the process.

> ...this third way of amnesty was consistent with a central feature of the African *Weltanschauung*—what we know in our languages as *ubuntu*, in the Nguni group of languages, or *botho*, in the Sotho languages. What is it that constrained so many to choose to forgive rather than to demand retribution, to be so magnanimous and ready to forgive rather than wreak revenge?
>
> *Ubuntu* is very difficult to render into a Western language. It speaks of the very essence of being human. ... It is to say, "My humanity is caught up, is inextricably bound up, in yours." We belong in a bundle of life. We say, "A person is a person through other persons." It is not, "I think therefore I am." It says rather: "I am human because

I belong, I participate, I share." A person with *ubuntu* is open and available to others, affirming of others, does not feel threatened that others are able and good, for he or she has a proper self-assurance that comes from knowing that he or she belongs in a greater whole and is diminished when others are humiliated or diminished, when others are tortured or oppressed, or treated as if they were less than who they are.[4]

The bold new possibility that South Africa chose for itself was at the same time a preservation of the core of identity of the people, a deep belonging to community, bonds that cannot be severed. Pumla Gobodo-Madikizela's essay *Forgiveness and the Maternal Body* explores "the process of forgiveness in the context of such irreparable loss."[5] Based on a profound sense of community, South Africa relied on dialogue to allow the victims and survivors "to revisit the sites of trauma," to feel again "the suffering of the victims," and to confront "perpetrators with their inhumanity as well as their humanity. Through dialogue, both victims and the greater society come to recognize perpetrators as human beings who failed morally...."[6]

In choosing dialogue, they chose to remember the full meaning of that word, to reenact, to bring together the shards of experience, to participate in the past in such a way that fully informs the present. In choosing dialogue, they chose accountability, to refrain from putting the perpetrator in the category of the nonhuman or totally other, to see the humanity of the person who has committed such ignominious deeds. In choosing dialogue, they invited "the perpetrator to negotiate the chasm between his monstrousness and the world of the forgiven."[7]

The preservation of common humanity and the transformation of individual lives and society cannot be understood apart from the actual stories of murder, terror, and inexplicable forgiveness. The following poem attempts to touch upon the experience of a perpetrator, "a black former police informant who infiltrated a group of seven young black activists from one of Cape Town's townships during apartheid rule," and the seven families with whom he met before the TRC.[8] A primary strategy of the apartheid government was to infiltrate groups of activists, train them to fight with weapons, and lure them into a police trap to kill them. This poem is based on the description of the TRC process provided in *Forgiveness and the Maternal Body*.

INIMBA

Seven mothers and their extended families
    mourning the deaths
of their seven sons meet with the young man, perpetrator,
police informant who turned his back
    on his people for profit,
for safety, for shame. Only the mothers speak when he asks
for their forgiveness. They tell him he sold his own blood
to the white apartheid government, he was a wolf.
He shakes as he listens, his face twitching, and pleads
haltingly, softly, addressing the mothers, "My parents,
I ask your forgiveness from the bottom of my heart."

It is not his words that move her. There is a long silence
after his plea. The whole story wells up without sound,
how limitless the losses, how unsayable the sins, and yet
she says, "You are the same age as my murdered son
Christopher. I want to tell you, my son, that I,
as Christopher's mother, I forgive you, my son."
She says "my son" and embraces him, presses his body
to her body, a child, her wayward child, a child forgiven.

Later, when they ask her how she could forgive him
she speaks of her womb, of the umbilical cord
that joins a mother to a child, of that feeling for a child,
how a mother knows her child's desperation or longing
for home when he is in trouble even a thousand miles away.
She speaks of the feeling in her body, she calls it
"inimba" umbilical tether, the cord that binds us all.

Much like the sense of *ubuntu*, the feeling of *inimba* exists at the very core of the mothers of the seven slain young men. They feel *inimba* as a bodily response to the young man's plea and it motivates them to be empathic and forgiving. They reach toward the perpetrator with radical forgiveness because they allow themselves to feel *inimba* in the womb of their being.

The preamble to the South African constitution reflects on past injustice and suffering and proclaims a new vision of unity and inclusion.

> We, the people of South Africa,
> Recognise the injustices of our past;
> Honour those who suffered for justice
> and freedom in our land;
> Respect those who have worked to build
> and develop our country; and
> Believe that South Africa belongs to all who live in it,
> united in our diversity.
> We therefore, through our freely elected representatives,
> adopt this Constitution as the supreme law of the
> Republic so as to
> Heal the divisions of the past and establish a society based
> on democratic values, social justice and fundamental
> human rights;
> Lay the foundations for a democratic and open society in
> which government is based on the will of the people and
> every citizen is equally protected by law; Improve the
> quality of life of all citizens and free the potential of
> each person...[9]

The constitution was published in the eleven official languages of the Republic and more than seven million copies were distributed. Its wise words were embodied in the Truth and Reconciliation process, which proved that the bold vision articulated in the constitution could be realized. The radical vision of a united South Africa and the healing of the wounds of apartheid are most powerfully seen in the actions of the family members of the killed and maimed who reached into the heart of their personal and social *ubuntu* and *inimba* to transform human fear and treachery into the possibility of grace and community. The attentiveness to both preservation and transformation that is so evident in the wise decisions of the new

Republic of South Africa is a key principle in the spiritual traditions of the religions of the world.

Preservation and Transformation in Spiritual Traditions

The number of religions and sects within religions is astounding. Religion seems to be a story of continual change and adaptation. Some would say this change in religious consciousness happens as a result of God's revelation. Others would point to the prophetic voices of reformers who believe their tradition has strayed from its original wisdom. Still others would explain these changes by articulating new cultural demands to which religion must respond. However, one thing is clear no matter how you explain the continual changes in the religious landscape. With every new religion, every new sect, or every process of reform within a religious tradition, there is a desire to retain or preserve some core truth from the past and a concomitant intention to transform the tradition with new consciousness, understanding, or practice.

Although we cannot trace one linear, historical process for the development of religion in general, the history of religions shows a complex evolution of several common elements over time. Each of these elements occurs because some new threshold of human consciousness is crossed. In the last chapter, our exploration of the turn toward inner wisdom and individual moral consciousness that occurred in the religions of the Axial Age is one of the clearest examples of crossing such a threshold in human consciousness. In the Axial Age, love of neighbor became inextricably bound with religious understandings of the transcendent. The focus of religion became less about understanding God than about doing good deeds, and less about sacrifice and ritual than about sharing bread and sheltering the homeless.

Many of the common elements that develop within religions can be viewed as complementary pairs. These pairs need to be held in tension or conversation within the tradition if the religion is to be fruitful and build up the human community. When one or the other element becomes overemphasized, there is often a movement to transform the tradition, to bring religion back into greater balance in a way that responds to new political or cultural circumstances. In other words, the change is not only a return to some important element of the past tradition but also a new synthesis of both elements of the pair in response to the particular historical experience. Thus, the change process is both conservative and transformative. It preserves some critical element of religious experience from the past and creates something new in response to the current experience. I will explore some of these common pairs of religious elements and give a few examples of reforms that attempt to bring greater balance among these elements.

Religion arises as part of our uniquely human consciousness. As far as we know, we are the only species that questions its beginning and end, its source and ultimate purpose, and answers this perplexing question with images and concepts of the transcendent. Karen Armstrong says, "Men and women started to worship gods as soon as they became recognizably human; they created religions at the same time as they created works of art."[10] David Chidester asserts that the "earliest records for the history of religions are bones. Evidence of the intentional, careful burial of human remains has been dated as far back as 100,000 years BCE."[11] Early burial sites reveal bones painted with red ochre, perhaps symbolizing blood and life, and corpses bound in the fetal position, perhaps symbolizing a hoped-for new birth.[12] From ancient cave paintings and archeological evidence of altars and sacrificial rites, it is evident the earliest response to the transcendent was awe, wonder, and fear.

TRANSCENDENCE AND IMMANENCE

These attitudes are still central aspects of religions today. However we imagine it, wonder is the experiential origin for our images and concepts about a higher power. Awe expresses the otherness of the transcendent, its power and immensity. It is not unusual for human beings to respond to great power with fear and trembling. The transcendent is mysterious, sometimes seems to act whimsically or inexplicably, and is ultimately unapproachable. Shaking in our proverbial boots, however, doesn't get us very far. Fear is debilitating if not counteracted by some level of confidence in life. Thus, the human experience of fear in the presence of incomprehensible omnipotence leads religions to devise ways to appease that power. Sacrifices and prescribed rituals arise as means of assuring that the rains fall, the crops grow, and new offspring are born. But transcendence of the divine is only part of the story. In human consciousness, there also arises a sense of unification with the divine. The divine is immanent, or within us, guiding us. God is close to us, loves us, and feels our suffering. With the realization of God's immanence, personal spirituality and devotion become heightened. Forms of mystical experience and meditation focus on accessing the "immortal spark at the core of the human person, which participated in—was of the same nature as—the immortal Brahman that sustained and gave life to the entire cosmos."[13]

The experience of the transcendent without any sense of immanence imprisons us in fear and subjects us to a scrupulous practice of ritual and sacrifice. Understanding the divine as immanent, without any sense of transcendence, removes the important dimension of the unknown and mysterious that undergirds our human quest to go beyond our present understanding. In the Hebrew tradition, we see this complementary pairing of transcendence and immanence in the two creation accounts that occur in the first chapters of the Book of Genesis. The second creation account that begins in Genesis 2:4b is the earlier one, probably written during the monarchy of kings David and Solomon. This was a time when there was a deep sense of Yahweh's guidance of the people through the king. God's covenant with the Israelites was for all ages, and there would always be a king to rule the people with justice and mercy. Out of this stable political structure, the Yahwist tradition portrays an immanent God who creates by hand, forms the animals and the human person out of the clay of the ground, breathes the divine spirit of life into the human being, and plants a garden in Eden. In this tradition, God is close to humankind, walks in the garden in the breezy time of the day, and calls out to the man and woman.

The first creation account in Genesis 1:1-2:4a is from the priestly tradition, probably written during the exile in Babylon, which was a time of upheaval, questioning, and suffering. God is portrayed as mighty and powerful. God creates by word. "Then God said, 'Let there be light,' and there was light" (Genesis 1:1). The glory and majesty of God are emphasized in this creation story, perhaps because the people needed to have confidence in a powerful God who could again deliver them from oppression in a foreign land. Although these two portrayals of God are radically different, both emphasize aspects of the human experience of the divine that need to be preserved. New stories of creation are written out of these disparate political contexts that require reflection on different dimensions of their understanding of God. The changing story of the Hebrew people transforms the memory of the past and brings new and powerful narratives into existence at the same time that it calls for the preservation of key aspects of the religious experience of the people.

Some of the other complementary paired aspects of religion include contemplation and action, the importance of sacred writings and the continuing experience of the community, faith and reason, external religious authority and internal personal authority of conscience, revealed law and natural law, right belief or assent to a creed and right relationship and action, religious laws and rules and the spirit of the law, and others.

PRESERVATION AND TRANSFORMATION IN CHRISTIANITY

There are many examples of movements within various spiritual traditions to preserve the core of the religion and, yet, respond boldly to a new cultural context. This process of preservation and transformation still functions in our current experience. For instance, Marcus Borg in *The Heart of Christianity* speaks of a paradigm shift in Christianity in North America today.[14] A new way of understanding what it means to be a Christian is emerging. In his description of the old and new paradigms of Christianity, he explains a basic change in emphasis from right belief to right relationship, from faith as creedal assent to faith as relationship with God and community that necessarily flows into compassionate service. His analysis of the current transformation reflects several of the paired aspects of religion articulated above. He believes one element of the pair has been overemphasized in the past and the complementary element needs to be reemphasized to respond to our contemporary challenges. Perhaps the single most important shift in emphasis is from seeing faith as a matter of intellectual or mental belief to seeing faith as a matter of trusting and acting with the heart.

> The virtual identification of faith with believing a set of statements is thus a serious impoverishment of the word "faith." ...Seeing the heart of Christianity requires recovering the rich meanings of faith, a recovery that leads to a relational understanding of faith and to an understanding of Christianity as a "way"—as the way of the heart.[15]

It is important to note that Borg calls the shift to this new paradigm a recovery of central elements at the heart of Christianity. These elements were eclipsed by the concerns and particular emphases of the last three centuries. In the new paradigm, critical forgotten components of Christianity are remembered again as the tradition responds with a broader vision to a set of new cultural circumstances. There is a creative advance that synthesizes in a transformative way the multiplicity of past aspects of the tradition.

PRESERVATION AND TRANSFORMATION IN ISLAM

Transformation is also occurring in Islam as it continues to be the fastest-growing and second largest religious tradition in the world today.[16] As with other spiritual traditions, a broad multiplicity of concerns faces Islam in the twenty-first century, including the application of the tradition to countless moral issues never before imagined, the diverse understandings of the relationship between government and religion, questions of religious pluralism and the rights of minorities from both Abrahamic traditions and others, and issues related to gender, roles, and rights. John Esposito accurately represents the diverse and often conflicting voices in the debates regarding change in Islam.

> The sacrosanct nature of tradition in Islam is of primary significance, it serves as a bedrock of faith, an inspirational reality for traditionalists, and a major hurdle for modern reformers. Two general approaches or attitudes to Islamic renewal and reform can be identified: (1) a traditionalist desire to restore an early Islamic ideal; and (2) a reformist call for renovation or reconstruction through Islamic, as distinct from Western, reform. Both approaches emphasize reliance on Islamic sources. A key difference between traditionalists and reformers is their understand-

ing and use of Islamic history and tradition as well as the nature and degree of change they advocate.[17]

Whether brought about by traditionalists or reformers, changes in the practice of Islam that preserve key themes and principles from the past and respond to the uniqueness of contemporary situations are being effected in large and small ways, from political structures to private family matters.

Throughout the world, religions are encountering opportunities to deepen the core values and fundamental principles of their traditions as they address the new cultural circumstances that require transformation and change. Perhaps one of the most significant aspects of the current interdependent and mobile world to which religions are called to respond is the reality of religious pluralism. In every nation and city, persons of diverse religious traditions are living and working side by side and relying on one another for professional services of every kind. In this context, many people and religions are grappling with how to understand the truth claims of each other's traditions. How can we speak with one another about religion in a way that does not polarize the human community? We are being called to dialogue among the diversity of religious traditions, to listen with sensitivity and openness to the distinctive beliefs of others. Each tradition must bring its most deeply held beliefs and be open to transformation as we learn new ways of understanding one another and living and working together.

The common religious principle to attend to preservation and transformation in the change process, to keep what is good from the past and move boldly toward the best possibility in the future, has many implications for how we go about deciding and for the basis upon which we make our judgments.

Principle Five Operating Procedures and Criteria

Mature decision-making often involves a complex process of balancing paradoxical concerns. The dual emphasis of this final principle on preservation and transformation is such a paradox. How can we focus on foundations, preserve traditions and values, and, at the same time, boldly embrace future possibilities? When we are faced with such a paradox, we often think we must choose a little from both poles of seeming opposites. The more accurate way to reflect on the paradox of preservation and transformation is to engage our most creative thinking in identifying how our positive core can be lived more fully through an innovative re-creation of our organizations or ourselves. By accepting the fullness and uniqueness of our positive core, and inhabiting the whole story that brings us to this moment, how do we live into the dream of the best possibility? How do we take all of who we are at the heart of our knowing and do the boldest, most creative thing we can do? The following operating procedures and criteria help us answer these central questions.

OPERATING PROCEDURE 5A:
BE ATTENTIVE TO ORIGINS AND FOUNDATIONS

To decide wisely, we must explore the positive core of our organization or ourselves. We must get to the foundation of who we are. In the last chapter, we explained briefly some aspects of the appreciative inquiry process that many organizations and individuals have used to become clearer about their values, best practices, strengths, and unique talents. Any process that facilitates listening to the central stories of success, fulfillment, service, and contribution is helpful in identifying the positive core or clarifying foundational values. In an organization, this listening process should be as broad as possible, including persons from all levels and departments as well as customers and suppliers. Communication of the central stories is very important because the values and strengths of an organization come alive in the concrete, specific stories that are shared. A set of values can seem abstract and lifeless until we see it embodied in courageous actions, exemplary service, innovative processes, and spirited team work.

For individuals, clarifying the positive core will be a process of in-depth reflection or interior listening. We might begin identification of our foundation by reflecting on these questions: (1) What are three of the most meaningful, alive, fulfilling times of my life? What happened, how did I feel, what contributions did I make? (2) Reflecting on these times and other key moments in my life, what do I know about my values, talents, strengths, abilities, gifts, and priorities? (3) Based on my reflections, how would I map, describe, or diagram the positive core or center of my being, using words, symbols, or images? Identifying my positive core as an individual may also involve talking with others about how they have experienced my talents, priorities, and values and my integration of this core into the various aspects of my life. Individuals are often surprised by what others see in them. A gift we might glimpse in ourselves or may be unsure about becomes clearer when others tell stories of how we may have convincingly exhibited this talent or value. As we consider a decision, we must ask how it is consistent with the core of who we are as individuals or organizations. Does this decision preserve what is most central? Is it congruent with my core values, vision, and talents?

Another way to become clearer about the positive core is to explore the origins and initial vision of the organization or to investigate one's early talents, interests, and focus as a youth. The founding documents and early history of an organization can provide inspiring examples of the values and vision that run through its veins. Analyze the founding documents, early board minutes, annual reports, and newsletters to identify the core values that were most important in the originating years of the organization. Talk to as many elders as possible about how things got started, what the original vision was, what the challenges were, and how they were surmounted. As an individual, explore family photo albums, home movies, and any saved drawings, projects, and papers from school. Review old journals, diaries, or yearbooks. Identify important interests, talents, values, and concerns from your years as a child and young adult.

In order to reflect on the origins and foundations of an organization in the decision-making process, the founding stories need to come alive for all employees. They need to be told repeatedly and in creative ways. Excerpts from founding documents can be put in the newsletter. Photos of founders, early buildings, processes, and products can be shared. An organizational museum or archive room can be created. Brief theatrical pieces about the founding days of the organization can be produced for important events. Video interviews with elders who talk about their positive experiences can be distributed electronically. At The College of St. Scholastica, where I serve on the Mission Integration Committee, "Living Our Mission" is one of the menu items on the college portal Web site. In this area, we regularly provide stories of persons who are putting the mission and values into practice in an exemplary way. There are also weekly reflections on the core values of the college. When there are regular reminders of the positive core, it is more likely people will think about the central values, vision, and strengths of the organization when important decisions are considered.

In order to reflect regularly on personal foundations, it is crucial to put our values and vision into a form we can revisit. I create a "positive, personal core map" each year that shows the relationships among my key values, strengths, and priorities. Although the values, strengths and priorities don't change from year to year, the prioritized order and interconnections vary. I put it on the first page of my journal so that I regularly consult it as I make decisions about how I spend my time and energy. In your office or work area, you may hang a visual symbol or image of your core values or a photo that reminds you of your critical priorities. You may write a letter to yourself about your foundational beliefs that you revisit weekly or monthly. There are many different ways to keep our positive core front and center in our considerations.

Living Out Our Foundational Values

Being attentive to origins and foundations is not about being static or supporting the status quo. Living out our individual or organizational founding values and vision to the fullest requires significant change in programs, processes, products, services, locations, structures, and the like as we put those values and visions into practice in a constantly changing world. Ultimately, reflection on origins and foundations means we remain true to ourselves as we respond to new challenges. We face new circumstances and make the needed changes because we are firmly grounded in a secure and unique identity. Our foundational values, vision, and strengths provide a stable base for confronting any new reality. When we preserve the positive core of our organization or ourselves, we recognize how it needs to be translated into new circumstances and we are open to the unfolding of the plenitude of its meaning for a new age.

The common principle to preserve and transform that is embedded in many of the religions of the world is consistent with the research of Jim Collins in *Good to Great*. His findings show how to "take a company with great results and turn it into an *enduring* great company of iconic stature. To make that final shift requires core values and a purpose beyond just making money combined with the key dynamic of preserve the core/stimulate progress."[18] This key dynamic is borne out repeatedly in organizations that excel. They regularly recall their founding purpose, tell the stories of their origin, reflect on the key motivations of their early history, and preserve the core values that provide direction. At the same time, they stimulate progress by living out their values in radically new ways.

One of the best individual examples of this paradox of preserving the core and being open to transformation is my friend Barry. I have been in a leadership group with him and two other men for more than a dozen years, meeting three or four weekends a year for intense dialogue on everything from servant leadership to shadow work, from re-creating our stories to deep listening processes. Barry embodies lifelong learning and compassionate care. He's been a team product manager at Proctor & Gamble Company, a recruiter at Management Recruiters, a sales engineer at Johnson Controls, co-owner and manager of a temporary services company, and a certified financial planner and agent with the Principal Financial Group.

He's had his share of scrapes and bumps, but his willingness to learn, his quickness to pick up skills and knowledge, and his sincere care for people have allowed him to be successful in new positions. In 2002, he began teaching business courses full-time at the University of Wisconsin Oshkosh and realized this was his true calling. Part of that realization came from reflecting on vocation in our group. Barry writes, "When our group reflected on *Let Your Life Speak* by Parker Palmer, it helped me get clarity on teaching being where my life was taking me. That was certainly a critical process in my discernment about my life's passion and work and allowed me to truly accept that path for my life."[19] His openness to, and excitement about, continual learning had finally brought him to a profession focused on education and care. He was a natural teacher, caring for students and sharing his many experiences related to all aspects of business and personal finances.

Barry taught for seven years but, because he did not have a doctoral degree, he wasn't in a tenure-track position and there were limits to the leadership roles he could fill. At forty-seven, Barry took the next step to preserve his positive core and stimulate progress. He entered a doctoral program in financial planning at Texas Tech University, one of only two doctoral programs in that field in the country at the time. He acted on his foundational love of learning and care for students and took the next bold step into his future. As he moves into the final semester of his program, he is excited about his research and is already scheduled for several job interviews across the country as undergraduate and graduate programs in financial planning continue to build. Barry believes the kind of consistent and deep reflection that our leadership group provided for us facilitated his decision to act on his core values in the boldest possible way.

OPERATING PROCEDURE 5B: PRACTICE RADICAL CREATIVITY

While the wise decision-making process asks hard questions about what is consistent with the origins and foundations of our organizations and ourselves, it also asks us to consider the boldest possibilities for living out our positive core. Wise decision-making requires that we practice radical creativity. Often this means not settling for the easy answer, and going beyond the assumptions and presuppositions of our present mental models. Peter Block says, "the future is created out of nothing. There's a void, a potential. Every time you have the courage to create an alternative future, you need that empty space, that space of potential."[20] The space of potential includes silence and chaos. To be wise decision-makers, we need to become more comfortable with creating that kind of space within ourselves and our organizations.

We need to welcome and respect the chaos, the not-knowing, the struggling with radically new ideas, and the conflicting perspectives that are spoken in a circle of trust. We must allow ourselves to simmer in this void for as long as it takes, to let the silence and emptiness of not knowing work their alchemy on our imaginations. We have to let go of our need to be right, to look good, and to have the answers. We must be vulnerable enough to see the treasures that come from the wild imaginations of others. We must have the courage to let go of our own interests, models, and certainties. We must meet new ideas that arise with the perspective of an "angel's advocate" rather than a devil's advocate. I have experienced so many creative suggestions shot down seconds after they were launched when someone said, "Well, let me play the devil's advocate on that idea." This usually results in the identification of all of the potential risks, all of the ways that things could go wrong, all of the difficulties that could be encountered, and all of the assumptions that support the status-quo. Without any of these reservations or apprehensions being tested, the idea is dismissed without cause and without a fair hearing. If we are going to practice radical creativity, we must play the angel's advocate more often. We must try to envision what could go right, how things could work out, and what the biggest benefits could be.

Create a space of welcome for off-beat, slightly wacky, and irreverent ideas and solutions. One of the key skills of radical creativity is the ability to ask the right questions and facilitate transparent, in-depth conversations in which people are willing to be vulnerable with their ideas. Block offers several key questions that open a space of risky creativity and transformation.

> Here are some thoughts about conversations that have the power to create an alternative future. One is the conversation of *possibility*. What's the possibility I came here to live into or to create?…There is a conversation of *commitment*. Commitment means, "What's the promise I'm willing to make with no expectation of return?"…There's a conversation of *gifts*, an incredible conversation…. Suppose our primary purpose in leading would be to bring the gifts of the margin into the center….The elegant thing about these conversations is that any one will do. They all carry the same spirit, the same love, and the same willingness to surrender to the unpredictability of the future.[21]

Nurturing Divergent Thinking

We have the power to create an alternative future for ourselves and our organizations. To make wise decisions that preserve the best of the past and step boldly into the future, we need to cultivate imaginative, divergent thinking. Most of our formal education focuses on convergent thinking—memorizing, recalling, and repeating what has already been discovered and tested. In many ways, formal education is passive, simply taking in models, concepts, and theories that have been developed by others. Radical creativity requires imaginative thinking, playing with possibilities, developing our capacities "to create new wholes out of preexisting elements, to explore the unstructured situation, to redefine the problem from a fresh angle, to generate the new, the unconventional, the original."[22] How do we go about stimulating our creativity and nurturing our divergent thinking? Here are several practical suggestions that apply both to internal personal reflection and organizational group reflection.

First, postpone judgment and evaluation of your own thoughts or those of others. Invite a diversity of ideas, play with them, try them out conceptually, and look for the positives and opportunities in them. Give new ideas some time to gestate before you write them off as unworkable. Second, regularly invite new ways of thinking and doing things. We all develop routines over time, standard ways we conceptualize projects and problems, habitual ways we respond to others, familiar topics and interests that we read and talk about. To invite creativity, we must consistently shake ourselves up, do things differently, listen deeply to those who don't think like us, engage in thinking and in doing things that are uncomfortable or at least diverge from our routine. Third, intentionally look at a question, issue, or solution from several different angles. An easy way to do this is to divide a sheet of paper into four quadrants and title the quadrants with different points of view that you will consider. They might be Right Now, In Seven Generations, Close In, Big Picture. They might be Risks, Benefits, Unforseeables, Certainties. They might be Values, Talents, Resources, Ethics. They might be Profits, Liabilities, People, Environment. They might be Thoughts, Feelings, Values, Gut Reaction. Spend time with each quadrant, but also visit each of the quadrants at least four times since your thinking in one quadrant will affect how you consider the other quadrants. If you are working with a team, another way of looking at an issue from multiple perspectives is to use a wheel model as described in *The Fifth Discipline Fieldbook*.

> Create a disk about eighteen inches in diameter from thick paper which can be written upon. Lay the wheel in the center of the table. Write a title or draw a symbol for

> the problem in the center of the wheel….Draw lines across the wheel is if cutting a pie, dividing the wheel into equal slices—one for each member of the team. Write everyone's name on a slice of the wheel….Then write up cards with the names or titles of eight or more key stakeholders, for the problem being explored.[23]

As you turn the wheel one space, each person in the team will have a chance to role-play the perspective of one of the eight or more key stakeholders. It is helpful if each person begins their reflection by stating the perspective they are taking, such as, "From my perspective as the production manager, I think one of the most important things we have to consider is…" or "From my viewpoint as a customer, the central question I would ask is…"

The three suggestions above are simply an introduction to the broad array of methods that can help you practice radical creativity. If you are interested in strengthening your creativity muscles, I suggest exploring (1) scenario planning, which opens up perspectives on multiple possible futures, (2) dialogue, which facilitates respectful, transformative conversations, and (3) the multitude of creativity tools. Thomas Chermack in *Scenario Planning in Organizations: How to Create, Use and Assess Scenarios* discusses the developmental and theoretical foundations of scenario planning and provides an excellent process for developing and applying scenarios.[24] William Isaacs in *Dialogue and the Art of Thinking Together* provides an in-depth overview of dialogue theory and practice along with many pertinent examples.[25]

For creativity tools, I would recommend the work of Edward de Bono, who is recognized as one of the leading international authorities in developing thinking skills, and Michael Michalko, who is one of the foremost practitioners of applying creative thinking to political and corporate issues.[26] A wise decision-making process must reflect on origins and foundations as well as explore radical creativity. Although there are countless techniques for incorporating these important perspectives, the key wisdom principle to preserve the best of the past and to be open to transformation can be synthesized into one fundamental challenge: to open a space where questions of values and possibilities can be deeply and respectfully explored in an atmosphere of trust and transparency. The principle to preserve and transform is further cemented by two criteria for judgment.

CRITERIA FOR JUDGMENT 5A: PRESERVE THE CORE FOCUS AND VISION

When we make decisions that preserve our core vision and values, we have a sense of congruence and integrity. We feel whole because there is a match between our soul and our actions, between what we really believe in and what we are doing. We have a deep satisfaction about our lives and our work. We've all seen people whose work matched their values and gifts. We come away from those encounters with a sense that the person was meant for this particular work. There's a fit between their heart and what they are doing, between their core values and where they put their energy every day. In teaching the course "Renewing the Inner Teacher," I have the opportunity to hear teachers talk about the connections between their soul and their work. For some, it is crystal clear that they are doing what they were called to do in life. They daily live out their deepest values. They couldn't imagine not being a teacher. They tell their success stories with tears streaming down their faces.

Linda tells me about her student Tara, who started second grade with very low reading and comprehension skills, an extremely negative attitude, and almost no friends. She talks about her morning meetings before school with Tara, reading together at her desk every Tuesday and Thursday morning; about the small library of books that Linda passed on to Tara because "I had a lot of doubles on my own shelves and the used book store just about gives these things away." She talks about the changes in Tara: the amazing jump in her reading ability, her animated participation in class discussion, and her new friends. Then there is the hair ribbon that she wears every Tuesday, a gift from Linda after Tara made her first oral book report. After hearing Linda's story, I know she was born to be a teacher.

For others, the story is different. Some talk of fatigue or burnout. They're not sure they can face another year or another difficult class. For some of them, it becomes clear that teaching doesn't fit their spirit. Work that fits with our passion and expresses our core values feeds our souls. Work that isn't congruent with our particular gifts and priorities depletes our energy and saps our joy in life. When we are involved in work that fits our core values, we often have a sense that we are making an important contribution. We are motivated to serve because our work is consistent with the priorities that are at the heart of who we are. The opposite is true as well. If we do something that goes counter to our central values, we lose part of our soul. We feel like our spirit is being crushed by the work. What is true for the individual is also true for the organization.

Ascension Health, the largest Catholic healthcare system in the United States (more than 500 locations in 20 states and the District of Columbia), is a powerful example of an organization that consistently focuses on foundational values as it changes to deliver evidence-based and person-centered healthcare.[27] I had the privilege of working with Sister Joyce DeShano, SSJ, when she was chairperson of the Board of Trustees for Ascension Health in its early years of formation. DeShano believed "the most important job of any organization was to be very clear about the core values that are at the heart and history of the organization and to make those values come alive."[28] A key dimension of her work was to activate the values focused on the selection process, finding values-based people to carry the mission and values into the future. When hiring leaders for the system, she strongly advocated for considering their values as important as their academic background or management experience. Her successors have continued the organizational focus on service of the poor, reverence, integrity, wisdom, creativity, and dedication. Ascension Health works hard to put these lofty words and concepts into concrete application.

INTEGRATING CORE VALUES IN TRANSFORMATIVE WAYS AT ASCENSION HEALTH

As Ascension Health has grown in the number of hospitals, clinics, associates, and corresponding complexity, it has continued to focus on the integration of its core values in transformative ways. In its recent strategic choices, the system places an even greater emphasis on ensuring those it serves have a consistently positive experience. The goal of 100 percent satisfaction has been expanded to include not only experiences in its hospitals but also its clinics. To support this goal, an interactive workshop called "Holistic Reverent Care"[29] was created to increase the emotional and spiritual intelligence of thousands of frontline associates and leaders. In 2011, a follow-up workshop was introduced that "gives additional depth, cultural competency, and skills to provide reverent care in difficult situations with a special focus on those who are poor and vulnerable."[30]

Ascension Health is intentionally focusing on preservation and transformation, persistently finding new ways to integrate the values that have been at its heart from its origin into cutting-edge research and health initiatives. Although innovation and transformation occur throughout the system, there is a particular team known as Transformational Development that "functions as Ascension Health's future-focused innovation agent."[31] One of its key projects explores ways of being more "proactive and supportive of those who live in poverty or are vulnerable by using what research has indicated is the only consistent common denominator: the cell phone."[32] The project is extending the basic social service information provided through the telephone to a much deeper level, using dedicated and specially trained, multilingual "navigators" to connect patients with needed health services and support. "Health navigators help individuals apply for programs such as Medicaid or prescription assistance, schedule appointments and pre-register patients, obtain transportation assistance if needed and receive mobile phone-based reminders regarding appointments and recommended follow-ups."[33]

One of the central values of Ascension Health has always been service of the poor, which they describe as "Healthcare That Leaves No One Behind."[34] There is a systemwide focus on providing for the vulnerable, helping them access the best care. They have identified several at-risk populations, not only the uninsured, but also those "who are vulnerable due to factors other than insurance coverage, including their economic situation, citizenship status, geographic location, health status, age, education level, or decision-making ability."[35] And Ascension Health doesn't stop at the domestic border. Through its Seton Institute, it "supports primary care projects and serves as a humanitarian early responder to emergencies in some of the world's poorest communities," most recently "supporting relief efforts in Haiti, Chile and Japan…"[36] These are only a few examples of the continuous focus on preserving its core values by translating them into innovative actions that transform the system and people's lives. The system even published the "Organizational Ethics Discernment Process,"[37] helping leaders explicitly reflect on mission, vision, and values as they are making decisions.

CRITERIA FOR JUDGMENT 5B:
MOVE TOWARD THE BOLDEST POSSIBILITY

The final criterion related to this principle of preserve and transform is to choose the boldest possibility, the option that stretches us toward the very best we can do and be, and the alternative that responds most audaciously to the creative pull. I turn again to Ascension Health for a clear example of responding to current challenges with radical creativity and choosing a bold possibility that is transforming how they provide holistic and compassionate care. This daring move incorporates several of the principles of wise decision-making that we have covered in previous chapters.

In 2011, Ascension Health began its "Enterprising Health" program, which brings together community teams to propose health-related businesses that will have an impact on the health of the community. The system has created a unique structure for broadening and deepening the listening process that pays particular attention to the marginalized and those whose voices are often not heard. Dr. Marilyn French Hubbard, executive director of Enterprise Health, describes it as "an opportunity for community members to be change agents for transforming their own health….to create businesses by people in the community that will have a sustainable and positive impact on health, wellness, disease management, and disease prevention."[38]

The experts in the Ascension Health system recognized that they didn't have all the answers. Scott Lambert, lead partner in the Transformational Development Team, says, "And in many cases, us trying to come up with the answers, we end up with answers that don't solve the needs of the community. So, the idea of having people from the actual grassroots community develop solutions that are sustainable as potential businesses that improve the health of the community and then to co-create those with the community was a very attractive idea for us."[39]

In April 2011, forty-six teams in Detroit, Michigan, developed proposals and competed for grants. They received extensive training in entrepreneurship and management and went through two rounds of judging. Thirteen teams were selected to test and further develop their concepts and on June 16, 2011, five teams were selected for focused support to help them launch or grow their businesses based on the "innovativeness of the business concept, potential impact on the health of the community, and viability/sustainability of the team and business model."[40] Three examples of the winning businesses are the Healthy Dollar, On Guard Detroit, and Change Game. Kathy Jackson explains that "Healthy Dollar is a dollar store. People love dollar stores, but it's bringing in fresh fruits and veggies. Just because you don't have a lot of money doesn't mean you can't have good quality things and feel good about yourself. And that's what we plan to do here and we will do it."[41]

On Guard Detroit works with students in K-12 schools in low-income environments. Physical activity and academic achievement are linked together in the program. Bobby Smith says, "We go in and teach kids the sport of fencing and then we'll link it to something educational in the science, technology, engineering, and mathematics area. What Ascension Health is doing well is they're talking to different groups in different areas and they are finding the answers across the catwalk. I applaud their audacity to push the envelope."[42] Change Game will help people take charge of managing their own health by making a game out of tracking their ongoing health information. The hope of the game developer is that a process that used to be tedious can be experienced as easy and even fun.[43]

Wise decisions will embody a creative response to the challenge that an individual or organization face, a fuller application of core values and vision in response to the current reality. This doesn't mean acting whimsically, with abandon, or without a careful weighing of liabilities. Rather, the wise decision will decisively grasp the future and respond to the lure of innovation, novelty, and human possibility. From a personal perspective, this means answering the question, "If I could take the gifts, talents, values at my core, the central uniqueness and identity of who I am, and really live this out, what would be the boldest possibility for my life?" What would I choose in this concrete situation with all of its particulars to move decisively toward the implementation of the largest vision for my life?

EBOO PATEL'S STORY OF
PRESERVATION AND TRANSFORMATION

It took several years and transformative experiences for Eboo Patel to step into a powerful vision that both embodied his spiritual roots and values and radically responded to the needs that he saw in the world. Enacting this principle of preservation and transformation, he chose a path of bold possibility and created an organization that is having a transformative effect on many young people. In *Acts of Faith*, Eboo tells his story:

> I am an American Muslim from India. My adolescence was a series of rejections, one after another, of the various dimensions of my heritage, in the belief that America, India, and Islam could not coexist within the same being. If I wanted to be one, I could not be the others. My struggle to understand the traditions I belong to as mutually enriching rather than mutually exclusive is the story of a generation of young people standing at the crossroads of inheritance and discovery, trying to look both ways at once.[44]

Through defining moments of struggle and insight, with support from parents, teachers, mentors, and friends, he came to value learning, his Muslim faith, and social justice. Putting these central dimensions of his life together, he created the Interfaith Youth Corps (IFYC) to bring "young people from different backgrounds to engage in social action and reflect on how their different traditions inspired that work."[45]

As is the case with many who claim bold possibilities, the universe itself seemed to support the development of Eboo's vision. He met Brother Wayne Teasdale, who served on the board of the Council for a Parliament of the World's Religions and arranged a trip to India for Eboo to meet with the Dalai Lama. In the audience, the Dalai Lama's message about the IFYC was very clear. He said, "Religions must dialogue, but even more, they must come together to serve others. Service is the most important. And common values… And as you study the other religions, you must learn more about your own and believe more in your own. This Interfaith Youth Corps is a very good project."[46]

On the same trip, Eboo stayed with his grandmother in Bombay. His understanding of his grandmother from her several visits with his family in the United States was of an old Muslim traditionalist. He dreaded her visits and did his best to avoid her. Eboo came to a fuller understanding of his grandmother's faith and his own call to social justice when he "woke up one morning to find a new woman in the apartment. She looked a little scared and disheveled" and was wearing one of his grandmother's much-too-large nightgowns.[47] When Eboo questioned his grandmother, she said she didn't know her real name but that the leader of the prayer house had brought her to the apartment for protection since she was being abused at home. When Eboo objected that the father or uncle of the woman might come looking for her, his grandmother said, "We will check the door before we answer it. And God is with us."[48] When Eboo insisted the arrangement was too risky for his grandmother, she revealed that she had been "doing this for forty-five years. That's more than twice as long as you've been on earth. This may be the fiftieth, sixtieth, hundredth person who has come here and been safe."[49] Eboo's call to social justice seemed to be rooted in a long tradition of service in his own family.

Eboo's vision is motivated by a passionate resolve to involve youth in their spiritual traditions and work together across those traditions to serve the dignity of the human community. He is painfully aware that young people can be trained to kill or to serve. He says, "Every time we read about a young person who kills in the name of God, we should recognize that an institution painstakingly recruited and trained that young person."[50] Eboo has created an institution that is recruiting and training young people to speak a new language "that allows us to emphasize our unique inspirations and affirm our universal values," that allows all of us to sing the common songs of human dignity and hope even as we each pray our unique prayers from many different spiritual traditions.[51] Creation of the IFYC and its continuing work is a bold and creative response to the challenges that face us in a world where differences in religion too often lead to misunderstanding, discrimination, and conflict. Wise decisions are choices for transformation that step into the boldest possibilities without forgetting the core values that are the inspiration for decisive action. Do not defer a dream. Do not fear the genius that lives at the core of who you are. Step boldly into your boldest future. Believe in possibility.

In Chapter Two, I introduced you to my gruff, hard-working grandfather. Our house was next door to his and it often seemed as if we lived in the shadow of his stern expectations. As a young child, I knew he cared about us, even though he was aloof and often corrected us. But I remember wishing there could somehow be more joy in his life. His days seemed so full of burdens and long hours of work. One day, I think I was about ten years old, he called me and my whole family to his back yard.

IN GRANDPA'S BACK YARD

Everything about him was mysterious
    to my child eyes. He shaved
with a straight razor. Slapped the cutting edge back and forth
in perfect rhythm against the leather strap to hone the blade,
held that sharp steel to his neck every morning.
    His body was fashioned
from hardwood; straight, strong, unyielding,
    not a bit of dance or flow.
He seldom smiled. One finger cut off
    above the knuckle. A hearing aid
that buzzed so loud, he just blankly nodded
    when you asked him a question.

He loved to work, even at eighty and ninety.
    Tended his acre of garden,
straight, long rows, every variety of vegetable
    evenly spaced and tasting
like Eden. On winter days that forced him inside,
    he would crack hickory nuts
with dogged persistence motivated by some
    non-negotiable quota divinely
revealed to him alone. Daily he would take his
    three Dutch prayer books
and walk to church to spend a few hours
    with the Lord. I don't know

if he was doing time for past sins or continuing
  his arguments before
the ultimate tribunal. Frayed collars and cuffs,
  patched black jacket,
one pocket ripped off. He never wore anything
  new; luxury and excess
were not allowed. Every night before he went
  to bed he drank one shot
of blackberry brandy from the bottle in his dresser,
  one shot no more no less.

And so I could hardly believe it when he called
  us all to his backyard
one bright summer afternoon. He had placed
  two flower stands
twenty feet apart. On one, balanced on a pivot,
  an old tarnished silver spoon
holding half a potato. On the other a wine glass
  glinting in sunlight.
With one quick flick of his finger, he sent
  the potato flying through space,
tumbling perfectly toward the other stand twenty feet away.
The half of potato round end down dropped
  exactly in the waiting wine glass.

He cackled, not a mild laugh, but glee bubbled
  out of him. Only once, no
repeat performance. Then, back to work, shovel
  on his shoulder to the garden.
Leaving us standing in the green grass with our
  questions. It was the first
and last time I heard my grandpa giggle but after that
  everything was possible.

This principle of preservation and transformation reminds us
that courageous decision-making is attentive to foundations and core
values while, at the same time, inviting bold innovation. It looks for
ways to incorporate the multiplicity of past experiences into new
possibilities. Wise decision-making also guards against the real pres-

sures of comfort and security that lead to inertia and block creative advance. It requires we be attentive to origins, founding experiences, and the core spirit of ourselves or our organizations. It also requires that we value and practice imaginal skills: alternative thinking, breaking set, deferring the habitual response, playing with a problem, making fresh associations, and exploring new metaphors and symbols. The wise decision comes from exercising the muscles of imagination personally and collectively so we step into our dreams, into our best possible future with boldness.

Questions for Reflection

What is one of the boldest steps I could take within the next few months in my personal or organizational life? How is this possibility connected to my core values and vision or my organization's core values and vision?

If I were to take the angel's advocate position about this bold step, what are all the things that could go right, all the positive consequences of this action? What are the risks related to this bold step? What are my fears and how can I address them?

How can I prepare to take this step? Who needs to be onboard or "with me" in nurturing this new direction?

An Assessment of Openness to Innovation

The following assessment may help you understand how well you are living with boldness and innovation. As you rate yourself, try to think of concrete examples in the last month of each of the areas that you are rating. If you are unable to recall specific examples, you may wish to rate yourself on the lower end of the scale. If you are able to articulate for yourself specific instances, you may wish to rate yourself on the higher end of the scale.

I make bold and innovative decisions.

High   9   8   7   6   5   4   3   2   Low

I welcome change.

High   9   8   7   6   5   4   3   2   Low

I invite and encourage diverse and creative perspectives, even when they may be contrary to my own.

High   9   8   7   6   5   4   3   2   Low

I plan regular learning activities and open myself to new experiences.

High   9   8   7   6   5   4   3   2   Low

I have made a significant change in my life within the past year that is both creative and consistent with my core values.

High   9   8   7   6   5   4   3   2   Low

EPILOGUE

The model for wise decision-making we have explored in this book is not a recipe or a formula. It isn't simply a tool that can be used successfully by anyone. There is an inextricable connection between the dimensions of the model and the character and skills of the person using it. An open-minded, flexible person will not be unduly challenged by broadening the listening process for decision-making. A person who has had limited experience with persons and perspectives from other cultures, races, or classes may have a difficult time inviting and sincerely listening to a diversity of viewpoints.

For a person who is comfortable with change and excited about the future, leading a bold visioning process will be enjoyable. A person who is steeped in tradition and fearful of change may be quite uncomfortable and unskilled in envisioning bold possibilities for the future. Using intuitive processes, visualization, and silence in the decision-making process will feel supportive for someone who is a cultural creative. A very rational person who has strong thinking skills may find it difficult to use methodologies of knowing that rely on intuition and feeling. In other words, practical wisdom and applying this wise decision-making model incorporates a way of being as well as a process of doing.

Wisdom as Doing and Being

Who we are as persons and how we grow play a large role in the way we make decisions and how we experience the various dimensions of this decision-making model. Each of us is challenged to continue to develop our strengths and to gently address those areas that challenge us. Only when we know our gifts and talents well do we have the confidence to work at those aspects of our personality and skills that need further growth.

As we use this model, some parts of it may feel like second nature to us while other parts will challenge us. As we implement aspects of the operating procedures and try to model them with others, we will develop skills, character traits, and virtues. If we genuinely reflect on the criteria that arise out of the wisdom principles of the religions of the world as we make decisions, we will be affected by their visions of the world. To make the best use of this model, we are required to intentionally develop our instrumental, interpersonal, imaginal, and systems skills. Instrumental skills are the basic skills related to work in the world: speaking and writing effectively, using the tools of our trade or occupation, calculating correctly, managing time and resources, using appropriate computer skills and software, and so forth. These skills will vary greatly from one occupation to another, although a broad set of instrumental skills is required for just getting along in our society.

Interpersonal skills include all of the dimensions of relating to one another, including listening, identifying feelings, expressing emotions, setting boundaries, resolving conflicts, reading nonverbal clues, accepting and giving positive and negative feedback, and accepting differences. Imaginal skills include all of the ways we vision, dream, connect with what is possible and creative, and plan the process of realizing something new. When we think of alternatives, identify our own assumptions, imagine possibilities, combine images and ideas in creative ways, suspend habitual ways of thinking or responding, we are exhibiting imaginal skills. Systems skills relate to understanding how the parts of a system relate to one another and how we navigate within its structures and play by its explicit and implicit rules. Systems in which we are involved may include our extended family, work team, department and larger organization, and political entities such as city, county, state, nation, not-for-profit organizations, or clubs. How do we shepherd a proposal for change through one of these systems? Who are the leaders and how should they be approached? What are the written and unwritten rules of engagement within the system?

Skills Related to Wisdom Principles

If we review the five wisdom principles of our model and their corresponding operating procedures and criteria, we can see how these different skill areas relate to wise decision-making. We can identify strengths and weaknesses within ourselves that may need to be nourished or addressed if we are to use the model effectively.

WISDOM PRINCIPLES	OPERATING PROCEDURES	CRITERIA FOR JUDGMENT CHOOSE WHAT…
Principle 1. Respect all persons.	OP 1A. Expand the listening process. OP 1B. Create seats at the table for the marginalized.	C 1A. Contributes to the common good. C 1B. Takes into account the poor and powerless.
Principle 2. Appreciate the wholeness of being human.	OP 2A. Explore all the ways of human knowing. OP 2B. Make room for silence.	C 2A. Values the whole person. C 2B. Brings balance and integration.
Principle 3. Recognize the interconnectedness of all reality.	OP 3A. Consider how systems will be impacted. OP 3B. Research effects on community and environment.	C 3A. Responds to needs of the whole community. C 3B. Attends to the long-term health of the earth.
Principle 4. Value inner wisdom and personal experience.	OP 4A. Reflect on experience deeply and broadly. OP 4B. Inquire into values, vision, and best practices.	C 4A. Addresses the full reality of the present experience. C 4B. Is most constructive to life.
Principle 5. Attend to preservation and transformation.	OP 5A. Be attentive to origins and foundations. OP 5B. Practice radical creativity.	C 5A. Preserves the core focus and vision. C 5B. Moves toward the boldest possibility.

For instance, principle one, "Respect for All Persons," and its corresponding operating procedure, "Expand the Listening Process," involve interpersonal skills, such as listening, expressing feelings, engaging with persons across lines of culture and class, understanding differences, and dealing with conflict. "Creating seats at the table for the marginalized" entails system skills related to the institutions, structures, and policies that keep some persons disenfranchised, poor, and without a voice in our society. Applying the criterion of what "contributes to the common good" requires the use of system skills as we weigh benefits and risks for the various stakeholders across our communities and make decisions that are sensitive to the interactions within the whole system. Choosing what "takes into account the poor and the powerless" requires the use of imaginal skills as we empathically enter into the experience of the broad array of persons that makes up our local, national, and global communities. These are a few examples of how developing various skills are important to fully implementing the wise decision-making model.

As we apply various aspects of the model, it is a good idea to think about the skills we need to strengthen. When we identify those skills and make intentional efforts to grow them, we have the best opportunity for making real progress in applying the model. When I was moving from a teaching role to higher education administration, it was clear to me that I needed to develop my ability to invite diverse perspectives and deal with conflict. These were interpersonal skills that were difficult for me, especially given my background of learning to avoid confrontation in my family of origin. I wrote down the kinds of actions I needed to take to improve these skills. I then kept track of how I was doing by reflecting weekly on my skill goals and my efforts and experiences. Slowly, I learned to listen more deeply, to avoid responding with my first thought, to specifically request opposing viewpoints so we could consider all the angles, and to create a container where my leadership team could speak freely and trust they would be heard. For me, the development of these model skills is a lifelong process. As my responsibilities and roles change, I identify new areas of instrumental, interpersonal, imaginal, and systems skills that I need to address.

Implementation in Small Steps

This wise decision-making model is best implemented in small steps, a few dimensions at a time. Depending upon the kind of decision you are facing, you may focus on one or two principles that relate to the specifics of the decision. You may try two or three of the suggestions from the operating procedures or focus on the application of a few of the criteria for judgment. At first, these steps might feel uncomfortable for you, your team, or your family. Slowly, applying the dimensions of the model will become less artificial. As others learn the various principles, operating procedures, and criteria of the model, they bring their own applications into the decision-making process. This isn't a "one-size-fits-all" model. You may need or want to customize the model for your own purposes and your own environment. The model isn't intended to be comprehensive; there are many additional principles that may be just as important to consider in your particular circumstances.

Approach the process of implementing the model as a never-ending journey, not a destination to reach. The greatest and most important journey is not measured across continents or up the greatest heights of mountains. It is the critical distance between our hearts, heads, and hands. The real work of practical wisdom is to translate what we know in our hearts into decisions and actions.

To apply the wisdom that comes from our core experiences of the preciousness of life to our everyday decisions is our most important challenge. The journey from heart to head and head to hands takes great courage. No model for wise decision-making can provide gumption and guts. We have to find those resources within us. Almost always, we need a community of support and affirmation to help us believe in our dreams and live them out. We need conversation partners who will listen to our stories of doubt in the dry desert times and our exclamations of joy in the mountain-top experiences of fulfillment. We need others to ask the questions that help us access our own inner wisdom and listen to our own inner teacher. We need the diverse perspectives of colleagues, friends, and sometimes, enemies, to help us recognize our own assumptions and mental models and open our minds and hearts to the broadest possibilities. Finally, we need practice, practice, and more practice. We will become wiser as we intentionally broaden our outlook, deepen our listening to diverse perspectives, use the many ways of knowing that are part of our human uniqueness, recognize the interdependent systems that affect our lives, explore our personal experience and values, and preserve the best of the past as we step boldly into the future. It's important to remember that we are not seeking certainty; we are simply taking the next step as wisely as we can. Remember the morning glory flowers, hanging on and reaching toward the light. And so do we. Decision by decision we take

> the next step without knowing
> everything, without certainty,
>
> on the steep climb feeling for footholds.
> Look for the circle, listen to the dream
> calling in your marrow, muscle, blood.
>
> Spiral toward hope, truth, bread,
> like the morning glories with their wise
> green hands climbing toward the light.

NOTES

Introduction

1. David La Chapelle, *Navigating the Tides of Change: Stories from Science, the Sacred, and a Wise Planet* (British Columbia: New Society Publishers, 2001), 7.

2. Ibid., 8.

3. Thomas H. Groome, *Sharing Faith: A Comprehensive Approach to Religious Education and Pastoral Ministry* (New York: HarperCollins Publishers, 1991), 29-30.

4. Stephen S. Hall, *Wisdom: From Philosophy to Neuroscience* (New York: Alfred A. Knopf, 2010), 34.

5. Thomas N. Martin and John C. Hafer, "Models of Emotional Intelligence, Spiritual Intelligence, and Performance: A Test of Tischler, Biberman, and McKeage," *Journal of Management, Spirituality and Religion*, 6:3 (2009): 249.

6. Jelaluddin Rumi, "A Great Wagon." *The Essential Rumi*, trans. Coleman Barks (New York: HarperCollins Publishers, 1995), 36.

7. Interview with Tom Wiig conducted by Gary Boelhower in Duluth, MN, July 9, 2010.

8. Ibid.

9. Mary Oliver, "The Summer Day." *House of Light* (Boston: Beacon Press, 1990), 60.

10. John Izzo, *The Five Secrets You Must Discover Before You Die* (San Francisco: Berrett-Koehler Publishers, 2008), 47.

11. Ibid., 48.

12. Parker J. Palmer, *A Hidden Wholeness: The Journey Toward an Undivided Life* (San Francisco: Jossey-Bass, 2004), 3.

13. Ibid., 17.

14. The Teacher Perceiver Interview and similar selection instruments based on a prescribed interview process for other profes-

sions were purchased by Gallup, which also provides training in the use of the instruments.

15. Parker J. Palmer, *Let Your Life Speak: Listening for the Voice of Vocation* (San Francisco: Jossey-Bass, 2000), 10.

16. Cynthia Bourgeault, *The Wisdom Jesus: Transforming Heart and Mind—A New Perspective on Christ and His Message* (Boston: Shambhala Publications, 2008), 24.

17. Robert K. Greenleaf, *The Servant as Leader* (Indianapolis: The Robert K. Greenleaf Center, 1970, 1991).

18. Ibid.; Bill George, *Authentic Leadership: Rediscovering the Secrets to Creating Lasting Value* (San Francisco: Jossey-Bass, 2004); Craig E. Johnson, *Meeting the Ethical Challenges of Leadership: Casting Light or Shadow* (Thousand Oaks, CA: Sage Publications, 2011); Daniel Goleman, Richard E. Boyatzis, and Annie McKee, *Primal Leadership: Realizing the Power of Emotional Intelligence* (Boston: Harvard Business Review Press, 2004).

19. Carl G. Jung, *Man and His Symbols* (New York: Dell Publishing, 1964), 174.

20. Palmer, *Let Your Life Speak*, 85-91.

21. Ibid., 88.

22. Saint Benedict, *Saint Benedict's Rule for Monasteries*, trans. Leonard J. Doyle (Collegeville, MN: The Liturgical Press, 1948).

23. Rainer Maria Rilke, *Letters to a Young Poet*, trans. M. D. Herter (New York: Norton, 1993), p. 35.

PRINCIPLE ONE: Respect All Persons

1. Deborah Adele, *The Yamas and Niyamas: Exploring Yoga's Ethical Practice* (Duluth, MN: On-word Bound Books, 2009), 36.

2. www.bodhicitta.net accessed on January 19, 2012.

3. Jack Kornfield, *The Wise Heart: A Guide to the Universal Teachings of Buddhist Psychology* (New York: BantamDell, 2008), 355.

4. Ibid., 12.

5. www.buddhistchannel.tv/index.php?id=18,1271,0,0,1,0 reportage on "The Golden Buddha at Wat Traimit" by Jeffrey Miller in *The Korean Times*, June 2, 2005, accessed on January 19, 2012.

6. Karen Armstrong, *Buddha* (New York: Penguin, 2001), 70.

7. Walpola Rahula, *What the Buddha Taught* (New York: Grove Press, 1974), 97.

8. The following listing of versions of the Golden Rule comes from www.scarboromissions.ca/Golden_rule/sacred_texts.php accessed on January 19, 2012.

9. Reza Aslan, *No god but God: The Origins, Evolution, and Future of Islam* (New York: Random House, 2006), 40.

10. Ibid., 60.

11. William Isaacs, *Dialogue and the Art of Thinking Together* (New York: Random House, 1999), 19.

12. Various guidelines for dialogue practice are discussed in William Isaacs, *Dialogue and the Art of Thinking Together* (New York: Random House, 1999), and Linda Ellinor and Glenna Gerard, *Dialogue: Rediscover the Transforming Power of Conversation* (New York: John Wiley & Sons, 1998).

13. www.tdindustries.com/AboutUs/ServantLeadership.aspx accessed on January 20, 2012.

14. Ibid.

15. From documentary film *The Test of Leadership* produced by Virginia Duncan Gilmore based on interviews with TDIndustries partners (Fond du Lac, WI: Virginia Duncan Gilmore, 1999).

16. http://www.tdindustries.com/AboutUs/Recognition.aspx accessed on January 20, 2012.

17. Interview with Scott Gradin conducted by Gary Boelhower in Duluth, MN, January 27, 2011.

18. Edgar H. Schein, *Process Consultation Revisited: Building the Helping Relationship*, New York: Addison-Wesley, 1999).

19. Interview with Robert Hartl conducted by Gary Boelhower in Duluth, MN, May 10, 2011.

20. Ibid.

21. Ibid.

22. *Saint Benedict's Rule for Monasteries*, 12-13.

23. Ibid., 13.

24. Andre L. Delbecq, "Bureaucracy, Leadership Style and Decision-Making," *Academy of Management Proceedings* (1963): 14.

25. John Rawls, *Justice as Fairness: A Restatement* (Cambridge, MA: Harvard University Press, 2001).

26. John Rawls, A *Theory of Justice* (Cambridge, MA: Harvard University Press, 1971), 14.

27. Ibid., 14-15.

28. Rawls, *Theory of Justice*, 103.

29. Amartya Sen, *The Idea of Justice* (Cambridge, MA: Harvard University Press, 2009), 18.

30. Laura Sewall, *Sight and Sensibility: The Ecopsychology of Perception* (New York: Putnam, 1999), 50.

31. My comments here on the development of inclusive organizations are based on Bailey W. Jackson, "Theory and Practice of Multicultural Organization Development," *The NTL Handbook of Organization Development and Change: Organizations, Principles and Practices*, eds. Brenda B. Jones and Michael Brazzel (San Francisco: Pfeiffer, 2006), 134-154.

32. Robert K. Greenleaf, *The Institution as Servant* (Indianapolis: The Robert K. Greenleaf Center, 1976), 11-15.

33. Gary J. Boelhower, "Values Integration: Putting Tires on Spirituality in Organizations," *Business Research Yearbook* 11 (2004): 1034.

34. From documentary film *The Test of Leadership* produced by Virginia Duncan Gilmore based on interviews with TDIndustries partners (Fond du Lac, WI: Virginia Duncan Gilmore, 1999).

35. *Facilities Council Handbook* (Ann Arbor, MI: University of Michigan, 2000), 3.

36. Sen, *Idea of Justice*, 20.

37. Ibid.

38. Ibid.

39. James Rachels and Stuart Rachels, *The Elements of Moral Philosophy* (New York: McGraw-Hill, 2010), 79.

40. William Clohesy, "Altruism and the Endurance of the Good," *Voluntas: International Journal of Voluntary and Nonprofit Organizations*, 11, 3 (2000): 239.

41. Rajendra S. Sisodia, David B. Wolfe and Jagdish N. Sheth, *Firms of Endearment: How World-Class Companies Profit from Passion and Purpose* (Upper Saddle River, NJ: Prentice Hall, 2007), xx.

42. Ibid., xxi-xxii.

43. Greenleaf, *Servant as Leader*, 7.

44. John Rawls, *Political Liberalism* (New York: Columbia University Press, 1993), 291, quoted in Amartya Sen, *The Idea of Justice* (Cambridge, MA: Harvard University Press, 2009), 59.

45. Sewall, *Sight and Sensibility*, 104.

46. Henri J. M. Nouwen, Donald P. McNeill and Douglas A. Morrison, *Compassion: A Reflection on the Christian Life* (New York: Doubleday, 1983).

47. http://www.100people.org accessed on January 20, 2012.

48. Sisodia, *Firms of Endearment*, 171-3.

49. Ibid., 173.

50. Ibid., 180-1.

51. Ibid., 178.

52. Ibid., 179.

PRINCIPLE TWO: Appreciate the Wholeness of Being Human

1. Palmer, *Let Your Life Speak*.

2. Axel Michaels, *Hinduism Past and Present*, trans. Barbara Harshav (Princeton, NJ: Princeton University Press, 2004), 4.

3. Ibid., 235-52.

4. Ibid., 252-59.

5. Ibid., 259-72.

6. Ibid., 272-80.

7. Robert C. Lester, *Buddhism: The Path to Nirvana* (San Francisco: Harper & Row, 1987), 12.

8. Huston Smith and Philip Novak, *Buddhism: A Concise Introduction* (San Francisco: HarperCollins, 2003), 66-7.

9. Ibid., 98.

10. Ibid., 16.

11. Ibid., 46-7.

12. Xinzhong Yao, *An Introduction to Confucianism* (Cambridge, UK: Cambridge University Press, 2000), 12-3.

13. Walter Brueggemann, *In Man We Trust: The Neglected Side of Biblical Faith* (Atlanta: John Knox Press, 1972), 15.

14. *Saint Benedict's Rule for Monasteries*, 22.

15. Ibid., 1.

16. Diana Chapman Walsh, *Trustworthy Leadership* (Ann Arbor, MI: Fetzer Institute, 2006), 6.

17. Parker J. Palmer, *To Know as We Are Known* (San Francisco: Harper and Row, 1983), 9.

18. Evelyn Fox Keller, *A Feeling for the Organism: The Life and Work of Barbara McClintock* (New York: W. H. Freeman, 1983); Sharon Bertsch McGrayne, *Nobel Prize Women in Science: Their Lives, Struggles, and Momentous Discoveries* (New York: Birch Lane Press, 1993); Joyce Tang, *Scientific Pioneers: Women Succeeding in Science* (Lanham, MD: University Press of America, 2006).

19. McGrayne, *Nobel Prize Women in Science*, 167.

20. Ibid., 170.

21. Evelyn Fox Keller, *A Feeling for the Organism: The Life and Work of Barbara McClintock* (New York: W. H. Freeman, 1983), 69.

22. Ibid., 198.

23. Judi Neal, *Edgewalkers: People and Organizations that Take Risks, Build Bridges, and Break New Ground* (Westport, CT: Praeger, 2006), 17.

24. Ibid., 16-9.

25. Ibid., 18.

26. Ibid., 19.

27. Marta Sinclair, "Misconceptions about Intuition," *Psychological Inquiry* 2, 4 (2010).

28. Ibid., 382.

29. Anna Katherine Montgomery, "A Creative Leap for New Orleans," *Journal of the Arts in Leadership and Organizational Learning* (2008), accessed at http://www.creativeleaps.org/news/200804/NewOrleans.htm.

30. Ibid.

31. David Creelman, "The Liberal Arts and Business," *Journal of the Arts in Leadership and Organizational Learning*, originally published in *Japanese for Works Magazine* (December 2007) accessed at http://www.creativeleaps.org/news/200804/LiberalArtsAndBusiness.htm.

32. Ibid.

33. Montgomery, "A Creative Leap for New Orleans."

34. Ibid.

35. David Pink, *A Whole New Mind* (New York: Penguin, 2005), 3.

36. Sewall, *Sight and Sensibility*, 84.

37. Candace Pert, *Your Body Is Your Subconscious Mind*, 3 CD Set Audio Recording (Boulder, CO: Sounds True, 2005).

38. Sewall, *Sight and Sensibility*, 145.

39. Palmer, *Let Your Life Speak*, 79.

40. David Whyte, *Midlife and the Great Unknown*, 2 CD Set Audio Recording (Boulder, CO: Sounds True, 2003).

41. Ibid.

42. Palmer, *Hidden Wholeness*, 19.

43. Ibid., 55.

44. Ibid., 51-69.

45. Interview with Robert Hartl conducted by Gary Boelhower in Duluth, MN, May 10, 2011.

46. David Whyte, *The Three Marriages: Reimagining Work, Self and Relationship* (New York: Penguin, 2009), 9.

47. Cecilia Chan, Petula Sik Ying Ho, and Esther Chow, "A Body-Mind-Spirit Model in Health: An Eastern Approach," *Social Work in Healthcare* 34 (2001): 26162.

48. Palmer, *Hidden Wholeness*, 8.

49. Ibid., 21.

PRINCIPLE THREE: Recognize the Interconnectedness of All Reality

1. Luther Standing Bear in *Land of the Spotted Eagle* quoted from John A. Grim, "Indigenous Traditions and Deep Ecology," *Deep Ecology and World Religions*, ed. David Landis Barnhill and Roger S. Gottlieb (Albany, NY: State University of New York Press, 2001), 35.

2. John A. Grim, "Indigenous Traditions and Deep Ecology," *Deep Ecology and World Religions*, ed. David Landis Barnhill and Roger S. Gottlieb (Albany, NY: State University of New York Press, 2001), 41-42.

3. Ibid., 50-51.

4. Robert Wolf, *Original Wisdom: Stories of an Ancient Way of Knowing* (Rochester, VT: Inner Traditions: 2001), 4.

5. Christopher Key Chapple, "Hinduism and Deep Ecology," *Deep Ecology and World Religions*, ed. by David Landis Barnhill and

Roger S. Gottlieb (Albany, NY: State University of New York Press, 2001), p. 61-62.

6. Michaels, *Hinduism*, 344.

7. Kornfield, *Wise Heart*, 356.

8. David Landis Barnhill, "Relational Holism," *Deep Ecology and World Religions*, ed. by David Landis Barnhill and Roger S. Gottlieb (Albany, NY: State University of New York Press, 2001), 87.

9. Mary Evelyn Tucker, "Confucianism and Deep Ecology," *Deep Ecology and World Religions*, ed. by David Landis Barnhill and Roger S. Gottlieb (Albany, NY: State University of New York Press, 2001), 130.

10. Ibid., 135.

11. Quoted in Nawal Amar, "Islam and Deep Ecology," *Deep Ecology and World Religions*, ed. by David Landis Barnhill and Roger S. Gottlieb (Albany, NY: State University of New York Press, 2001), 196-97.

12. Ibid., 197.

13. Eric Katz, "Faith, God and Nature: Judaism and Deep Ecology," *Deep Ecology and World Religions*, ed. by David Landis Barnhill and Roger S. Gottlieb (Albany, NY: State University of New York Press, 2001), 155.

14. Amar, "Islam and Deep Ecology," 206-7.

15. Ibid., 202.

16. Peter M. Senge, *The Fifth Discipline: The Art and Practice of The Learning Organization* (New York: Doubleday, 1990), 7.

17. Bill Plotkin, *Soulcraft: Crossing into the Mysteries of Nature and Psyche* (Novato, CA: New World Library, 2003).

18. John A. Vucetich, *Winter Study 2011: Notes from the Field*, p. 17 available from Isle Royale National Park, information available on the blog www.isleroyalewolf.org.

19. Rolf O. Peterson, *The Wolves of Isle Royale: A Broken Balance* (Ann Arbor, MI: The University of Michigan Press, 2007).

20. Ibid., 192.

21. Quoted from an exhibit at Isle Royale, Windigo visitor center, July 2011.

22. Fred Kofman, *Conscious Business: How to Build Value Through Values* (Boulder, CO: Sounds True, 2006), 205.

23. From the Pegasus Communications website: www.pegasus com.com/systems-thinking.html accessed on November 17, 2011.

24. Ann McGee-Cooper, Gary Looper and Duane Trammell, *Being the Change: Profiles from Our Servant Leadership Learning Community* (Dallas: AMCA, 2007), 29.

25. Ibid., 30.

26. Sisodia, *Firms of Endearment*, xxviii.

27. Ibid.

28. http://povertydata.worldbank.org/poverty/home

29. United Nations Development Programme, *Human Development Report 2011, Sustainability and Equity: A Better Future for All* (New York: Palgrave Macmillan, 2011) available at http://hdr.undp. org/en/media/HDR_2011_EN_Summary.pdf.

30. Ibid., summary page.

31. Ibid., 14.

32. David Suzuki and Amanda McConnell, *The Sacred Balance: Rediscovering Our Place in Nature* (New York: Prometheus, 1997), 18.

33. Ibid., 38.

34. Edward Broughton, "The Bhopal Disaster and Its Aftermath: A Review," *Environmental Health* 4, 6 (2005).

35. "Plans to Lift Radioactive Contamination Controls on UK Sheep Farms," *The Guardian*, November 17, 2011.

36. Suzuki, *Sacred Balance*, 27.

37. Sisodia, *Firms of Endearment*, xx-xxi.

38. Ibid., xxii.

39. Ibid., 31.

40. Ibid., 19.

41. Marcus J. Borg, *The Heart of Christianity: Rediscovering a Life of Faith* (San Francisco: HarperCollins, 2003), 140.

42. Pratima Bansal and Kendall Roth, "Why Companies Go Green: A Model of Ecological Responsiveness," *Academy of Management Journal* 43, 4 (2000).

43. Chris Laszlo and Nadya Zhexembayeva, *Embedded Sustainability: The Next Big Competitive Advantage*, (Sheffield, UK: Greenleaf, 2011). and Hunter Lovins and Boyd Cohen, *Climate Capitalism: Capitalism in the Age of Climate Change* (New York: Hill and Wang), 2011.

44. Bansal, "Why Companies Go Green," 728.

45. Sisodia, *Firms of Endearment*, 178.

46. www.greenchoices.org accessed on November 22, 2011.

47. Sisodia, *Firms of Endearment*, 55.

48. Ibid., 55.

49. Ibid.

50. Ibid., 92.

51. Ibid., 68-69.

52. Ibid., 84.

53. Ibid., 91.

54. Susan Arterian Chang, "Best Job in the Neighborhood—And They Own It," *YES! Magazine*, online, Fall 2011.

55. Ibid.

56. John Kania and Mark Kramer, "Collective Impact," *Stanford Social Innovation Review* Winter 2011.

57. Ibid.

58. David Abram, *Becoming Animal: An Earthly Cosmology* (New York: Pantheon Random House, 2010), 128.

59. Ibid., 3.

60. Suzuki, *Sacred Balance*, 4.

61. Ibid.

62. www.deloitte.com accessed on November 23, 2011.

63. Sisodia, *Firms of Endearment*, 182.

64. Ibid., 183.

65. Ibid., 185.

66. Ibid.

67. Paula Underwood, *Three Native American Learning Stories* (Bayfield, CO: A Tribe of Two Press, 2002) 34.

PRINCIPLE FOUR: Value Inner Wisdom and Personal Experience

1. Virginia L. Duncan (Gilmore), "The Heroine's Journey" (unpublished paper, 1996) 2-3.

2. Palmer, *Hidden Wholeness*, 33.

3. Duncan, "Heroine's Journey," 28-9.

4. Ibid., 57.

5. Ibid., 49-50.

6. Palmer, *Hidden Wholeness*, 17.

7. Karen Armstrong, *The Great Transformation: The Beginning of Our Religious Traditions* (New York, Anchor Books, 2006), xvi.

8. Ibid., xviii.

9. Ibid., 92.

10. Ibid., 98.

11. Ibid., 145.

12. Ibid., 146.

13. Ibid., 283-90.

14. Ibid., 329.

15. Ibid., 334.

16. Ibid., 151, 153.

17. Ibid., 137.

18. Ibid., 81.

19. Ibid., 139.

20. Ibid.

21. Ibid.

22. Ibid., 237.

23. Ibid., 244.

24. Ibid., 246.

25. Ibid., 106.

26. Ibid., 216.

27. Brueggemann, *In Man We Trust*.

28. John Esposito, *Islam: The Straight Path* (New York: Oxford University Press, 2005), 227.

29. Ibid., 85.

30. Jonathan Brockopp, "Taking Life and Saving Life," in *Islamic Ethics of Life*, ed. Jonathan Brockopp (Columbia, SC: University of South Carolina Press, 2003), 15-16.

31. Vardit Rispler-Chaim, "The Right Not to Be Born," in *Islamic Ethics of Life*, ed. Jonathan Brockopp (Columbia, SC: University of South Carolina Press, 2003), 83.

32. A. Kevin Reinhart, "The Past in the Future of Islamic Ethics," in *Islamic Ethics of Life*, ed. Jonathan Brockopp (Columbia, SC: University of South Carolina Press, 2003), 218.

33. Sujezana Akpinar, "The Ethics of Islam," *Religion East & West* 10 (2010), 113-19.

34. Esposito, *Islam*, 107.

35. Ibid., 108.

36. Armstrong, *Buddha*, 176.

37. Bhikkhu Bodhi, ed., *In the Buddha's Words: An Anthology of Discourses from the Pali Canon* (Boston: Wisdom Publications, 2005), 89-90.

38. Unpublished report by Ann McGee Cooper based on presentation by Mac Tristan of the Carrollton Police Department at the Dallas Servant Leadership Learning Circle in March 2009.

39. Ibid.

40. Ibid.

41. My understanding and facilitation of the clearness circle relies heavily on Parker Palmer's books *The Courage to Teach* and *A Hidden Wholeness* and experiences with him in retreats, as well as the many clearness circles that I have facilitated.

42. Parker J. Palmer, "The Clearness Committee: A Communal Approach to Discernment," *The Courage To Teach: A Guide for Reflection and Renewal* by Rachel Livsey (San Francisco: Jossey-Bass, 1999), 43.

43. Palmer, *Hidden Wholeness*, 64.

44. www.couragerenewal.org

45. I have been honored to serve on the Sophia Foundation board since the inception of the foundation. For more information, www.fdlareafoundation.com/sophiafoundation.html.

46. Daniel Maguire, *Ethics: A Complete Method for Moral Choice* (Minneapolis: Fortress Press, 2010), 206.

47. David Cooperrider and Diana Whitney, *Appreciative Inquiry: A Positive Revolution in Change* (San Francisco: Berrett-Koehler, 2005).

48. Ibid., 9.

49. Ibid., 14.

50. Ibid., 9.

51. This is the story as I remember Bob telling it during our session.

52. Cooperrider, *Appreciative Inquiry*, 9.

53. Interview by phone with Judith Neal conducted by Gary Boelhower, July 26, 2010.

54. Sewall, *Sight and Sensibility*, 165.

55. Ibid, 164.

56. Maguire, *Ethics*, 71.

57. Ibid., 30.

PRINCIPLE FIVE: **Attend to Preservation and Transformation**

1. Desmond Tutu, *No Future Without Forgiveness* (New York: Doubleday, 1999), 19.

2. Ibid., 30.

3. Ibid.

4. Ibid., 4.

5. Pumla Gobodo-Madikizela, *Forgiveness and the Maternal Body: An African Ethics of Interconnectedness*, Essays on Exploring a Global Dream (Ann Arbor: Fetzer Institute, 2011), 3.

6. Ibid.

7. Ibid., 4.

8. Ibid., 5.

9. www.info.gov.za/documents/constitution/1996/index.htm accessed on January 28, 2012.

10. Karen Armstrong, *A History of God* (New York: Ballantine, 1993), xix.

11. David Chidester, *Patterns of Transcendence* (Stamford, CT: Wadsworth, 2002), 1.

12. Ibid.

13. Armstrong, *Great Transformation*, 151.

14. Borg, *Heart of Christianity*.

15. Ibid., 27.

16. Esposito, *Islam*, 270.

17. Ibid., 228.

18. Jim Collins, *Good to Great: Why Some Companies Make the Leap…and Others Don't* (New York: HarperCollins, 2001), 14.

19. Barry Mulholland email, January 11, 2012.

20. From the foreword to *The Spirit of Servant-Leadership*, ed. Shann Ray Ferch and Larry C. Spears (New York/Mahwah, NJ: Paulist Press, 2011), xviii.

21. Ibid., xxiv-vi.

22. Janet Kalven, Larry Rosen and Bruce Taylor, *Value Development: A Practical Guide*, New York/Mahwah, NJ: Paulist Press, 1982), 125.

23. Peter Senge, Art Kleiner, Richard Ross, Bryan Smith, Charlotte Roberts, *The Fifth Discipline Fieldbook* (New York: Doubleday, 1994), 273.

24. Thomas Chermack, *Scenario Planning in Organizations: How to Create, Use and Assess Scenarios* (San Francisco: Berrett-Koehler, 2011).

25. Isaacs, *Dialogue.*

26. Edward de Bono, *Creativity Workout: 62 Exercises to Unlock Your Most Creative Ideas* (Berkeley, CA: Ulysses Press, 2008) and Michael Michalko, *Thinkertoys: A Handbook of Creative Thinking Techniques* (Berkeley, CA: Ten Speed Press, 2006).

27. www.AscensionHealth.org accessed on January 28, 2012.

28. From documentary film *The Test of Leadership* produced by Virginia Duncan Gilmore based on interviews with Joyce DeShano (Fond du Lac, WI: Virginia Duncan Gilmore, 1999).

29. www.AscensionHealth.org accessed on January 28, 2012.

30. Ascension Health 2011 Annual Report, available at www.AscensionHealth.org accessed on January 28, 2012.

31. Ibid.

32. Ibid.

33. Ibid.

34. Ibid.

35. Ibid.

36. Ibid.

37. www.AscensionHealth.org accessed on January 28, 2012.

38. Enterprising Health video in 2011 Ascension Health Annual Report, available at www.AscensionHealth.org accessed on January 28, 2012.

39. Ibid.

40. Ibid.

41. Ibid.

42. Ibid.

43. Ibid.

44. Eboo Patel, *Acts of Faith* (Boston: Beacon Press, 2007), xvii.

45. Ibid., 115.
46. Ibid., 96.
47. Ibid., 98.
48. Ibid.
49. Ibid., 99.
50. Ibid., 149.
51. Ibid.

BIBLIOGRAPHY

Abram, David. *Becoming Animal: An Earthly Cosmology*, New York: Pantheon Random House, 2010.

Adele, Deborah. *The Yamas and Niyamas: Exploring Yoga's Ethical Practice*. Duluth, MN: On-word Bound Books, 2009.

Akpinar, Sujezana. "The Ethics of Islam." *Religion East & West* 10 (2010): 113-19.

Amar, Nawal. "Islam and Deep Ecology." *Deep Ecology and World Religions*, edited by David Landis Barnhill and Roger S. Gottlieb, 193-211. Albany, NY: State University of New York Press, 2001.

Armstrong, Karen. *The Great Transformation: The Beginning of Our Religious Traditions*. New York: Anchor Books, 2006.

————. *Buddha*. New York: Penguin, 2001.

————. *A History of God*. New York: Ballantine, 1993.

Aslan, Reza. *No god but God: The Origins, Evolution, and Future of Islam*. New York: Random House, 2006.

Bansal, Pratima and Kendall Roth. "Why Companies Go Green: A Model of Ecological Responsiveness." *Academy of Management Journal*, 43, 4 (2000): 717-36.

Barnhill, David L. "Relational Holism." *Deep Ecology and World Religions*, edited by David Landis Barnhill and Roger S. Gottlieb, 77-106. Albany, NY: State University of New York Press, 2001.

Benedict of Nursia. *Saint Benedict's Rule for Monasteries*. Translated by Leonard J. Doyle. Collegeville, MN: The Liturgical Press, 1948.

Bodhi, Bhikkhu, ed. *In the Buddha's Words: An Anthology of Discourses from the Pali Canon*. Boston: Wisdom Publications, 2005.

Boelhower, Gary J. "Values Integration: Putting Tires on Spirituality in Organizations." *Business Research Yearbook* 11 (2004): 1033-37.

Borg, Marcus J. *The Heart of Christianity: Rediscovering a Life of Faith.* San Francisco: HarperCollins, 2003.

Bourgeault, Cynthia. *The Wisdom Jesus: Transforming Heart and Mind—a New Perspective on Christ and His Message.* Boston: Shambhala Publications, 2008.

Brockopp, Jonathan. "Taking Life and Saving Life." *Islamic Ethics of Life*, edited by Jonathan Brockopp. Columbia, SC: University of South Carolina Press, 2003.

Broughton, Edward. "The Bhopal Disaster and Its Aftermath: A Review." *Environmental Health* 4 (2005): 6.

Brueggemann, Walter. *In Man We Trust: The Neglected Side of Biblical Faith.* Atlanta: John Knox Press, 1972.

Chan, Cecilia, Petula Sik Ying Ho and Esther Chow. "A Body-Mind-Spirit Model in Health: An Eastern Approach." *Social Work in Healthcare* 34 (2001): 261-82.

Chang, Susan Arterian. "Best Job in the Neighborhood—And They Own It" *YES! Magazine*, Fall 2011, online.

Chapple, Christopher K. "Hinduism and Deep Ecology." *Deep Ecology and World Religions*, edited by David Landis Barnhill and Roger S. Gottlieb, 59-76. Albany, NY: State University of New York Press, 2001.

Chermack, Thomas. *Scenario Planning in Organizations: How to Create, Use and Assess Scenarios.* San Francisco: Berrett-Koehler, 2011.

Chidester, David. *Patterns of Transcendence.* Stamford, CT: Wadsworth, 2002.

Clohesy, William. "Altruism and the Endurance of the Good." *Voluntas: International Journal of Voluntary and Nonprofit Organizations* 11, 3 (2000): 237-53.

Collins, Jim. *Good to Great: Why Some Companies Make the Leap…and Others Don't.* New York: HarperCollins, 2001.

Cooperrider, David, and Diana Whitney. *Appreciative Inquiry: A Positive Revolution in Change.* San Francisco: Berrett-Koehler, 2005.

Creelman, David. "The Liberal Arts and Business." *Journal of the Arts in Leadership and Organizational Learning*, originally published in *Japanese for Works Magazine*, December 2007, accessed at www.creativeleaps.org/news/200804/LiberalArtsAndBusiness.htm.

de Bono, Edward. *Creativity Workout: 62 Exercises to Unlock Your Most Creative Ideas*. Berkeley, CA: Ulysses Press, 2008.

Delbecq, Andre L. "Bureaucracy, Leadership Style and Decision-Making." *Academy of Management Proceedings*, (1963): 14-38.

Ellinor, Linda, and Glenna Gerard. *Dialogue: Rediscover the Transforming Power of Conversation*. New York: John Wiley & Sons, 1998.

Enterprising Health video in 2011 Ascension Health Annual Report, available at www.AscensionHealth.org.

Esposito, John. *Islam: The Straight Path*. New York: Oxford University Press, 2005.

Facilities Council Handbook. Ann Arbor, MI: University of Michigan Press, 2000.

George, Bill. *Authentic Leadership: Rediscovering the Secrets to Creating Lasting Value*. San Francisco: Jossey-Bass, 2004.

Gobodo-Madikizela, Pumla. *Forgiveness and the Maternal Body: An African Ethics of Interconnectedness*. Essays on Exploring a Global Dream. Ann Arbor, MI: Fetzer Institute, 2011.

Goleman, Daniel, Richard E. Boyatzis, and Annie McKee. *Primal Leadership: Realizing the Power of Emotional Intelligence*. Boston: Harvard Business Review Press, 2004.

Greenleaf, Robert K. *The Institution as Servant*. Indianapolis: The Robert K. Greenleaf Center, 1976.

————. *The Servant as Leader*. Indianapolis: The Robert K. Greenleaf Center, 1970.

Grim, John A. "Indigenous Traditions and Deep Ecology." *Deep Ecology and World Religions*, edited by David Landis Barnhill and Roger S. Gottlieb, 35-57. Albany, NY: State University of New York Press, 2001.

Groome, Thomas H. *Sharing Faith: A Comprehensive Approach to Religious Education and Pastoral Ministry*. New York: HarperCollins Publishers, 1991.

Hall, Stephen S. *Wisdom: From Philosophy to Neuroscience*. New York: Alfred A. Knopf, 2010.

Isaacs, William. *Dialogue and the Art of Thinking Together*. New York: Random House, 1999.

Izzo, John. *The Five Secrets You Must Discover Before You Die*. San Francisco: Berrett Koehler Publishers, 2008.

Jackson, Bailey W. "Theory and Practice of Multicultural Organization Development." *The NTL Handbook of Organization Development and Change: Organizations, Principles and Practices*, edited by Brenda B. Jones and Michael Brazzel, San Francisco: Pfeiffer, 2006.

Johnson, Craig E. *Meeting the Ethical Challenges of Leadership: Casting Light or Shadow*. Thousand Oaks, CA: Sage Publications, 2011.

Jung, Carl G. *Man and His Symbols*. New York: Dell Publishing, 1964.

Kalven, Janey, Larry Rosen and Bruce Taylor. *Value Development: A Practical Guide*. New York/Mahwah, NJ: Paulist Press, 1982.

Kania, John, and Mark Kramer. "Collective Impact." *Stanford Social Innovation Review* 9, 1, Winter, 2011: 36-41.

Katz, Eric. "Faith, God and Nature: Judaism and Deep Ecology." *Deep Ecology and World Religions*, edited by David Landis Barnhill and Roger S. Gottlieb, 153-67. Albany, NY: State University of New York Press, 2001.

Keller, Evelyn Fox. *A Feeling for the Organism: The Life and Work of Barbara McClintock*. New York: W. H. Freeman, 1983.

Kofman, Fred. *Conscious Business: How to Build Value Through Values*. Boulder, CO: Sounds True, 2006.

Kornfield, Jack. *The Wise Heart: A Guide to the Universal Teachings of Buddhist Psychology*. New York: BantamDell, 2008.

La Chapelle, David. *Navigating the Tides of Change: Stories from Science, the Sacred, and a Wise Planet*. British Columbia: New Society Publishers, 2001.

Laszlo, Chris and Nadya Zhexembayeva. *Embedded Sustainability: The Next Big Competitive Advantage*. Sheffield, UK: Greenleaf, 2011.

Lester, Robert C. *Buddhism: The Path to Nirvana*. San Francisco: Harper & Row, 1987.

Lovins, Hunter, and Boyd Cohen. *Climate Capitalism: Capitalism in the Age of Climate Change*. New York: Hill and Wang, 2011.

Maguire, Daniel. *Ethics: A Complete Method for Moral Choice*. Minneapolis: Fortress Press, 2010.

Martin, Thomas N., and John C. Hafer. "Models of Emotional Intelligence, Spiritual Intelligence, and Performance: A Test of

Tischler, Biberman, and McKeage." *Journal of Management, Spirituality and Religion*, 6, 3 (2009): 247-57.

McGee-Cooper, Ann, Gary Looper and Duane Trammell. *Being the Change: Profiles from Our Servant Leadership Learning Community*. Dallas: AMCA, 2007.

McGrayne, Sharon Bertsch. *Nobel Prize Women in Science: Their Lives, Struggles, and Momentous Discoveries*. New York: Birch Lane Press, 1993.

Michaels, Alex. *Hinduism Past and Present*. Translated by Barbara Harshav. Princeton, NJ: Princeton University Press, 2004.

Michalko, Michael. *Thinkertoys: A Handbook of Creative Thinking Techniques*. Berkeley, CA: Ten Speed Press, 2006.

Miller, Jeffrey. "The Golden Buddha at Wat Traimit." *The Korean Times*, June 2, 2005, accessed at www.buddhistchannel.tv/index.php?id=18,1271,0,0,1,0 on January 19, 2012.

Montgomery, Anna K. "A Creative Leap for New Orleans." *Journal of the Arts in Leadership and Organizational Learning* (2008), accessed at www.creativeleaps.org/news/200804/NewOrleans.htm.

Neal, Judi. *Edgewalkers: People and Organizations that Take Risks, Build Bridges, and Break New Ground*. Westport, CT: Praeger, 2006.

Nouwen, Henri J. M., Donald P. McNeill and Douglas A. Morrison. *Compassion: A Reflection on the Christian Life*. New York: Doubleday, 1983.

Oliver, Mary. "The Summer Day." *House of Light*. Boston: Beacon Press, 1990.

Palmer, Parker J. *A Hidden Wholeness: The Journey Toward an Undivided Life*. San Francisco: Jossey-Bass, 2004.

―――. *Let Your Life Speak: Listening for the Voice of Vocation*. San Francisco: Jossey-Bass, 2000.

―――. "The Clearness Committee: A Communal Approach to Discernment." *The Courage To Teach: A Guide for Reflection and Renewal*, Rachel Livsey. San Francisco: Jossey-Bass, 1999.

―――. *To Know as We Are Known*. San Francisco: Harper and Row, 1983.

Patel, Eboo. *Acts of Faith*. Boston: Beacon Press, 2007.

Pert, Candace. *Your Body Is Your Subconscious Mind* (3 CD Set Audio Recording). Boulder, CO: Sounds True, 2005.

Peterson, Rolf O. *The Wolves of Isle Royale: A Broken Balance*. Ann Arbor, MI: The University of Michigan Press, 2007.

Pink, David. *A Whole New Mind*. New York: Penguin, 2005.

"Plans to Lift Radioactive Contamination Controls on UK Sheep Farms." *The Guardian*, November 17, 2011.

Plotkin, Bill. *Soulcraft: Crossing into the Mysteries of Nature and Psyche*. Novato, CA: New World Library, 2003.

Rachels, James, and Stuart Rachels. *The Elements of Moral Philosophy*. New York: McGraw-Hill, 2010.

Rahula, Walpola. *What the Buddha Taught*. New York: Grove Press, 1974.

Rawls, John. *Justice as Fairness: A Restatement*. Cambridge, MA: Harvard University Press, 2001.

———. *Political Liberalism*. New York: Columbia University Press, 1993.

———. *A Theory of Justice*. Cambridge, MA: Harvard University Press, 1971.

Reinhart, A. Kevin. "The Past in the Future of Islamic Ethics." *Islamic Ethics of Life*, edited by Jonathan Brockopp, 214-19. Columbia, SC: University of South Carolina Press, 2003.

Rilke, Rainer Maria. *Letters to a Young Poet*, translated by M. D. Herter. New York: Norton, 1993.

Rispler-Chaim, Vardit. "The Right Not to Be Born." *Islamic Ethics of Life*, edited by Jonathan Brockopp, 81-102. Columbia, SC: University of South Carolina Press, 2003.

Rumi, Jelaluddin "A Great Wagon." *The Essential Rumi*, translated by Coleman Barks. New York: HarperCollins Publishers, 1995.

Schein, Edgar H. *Process Consultation Revisited: Building the Helping Relationship*. New York: Addison-Wesley, 1999.

Sen, Amartya. *The Idea of Justice*. Cambridge, MA: Harvard University Press, 2009.

Senge, Peter M., Art Kleiner, Richard Ross, Bryan Smith, and Charlotte Roberts. *The Fifth Discipline Fieldbook*. New York: Doubleday, 1994.

Senge, Peter M. *The Fifth Discipline: The Art and Practice of the Learning Organization*. New York: Doubleday, 1990.

Sewall, Laura. *Sight and Sensibility: The Ecopsychology of Perception*. New York: Putnam, 1999.

Sinclair, Marta. "Misconceptions about Intuition." *Psychological Inquiry* 21, 4 (2010): 378-86.

Sisodia, Rajendra S., David B. Wolfe and Jagdish N. Sheth. *Firms of Endearment: How World-Class Companies Profit from Passion and Purpose*. Upper Saddle River, NJ: Prentice Hall, 2007.

Smith, Huston, and Philip Novak. *Buddhism: A Concise Introduction*. San Francisco: HarperCollins, 2003.

Suzuki, David, and Amanda McConnell. *The Sacred Balance: Rediscovering Our Place in Nature*. New York: Prometheus, 1997.

Tang, Joyce. *Scientific Pioneers: Women Succeeding in Science*. Lanham, MD: University Press of America, 2006.

The Test of Leadership. DVD. Produced by Virginia Duncan Gilmore, Fond du Lac, WI: 1999.

Tucker, Mary Evelyn. "Confucianism and Deep Ecology." *Deep Ecology and World Religions*, edited by David Landis Barnhill and Roger S. Gottlieb, 127-52. Albany, NY: State University of New York Press, 2001.

Tutu, Desmond. *No Future Without Forgiveness*. New York: Doubleday, 1999.

Underwood, Paula. *Three Native American Learning Stories*. Bayfield, CO: A Tribe of Two Press, 2002.

United Nations Development Programme, *Human Development Report 2011, Sustainability and Equity: A Better Future for All*. New York: Palgrave Macmillan, 2011. Available at http://hdr.undp.org/en/media/HDR_2011_EN_Summary.pdf.

Vucetich, John A. *Winter Study 2011: Notes from the Field*. Available from Isle Royale National Park, information available on the blog www.isleroyalewolf.org.

Walsh, Diana Chapman. *Trustworthy Leadership*. Ann Arbor, MI: Fetzer Institute, 2006.

Whyte, David. *Midlife and the Great Unknown* (2 CD Set Audio Recording). Boulder, CO: Sounds True, 2003.

Wolf, Robert. *Original Wisdom: Stories of an Ancient Way of Knowing*. Rochester, VT: Inner Traditions, 2001.

Xinzhong Yao. *An Introduction to Confucianism*. Cambridge, UK: Cambridge University Press, 2000.

INDEX